1994

# Multimedia Law Handbook

a practical guide
for
developers
and
publishers

1994

# Multimedia Law Handbook

a practical guide
for
developers
and
publishers

J. Dianne Brinson

Mark F. Radcliffe

LADERA PRESS

John Zussman, Logical Arts, project management
Pamela Shandrick, editing
Bernadette Castor, cover design
Hal Lewis, book design
Donna Kelley and Chistopher Glazek, production

This publication is designed to provide accurate and authoritative information in regard to the subject matter covered. It is sold with the understanding that the publisher is not engaged in rendering legal, accounting, or other professional service. If legal advice or other expert assistance is required, the services of a competent professional person should be sought.

*Library of Congress Cataloging in Publication Data*
Brinson, J. Dianne
    Multimedia law handbook: a practical guide for developers and publishers / J. Dianne Brinson
    and Mark F. Radcliffe.
        p. cm.
        Includes bibliographical references.
        Preassigned LCCN: 93-80463
        ISBN 0-9639173-0-7

    1. Multimedia systems—Law and legislation—United States. 2. Multimedia systems industry—
    Law and legislation—United States. I. Radcliffe, Mark F.   II. Title.

    KF309.5.M8B75 1994          343.7309'99
                                QBI93-22248

# Contents

 INTERACTIVE
MULTIMEDIA
ASSOCIATION

This Special IMA Edition of the Multimedia Law Handbook is made possible by arrangement between the Interactive Multimedia Association and Ladera Press. Its distribution is underwritten by Eastman Kodak Company and ITC, and the IMA gratefully acknowledges their support.

Based in Annapolis, MD, the Interactive Multimedia Association is the oldest, largest and most active trade association devoted to multimedia, tackling issues including application portability and interoperability, intellectual property rights and technology convergence. Its mission is to promote successful application of interactive multimedia in business and consumer markets, and to reduce key barriers to the widespread use of interactive multimedia technologies and applications.

The IMA is a leader in bringing to light the problems associated with overly broad and obvious patent claims, and the association continues to work toward patent policy and procedure reform, including better trained examiners, an improved database of software prior art and pre-grant publication. The IMA also has been instrumental in the development of recommended practices contributing to cross-platform portability of multimedia data and applications.

Membership in the IMA ranges from $500 to $10,000 annually based on company revenue. Sponsorship is $50,000 annually, and non-profit membership is also available.

For further information on the Interactive Multimedia Association, please contact the IMA by telephone at (410) 626-1380, or by fax at (410) 263-0590. For more immediate response, call the IMA FAXBack System from the handset of a fax machine at (410) 268-2100 to immediately request faxed documents on the association's key initiatives and services, or to receive a membership application. You may also write to the IMA at 48 Maryland Avenue–Suite 202, Annapolis, MD 21401-8011.

# Acknowledgements

We would like to extend our profound thanks to all of the individuals who generously provided their assistance in writing this book. In many ways, this book was a collaborative project. It depended on the willingness of many people to provide us with information and keep us informed of the almost daily changes in this area. We wish to thank particularly Craig Sheumaker, for urging us to undertake the project, and the partners of Ware & Freidenrich (now Gray Cary Ware & Freidenrich) and its Multimedia Law Group, who generously agreed to permit our use of the form contracts in Appendix B. We also wish to thank Mary Clyde, who spent her weekends organizing the appendices, and Rose Ann Billingsley, who helped us with proofreading.

This book includes our opinions. They should not be interpreted as those of Gray Cary Ware & Freidenrich or its clients. We have done our best to accurately reflect the practices in this rapidly evolving industry, but any errors are solely our responsibility.

We would like to thank the following individuals for their assistance:

*Warren Adler*   Directors Guild of America

*Sueann Ambron*   Paramount Communications, Inc.

*Ed Bernstein*   The Software Toolworks, Inc.

*Joel Block*   Writers Guild of America

*Brian Blum*   The Software Toolworks, Inc.

*John Campbell*   Media Vision Technology, Inc.

*Vincent Castellucci*   The Harry Fox Agency, Inc.

*Dominique Claessens*   Image Smith, Inc.

*Gary Culpepper*   Law Offices of Gary Culpepper

*Richard Curtis*   Richard Curtis Associates

*Bob Derber*   Maxis

*John Evershed*   Mondo Media

*Darlene deMontfreid*   Media Vision Technology, Inc.

*Halle Eavelyn*   Hyperbole

*Dick Gabriel*   American Federation of Musicians

*Ted Grabowski*   The Software Toolworks, Inc.

*Craig Harding*   Kaleida Labs, Inc.

*Bob Kohn*   Borland International, Inc.

*Rockley Miller*   Multimedia Monitor

*Jake Myrick*   Image Smith, Inc.

*Jim Myrick*   Image Smith, Inc.

*Deirdre O'Malley*   Mondo Media

*Jeannine Parker*   IICS

*Randy Parker*   Clearing House, Ltd.

*Michael Prohaska*   Screen Actors Guild

*Greg Roach*   Hyperbole

*Jim Roberts*   Image Smith, Inc.

*Lionel Sobel*   Loyola Law School

*Joey Tamer*   S.O.S., Inc.

*Allen Thygessen*   Media Vision Technology, Inc.

*Karen Stuart*   AFTRA

*Chuck Warn*   Warn Communications Group

# Introduction

The purpose of this book is to give multimedia developers and publishers a basic understanding of the legal issues involved in developing and distributing multimedia works. Reading this book will not make you a lawyer (the authors don't want more competition in their field), but it will enable you to ask appropriate questions and take steps to protect your interests.

The creation and distribution of an interactive multimedia work is a complex process. It involves a number of legal issues:

- Contracting with employees, independent contractors, and consultants for the creation of your multimedia work.

- Avoiding infringement of others' intellectual property rights.

- Obtaining licenses to use content owned by others.

- Complying with union rules.

- Contracting for sale or distribution of your multimedia work.

- Protecting the intellectual property rights in your multimedia work.

These legal issues are frequently as important to a multimedia developer as the technological and creative issues involved in multimedia projects.

A multimedia developer who fails to obtain the necessary rights to use material owned by others can incur liability for hundreds of thousands or even millions of dollars in damages.

*Productions, Inc. created an interactive multimedia training work called You Can Do It. The script was written by a freelance writer. You Can Do It includes an excerpt from a recording of Julie Andrews singing Climb Every Mountain. It ends with a photograph of Lauren Bacall shown above the words, "Good luck."*

In this example, if the Productions staff did not obtain permission to use the recording of *Climb Every Mountain* or the photo of Lauren Bacall, *Do It* infringes three copyrights: the copyright on the song, the copyright on the Julie Andrews recording of the song, and the copyright on the photograph. In addition, the use of the photograph violates Ms. Bacall's rights of publicity and privacy. If Productions did not acquire ownership of the script from the freelance writer, Productions does not have clear title to *Do It*, and distribution of *Do It* may infringe the writer's copyright in the script.

## How To Use This Book

The approach taken in this book is what lawyers call "preventive law"—working from a base of knowledge of the applicable law to create strategies and procedures that will help you avoid future lawsuits and legal complications.

Part 1 of this book ("Building Blocks," Chapters 1–5) will give you an understanding of the U.S. legal system and legal terminology, and of the fundamentals of copyright, patent, trademark, and trade secret law. A primer on contracts law is also included.

Part 2 of the book ("Production Relationships," Chapters 6–8) gives you guidelines for setting up development agreements with clients, and for ensuring that you get ownership of material created for your multimedia works by employees and independent contractors.

In Part 3 ("Other Production Issues," Chapters 9–14), you'll learn how to determine when you need permission to use preexisting content in your multimedia works and how to get licenses to use works owned by others. The industries that are your most likely sources for preexisting content are described in this section. The laws of publicity, privacy, and libel are covered in this section, as are union issues.

Part 4 ("Post-Production Issues," Chapters 15–19) is devoted to legal issues that come up after your multimedia work is finished. Topics include how to choose a name for your product, how to protect your own intellectual property rights, sales law, and distribution agreements. Special concerns of multimedia publishers are also covered in this section.

In the Appendices, we have included sample contracts to assist you in understanding the issues. We have also included information on resource organizations, as well as provisions from the Copyright Act and copies of copyright registration forms.

# 1

## Building Blocks

# 1

## The U.S. Legal System

In the United States, laws are made at the federal and state levels. Laws adopted by legislative bodies—Congress and state legislatures—are called "statutes."

The federal and state courts enforce statutes. They also create law.

This chapter describes some of the basic concepts of our legal system, and the roles played by legislatures and courts.

### Federal Statutes

The U.S. Constitution gives Congress the power to enact federal laws ("statutes") on certain subjects.

The Copyright Act (discussed extensively in Chapter 2) is one example of a statute adopted by Congress. Congress's power to enact the Copyright Act stems from Article I, Section 8, of the Constitution, which authorizes Congress to establish laws giving "authors and inventors the exclusive right to their respective writings and discoveries" to encourage progress in the arts and sciences.

According to the Constitution, all powers not expressly delegated to Congress are reserved to the states. The "commerce clause" of the Constitution (which concerns interstate commerce) is generally viewed as giving Congress broad power to regulate matters affecting interstate commerce—trademarks used in interstate commerce, for example.

Federal law-making begins when a member of the Senate or the House of Representatives introduces a bill. Most bills are referred to standing committees (for example, the House Committee on the Judiciary) and to subcommittees for study. Bills are later brought before the Senate or House for debate and vote. Differences between the Senate and House versions of a bill are resolved in joint conference committees.

After the House and Senate have approved a uniform version of the bill, the bill is sent to the President. If the President signs the bill, it becomes law. If the President vetoes the bill, it becomes law only if the Senate and House override the veto. This requires the consent of two-thirds of the members of the Senate and House.

## State Statutes

State legislatures can pass laws on matters for which they share jurisdiction with Congress. Trademark law is an example of a shared jurisdiction. In other matters, the federal government has taken exclusive jurisdiction. Copyright is an example: The Copyright Act prohibits the states from granting copyright-like protection.

States can also pass laws on matters in which the Constitution does not grant jurisdiction to the federal government.

State law-making occurs through a process that is similar to the federal process.

## The Courts

The courts enforce statutes and interpret them. They also invalidate unconstitutional statutes, and make law in areas not covered by statutes. Here are some examples of the four main roles played by our courts:

- *Enforcement.* The Copyright Act gives a copyright owner the exclusive right to reproduce the owner's work. A copyright infringement suit is an example of court *enforcement* of a statute. (Copyright infringement is discussed in "Infringement," Chapter 2.)

- *Interpretation.* According to the Copyright Act, the copyright in a work created by an employee within the scope of his or her employment is owned by the employer. The Copyright Act does not define the term "employee." The Supreme Court case that defines the term is an example of court *interpretation* of a statute. (That case is discussed in the "The Work Made for Hire Rule," Chapter 4.)

- *Invalidation.* The courts invalidate unconstitutional laws. Unconstitutional laws are laws that conflict with provisions of the Constitution. The Constitution is the supreme law of the United States. Many "constitutionality" cases involve claims that a law violates the Constitution's Bill of Rights (the first ten amendments). In *Roe v. Wade*, the Supreme Court invalidated a state statute restricting women's access to abortion. According to the Court, the statute violated a pregnant woman's constitutional right of privacy.

- *Making Law.* The courts create the law for "common law" subject areas. Common law covers areas not covered by statutes. In many states, for example, individuals' rights of privacy and publicity (discussed in "The Rights of Publicity and Privacy," Chapter 13) are protected under common law rather than under statutory laws.

## Types of Courts

There are several types of courts. The federal and state court systems consist of two levels of courts: trial courts and appellate courts. Cases are tried in trial courts. Appellate courts review the decisions of the trial courts. (Appellate and trial courts are discussed in "Civil Lawsuits," later in this chapter.)

The federal court system is divided into 13 judicial circuits. Eleven of the circuits are numbered. Each of the numbered circuits contains more than one state. The Ninth Circuit, for example, covers California, Oregon, Washington, Idaho, Nevada, Arizona, Alaska, and Hawaii. The 12th and 13th circuits are the District of Columbia Circuit and the Federal Circuit. The Federal Circuit handles appeals in patent cases and Claims Court cases.

Each federal circuit has one appellate court. These courts are known as Courts of Appeals or Circuit Courts. The Supreme Court reviews the decisions of the Courts of Appeals.

Each federal circuit is divided into judicial districts. A district can be as small as one city or as large as an entire state. The trial courts are known as the United States District Courts.

## Jurisdiction

The federal courts have jurisdiction over cases involving federal statutes (the Copyright Act, for example) and other "federal questions." They also have jurisdiction over cases in which the party filing the suit and the party being sued reside in different states. This type of federal jurisdiction is known as "diversity" jurisdiction.

Other types of cases must be brought in state court.

## Civil and Criminal Cases

A criminal case is brought by the federal government or a state to prosecute a defendant (the party sued) for violations of the government's criminal laws. Murder and burglary are examples of violations of criminal laws. If the defendant in a criminal case is found guilty by the jury, he or she is sentenced by the court to serve a jail sentence or pay a fine as punishment for the crime.

A civil case is a case brought by one party (the "plaintiff") against another party (the "defendant") to resolve a legal dispute involving rights based on statutory law or common law. A copyright infringement case is an example of a civil case involving statutory law. A suit seeking damages for a writer's breach of a contract (in which the writer promised to create a script for a movie but failed to do so) is an example of a civil case involving common law rights. (Breach of contract is discussed in "What Is a Contract?," Chapter 5.)

While certain violations of the Copyright Act and the Lanham Act (the federal trademark statute) are criminal violations, multimedia developers and publishers will be concerned primarily with civil cases.

### Civil Lawsuits

There are several stages in civil lawsuits, from initiation to trial and then on to stages of appeal. We'll discuss these stages in this section.

#### *Initiation*

A civil lawsuit is initiated when the plaintiff files a "complaint" against the defendant alleging that the defendant has wronged the plaintiff in some way recognized by the law. In most civil lawsuits, the plaintiff asks the court to award the plaintiff "damages" (a remedy for the defendant's wrongdoing—usually money) or to order the defendant to do something.

The defendant responds to the allegations in the complaint by filing an "answer" (a document in which the defendant admits or denies the complaint's allegations and states defenses). The defendant can also file a "counterclaim" against the plaintiff (allegations that the plaintiff has wronged the defendant).

#### *Trial*

If the parties do not "settle" the case (reach their own agreement on how to resolve the dispute), the case eventually goes to trial. In most types of civil cases, the Constitution gives the parties a right to a jury trial. The role of the jury is to decide questions of fact. However, in some complex cases, the parties choose to dispense with the jury and have the case decided by the trial judge.

#### *Appeal*

If the losing party in a civil lawsuit is not satisfied with the decision of the trial court, the losing party can appeal the case to the appropriate appellate court.

In the federal court system, the appeal generally must be filed with the Court of Appeals for the judicial circuit in which the trial was held. A case tried in the United States District Court for the Northern District of California, for example, must be appealed to the Court of Appeals for the Ninth Circuit.

An appellate court's job in reviewing a trial court's decision is to look for "mistakes of law" made by the trial court. Appellate courts do not "second guess" factual issues decided by trial courts. In our legal system, factual issues are supposed to be resolved by the jury, not by the appellate court. So long as there is adequate factual evidence to support the verdict, an appellate court will not reverse a trial court's decision or "remand" the case (send it back to the trial court for retrial) unless they find that the trial court made a "mistake of law."

Filing an appeal is probably a waste of money unless a losing party can reasonably hope to convince the appellate judges that there is insufficient evidence to support the trial court's decision, or that the trial court misapplied the law.

*Plaintiff's lawsuit alleges that Defendant infringed the copyright on Plaintiff's song by copying the melody of the song. The jury found that Defendant did not infringe Plaintiff's copyright. If the jury reached its decision after being told by the judge that a song's melody is not protected by copyright (a mistake in the applicable law, copyright law), Plaintiff has a good basis for appeal. However, if the jury reached its decision after listening to Defendant's song and concluding that the melody of Defendant's song is not similar to the melody of Plaintiff's song, Plaintiff does not have a strong basis for appeal. (Whether or not the songs have similar melodies is a factual determination.)*

Appellate courts generally issue written opinions explaining how they reached their conclusions on whether to affirm (uphold), reverse, or remand a case. These opinions are important parts of the development of the law because our legal system is based on "precedent" (reliance on previously decided cases). (The role of precedent is discussed in "Precedent," later in this chapter.)

### Supreme Court Review

There are two ways to get a case reviewed by the U.S. Supreme Court: by appeal and by *certiorari*. The losers in certain types of cases—for example, cases involving claims that state statutes are unconstitutional—have a right to appeal to the Supreme Court.

For most cases, though, there is no right of appeal to the Supreme Court. However, a party who has lost a case at the federal Court of Appeals level can file a petition for *certiorari* with the Supreme Court. A petition for *certiorari* is a document explaining why the Supreme Court should review a case. If the Supreme Court grants *certiorari*, the appeal proceeds. If the Court denies it, the Court of Appeals' decision stands.

Thousands of petitions for *certiorari* are filed each year and most are denied. The Supreme Court is likely to grant *certiorari* on a case only if the case involves a matter of national interest or the Court believes that it must decide the case to resolve conflicts among the Circuit Courts and create uniformity in federal law.

## Precedent

An appellate court's decision on an issue is binding on lower courts in the appellate court's jurisdiction. Thus, an appellate court's decisions are "precedent" that the lower courts in the appellate court's jurisdiction must follow (apply).

> *In Effects Associates, Inc. v. Cohen, the United States Court of Appeals for the Ninth Circuit held that the grant of a nonexclusive copyright license can be implied from the copyright owner's conduct. (Implied licenses are discussed in "Implied Licenses," Chapter 8.) This decision is binding on the federal district courts located in the Ninth Circuit. Those courts are not free to decide that a nonexclusive copyright license cannot be implied from conduct.*

A lower court's decision is not binding on a higher court. In fact, appellate courts frequently reverse decisions made by trial courts to correct the trial courts' "mistakes of law."

Because the United States Supreme Court is the "highest court in the land," the Supreme Court's decisions are binding on all courts in the United States.

> *In Community for Creative Non-Violence v. Reid, the Supreme Court decided how to apply the Copyright Act's "work made for hire" rule to works created by independent contractors. That decision is binding on all courts in the United States. (Work made for hire is discussed in "The Work Made for Hire Rule," Chapter 4.)*

A court's decision may "be persuasive" outside its region. For a decision to "be persuasive" means that other courts, while not compelled to follow it, choose to follow it. For example, if the Court of Appeals for the Eleventh Circuit has never decided whether a nonexclusive copyright license can be implied from the copyright owner's conduct but the Ninth Circuit has, the Eleventh Circuit may reach the same conclusion as the Ninth Circuit when it decides that issue because it believes that the Ninth Circuit's decision was correct.

Earlier court decisions are generally "followed" by the deciding court in all later cases involving the same issue. For example, if the Ninth Circuit decides a case that involves the same legal issues that were involved in a previous case, it is likely to decide those issues as it did in the previous case.

The reliance that our courts put on previously decided cases in deciding new cases is known as *stare decisis*. That is Latin for "let the decision stand." The doctrine of *stare decisis* does not prevent a court from "overruling" its own previously decided cases. However, *stare decisis* discourages rapid and radical changes in the law. As Supreme Court Justice William O. Douglas once wrote in the *Columbia Law Review*, "*stare decisis* provides some moorings so that men may trade and arrange their affairs with confidence....It is the strong tie which the future has to the past."

The doctrine of *stare decisis* is the reason that an attorney performs legal research hoping to find cases supporting the attorney's position on a legal issue.

## Finding the Law

Because law is made by the courts on a precedent basis following the doctrine of *stare decisis*, and also made by Congress and the state legislatures, knowing the law on a given topic generally requires a review of both statutory law and case law.

### Statutes

Federal and state statutory laws can be found by consulting published "codifications" of laws in law libraries maintained by law schools, law firms, courts, and bar associations. To find a federal law such as the Copyright Act, for example, you would look in the United States Code, which is divided into "titles." Federal and state statutory laws can also be obtained "on-line" from Westlaw or Lexis, two computerized legal research services.

Recently adopted laws may not be included in the published codifications of statutes. While the publishers of these codifications add new material regularly (in "pocket parts" inserted at the back of appropriate volumes), even the pocket parts may not include laws adopted in the most recent session of the legislature.

### Court Decisions

Court decisions (also known as "case law") can be found in publications called "reporters." For example, decisions of the United States Supreme Court are published in the *United States Reports*, the *Supreme Court Reporter*, and the *Lawyers Edition* (three different "reporters" from three different publishers).

These decisions are also available from computerized services such as Westlaw and Lexis, which provide on-line research assistance for locating cases on desired topics. "Digests" that divide decided cases into topics are also helpful for locating relevant cases. Other research resources help lawyers determine whether cases in which they are interested have been reversed by a higher court or overruled (modified by a later decision of the same court).

Various publishing companies publish "annotated" statutory codes, which bring statutes and relevant court decisions together in one source. West Publishing Company, for example, publishes the *United States Code Annotated*, which lists the court decisions enforcing or interpreting each provision of the United States Code.

## Arbitration

The parties to a dispute sometimes choose to resolve a dispute through arbitration rather than through court litigation. In arbitration, a dispute is resolved by a neutral arbitrator rather than by a judge or jury.

Arbitration is generally quicker and cheaper than court litigation. Specially qualified arbitrators are often used to resolve technical disputes.

Both parties must agree to submit their dispute to arbitration. Many contracts require that disputes be resolved through arbitration rather than through litigation.

In the United States, many arbitration cases are handled by arbitrators approved by the American Arbitration Association, which has offices in a number of cities. Arbitration is similar to a trial in that both parties present their cases to the arbitrator, who renders a decision. Appeals of arbitrators' decisions are generally possible only if the arbitration was conducted improperly.

## Government Offices and Agencies

Government offices and agencies play an important role in our legal system. The Copyright Office and the U.S. Patent and Trademark Office are the key federal government offices for multimedia developers and publishers. (The Copyright Office is discussed in "Copyright Protection," Chapter 16. The U.S. Patent and Trademark Office is discussed in "Patent Law" and "Trademark Law," Chapter 3.)

# 2

## Copyright Law

There are four major intellectual property laws in the United States that are important for multimedia developers and publishers:

- Copyright law.

- Patent law.

- Trademark law.

- Trade secret law.

In this chapter, we discuss copyright law, the most important of the intellectual property laws for developers and publishers of multimedia works. Patent law, trademark law, and trade secret law are discussed in Chapter 3.

Ownership of copyrights and other intellectual property is discussed in Chapter 4. In Chapter 16, we discuss ways in which you can use the four intellectual property laws to protect your multimedia works.

Other laws that create rights somewhat like intellectual property law rights—privacy, publicity, and dilution laws—are discussed in Chapters 13 and 15.

### Introduction

Copyright law in the U.S. is based on the Copyright Act of 1976, a federal statute that went into effect on January 1, 1978. We'll refer to this statute throughout the book as the Copyright Act. Excerpts from the Copyright Act appear in Appendix A.

States cannot enact their own laws to protect the same rights as the rights provided by the Copyright Act. For example, a state cannot pass a law to extend copyright protection on works in the state beyond the term of protection given by the Copyright Act. State "copyright" laws exist, but they are limited to works that cannot be protected under federal copyright law. (Requirements for federal protection are discussed in "Standards," later in this chapter.)

Copyright law is important for multimedia developers and publishers for two reasons:

- Original multimedia works are protected by copyright. The Copyright Act's exclusive rights provision gives developers and publishers the right to control unauthorized exploitation of their works. (Steps to maximize your protection are discussed in "Copyright Protection," Chapter 16.)

- Multimedia works are created by combining "content"—music, text, graphics, illustrations, photographs, software—that is protected under copyright law. Developers and publishers must avoid infringing copyrights owned by others, as explained in Chapter 9.

## Types of Works Protected by Copyright

Copyright law protects "works of authorship." The Copyright Act states that works of authorship include the following types of works:

- *Literary works.* Novels, nonfiction prose, poetry, newspaper articles and newspapers, magazine articles and magazines, computer software, software documentation and manuals, training manuals, manuals, catalogs, brochures, ads (text), and compilations such as business directories.

- *Musical works.* Songs, advertising jingles, and instrumentals.

- *Dramatic works.* Plays, operas, and skits.

- *Pantomimes and choreographic works.* Ballets, modern dance, jazz dance, and mime works.

- *Pictorial, graphic, and sculptural works.* Photographs, posters, maps, paintings, drawings, graphic art, display ads, cartoon strips and cartoon characters, stuffed animals, statues, paintings, and works of fine art.

- *Motion pictures and other audiovisual works.* Movies, documentaries, travelogues, training films and videos, television shows, television ads, and interactive multimedia works.

- *Sound recordings.* Recordings of music, sounds, or words.

- *Architectural works.* Building designs, whether in the form of architectural plans, drawings, or the constructed building itself.

## Standards

To receive copyright protection, a work must be "original" and must be "fixed" in a tangible medium of expression. Certain types of works are not copyrightable.

## Originality

The originality requirement is not stringent: A work is original in the copyright sense if it owes its origin to the author and was not copied from some preexisting work. A work can be original without being novel or unique.

·· · *Betsy's book How to Lose Weight is original in the copyright sense so long as Betsy did not* · *create her book by copying existing material—even if it's the millionth book to be written* · *on the subject of weight loss.*

Only minimal creativity is required to meet the originality requirement. No artistic merit or beauty is required.

A work can incorporate preexisting material and still be original. When preexisting material is incorporated into a new work, the copyright on the new work covers only the original material contributed by the author.

·· · *Developer's multimedia work incorporates a number of photographs that were made by* · *Photographer (who gave Developer permission to use the photographs in the multimedia* *work). The multimedia work as a whole owes its origin to Developer, but the photographs* *do not. The copyright on the multimedia work does not cover the photographs, just the* *material created by Developer.*

Facts owe their origin to no one and so are not original. A compilation of facts (a work formed by collecting and assembling data) is protected by copyright only to the extent of the author's originality in the selection, coordination, and arrangement of the facts.

·· · *Ralph created a neighborhood phone directory for his neighborhood by going door-to-door* · *and getting his neighbors' names and phone numbers. The directory's facts (names and* *phone numbers) are not original. Ralph's selection of facts was not original (he "selected"* *every household in the neighborhood). His coordination and arrangement of facts (alpha-* *betical order by last name) is routine rather than original. The directory is not protected* *by copyright.*

## Fixation

According to Section 101 of the Copyright Act, a work is "fixed" when it is made "suffi-ciently permanent or stable to permit it to be perceived, reproduced, or otherwise communi-cated for a period of more than transitory duration." It makes no difference what the form, manner, or medium. An author can "fix" words, for example, by writing them down, typing them on an old-fashioned typewriter, dictating them into a tape recorder, or entering them into a computer. A live television broadcast is "fixed" if it is recorded simultaneously with the transmission.

### Uncopyrightable Works

Works prepared by federal government officers and employees as part of their official duties are not protected by copyright. Consequently, federal statutes (the Copyright Act, for example) and regulations are not protected by copyright. This rule does not apply to works created by state government officers and employees.

The design of a useful article is protected by copyright only if, and to the extent that, the design "incorporates pictorial, graphic, or sculptural features that can be identified separately from, and are capable of existing independently of, the utilitarian aspects of the article." For example, while a "normal" belt buckle is not protected, a three-dimensional belt-buckle design with a dolphin shape qualifies for limited protection.

Uncopyrightable works and works for which copyright protection has ended are referred to as "public domain" works. (These works are discussed in "Public Domain Works," Chapter 9.)

## Procedure for Getting Protection

Copyright protection arises automatically when an original work of authorship is fixed in a tangible medium of expression. Registration with the Copyright Office is optional (but you have to register before you file an infringement suit).

The use of copyright notice is optional for works distributed after March 1, 1989. Copyright notice can take any of these three forms:

- "©" followed by a date and name.
- "Copyright" followed by a date and name.
- "Copr." followed by a date and name.

The benefits of registering a copyright and using copyright notice and how to register are discussed in Chapter 16. The role of notice for works distributed prior to March 1, 1989, is discussed in "Public Domain Works," Chapter 9.

## The Exclusive Rights

A copyright owner has five exclusive rights in the copyrighted work:

- *Reproduction Right.* The reproduction right is the right to copy, duplicate, transcribe, or imitate the work in fixed form.

- *Modification Right.* The modification right (also known as the derivative works right) is the right to modify the work to create a new work. A new work that is based on a preexisting work is known as a "derivative work."

- *Distribution Right.* The distribution right is the right to distribute copies of the work to the public by sale, rental, lease, or lending.

- *Public Performance Right.* The public performance right is the right to recite, play, dance, act, or show the work at public place or to transmit it to the public. In the case of a motion picture or other audiovisual work, showing the work's images in sequence is considered "performance."

- *Public Display Right.* The public display right is the right to show a copy of the work directly or by means of a film, slide, or television image at a public place or to transmit it to the public. In the case of a motion picture or other audiovisual work, showing the work's images out of sequence is considered "display."

The exclusive rights are discussed in more detail in "Myths," Chapter 9, and in the "Determining What Rights You Need," Chapter 10.

## Infringement

Anyone who violates any of the exclusive rights of a copyright owner is an infringer.

*Developer scanned Photographer's copyrighted photograph, altered the image by using digital editing software, and included the altered version of the photograph in a multimedia work that Developer sold to consumers. If Developer used Photographer's photograph without permission, Developer infringed Photographer's copyright by violating the reproduction right (scanning the photograph), the modification right (altering the photograph), and the distribution right (selling the altered photograph as part of the multimedia work).*

A copyright owner can recover actual or, in some cases, statutory damages from an infringer (see "Copyright Protection," Chapter 16). The federal district courts have the power to issue injunctions (orders) to prevent or restrain copyright infringement and to order the impoundment and destruction of infringing copies.

## Duration of the Rights

For works created on and after January 1, 1978, the copyright term for works created by individuals is the life of the author plus 50 years.

The copyright term for "works made for hire" is 75 years from the date of first "publication" (distribution of copies to the general public) or 100 years from the date of creation, whichever expires first. Works made for hire are works created by employees for employers and certain types of specially commissioned works (see "The Work Made for Hire Rule," Chapter 4).

The duration of copyright for pre-1978 works is discussed in "Public Domain Works," Chapter 9.

## Limitations on the Exclusive Rights

The copyright owner's exclusive rights are subject to a number of exceptions and limitations that give others the right to make limited use of a copyrighted work. Major exceptions and limitations are outlined in this section. (They are discussed in detail in "When You Don't Need a License," Chapter 9.)

### Ideas

Copyright protects only against the unauthorized taking of a protected work's "expression." It does not extend to the work's ideas, procedures, processes, systems, methods of operation, concepts, principles, or discoveries.

### Facts

A work's facts are not protected by copyright, even if the author spent large amounts of time, effort, and money discovering those facts. Copyright protects originality, not effort or "sweat of the brow."

### Independent Creation

A copyright owner has no recourse against another person who, working independently, creates an exact duplicate of the copyrighted work. The independent creation of a similar work or even an exact duplicate does not violate any of the copyright owner's exclusive rights.

### Fair Use

The "fair use" of a copyrighted work, including use for purposes such as criticism, comment, news reporting, teaching, scholarship, or research, is not an infringement of copyright. Copyright owners are, by law, deemed to consent to fair use of their works by others.

The Copyright Act does not define fair use. Instead, whether a use is fair use is determined by balancing these factors:

- The purpose and character of the use.
- The nature of the copyrighted work.

- The amount and substantiality of the portion used in relation to the copyrighted work as a whole.

- The effect of the use on the potential market for, or value of, the copyrighted work.

## International Protection

U.S. authors automatically receive copyright protection in all countries that are parties to the Berne Convention for the Protection of Literary and Artistic Works, or parties to the Universal Copyright Convention (UCC). Most countries belong to at least one of these conventions. Members of the two international copyright conventions have agreed to give nationals of member countries the same level of copyright protection they give their own nationals.

*Publisher has discovered that bootleg copies of one of its multimedia works are being sold in England. Because the United Kingdom is a member of the Berne Convention and the UCC, Publisher's work is automatically protected by copyright in England. When Publisher files a copyright infringement action in England against the bootlegger, Publisher will be given the same rights that an English copyright owner would be given.*

Works of foreign authors who are nationals of Berne- or UCC-member countries automatically receive copyright protection in the U.S., as do works first published in a Berne Convention or UCC country. Unpublished works are subject to copyright protection in the U.S. without regard to the nationality or domicile of the author.

# 3

## Patent, Trademark, and
## Trade Secret Law

While copyright law is the most important intellectual property law for protecting rights in multimedia works, you need to know enough about patent, trademark, and trade secret law to avoid infringing intellectual property rights owned by others and to protect your multimedia works. These three intellectual property laws are discussed in this chapter.

In Chapter 16, we discuss ways in which you can use these three laws and copyright law to protect your multimedia works. Ownership of intellectual property is discussed in Chapter 4.

Choosing product names is covered in Chapter 15.

## Patent Law

Patent law in the U.S. is based on a federal statute, the Patent Act. States are prohibited from granting protection similar to that provided by the Patent Act.

### Types of Works Protected

Patent law protects inventions and processes ("utility" patents) and ornamental designs ("design" patents).

Inventions and processes protected by utility patents can be electrical, mechanical, or chemical in nature. Examples of works protected by utility patents are a microwave oven, genetically engineered bacteria for cleaning up oil spills, a computerized method of running cash management accounts, and a method for curing rubber.

Examples of works protected by design patents are a design for the sole of running shoes, a design for sterling silver tableware, and a design for a water fountain.

### Standards

There are strict requirements for the grant of utility patents and design patents. We'll discuss the requirements in this section.

#### Utility Patents

To qualify for a utility patent, an invention must be new, useful, and "nonobvious."

To meet the novelty requirement, the invention must not have been known or used by others in this country before the applicant invented it, and it also must not have been patented or described in a printed publication in the U.S. or a foreign country before the applicant invented it. The policy behind the novelty requirement is that a patent is issued in exchange for the inventor's disclosure to the public of the details of his invention. If the inventor's work is not novel, the inventor is not adding to the public knowledge, so the inventor should not be granted a patent.

Meeting the useful requirement is easy for most inventions. An invention is useful if it can be applied to some beneficial use in society.

To meet the nonobvious requirement, the invention must be sufficiently different from existing technology and knowledge so that, at the time the invention was made, the invention as a whole would not have been obvious to a person having ordinary skill in that field. The policy behind this requirement is that patents should only be granted for real advances, not for mere technical tinkering or modifications of existing inventions.

It is difficult to obtain a utility patent. Even if the invention or process meets the requirements of novelty, utility, and nonobviousness, a patent will not be granted if the invention was patented or described in a printed publication in the U.S. or a foreign country more than one year before the application date, or if the invention was in public use or on sale in the U.S. for more than one year before the application date.

If you think your multimedia work involves technology that might be patentable, you should contact a patent attorney before you display or distribute your work. In the multimedia field, an example of an invention that might be patentable is a software engine for multimedia works. An example of a process that might be patentable is an instructional method for using interactive video technology in classrooms (Optical Data Corporation was recently granted two patents covering such a process).

Unrealized mental conceptions are not patentable. Methods of transacting business and printed matter without physical structure are not patentable. Discoveries of scientific principles, laws of nature, and natural phenomena are not patentable (although applications of such discoveries are). The discovery of a new use for an old product is not patentable.

### Design Patents

To qualify for a design patent, a design must be new, original, and ornamental. Design patents may be an option for protecting some elements of multimedia works (user interfaces, for example, which can also be protected through copyright law). However, design patents are considered rather weak intellectual property protection, and owners of design patents rarely sue to enforce their patents against infringers.

## Procedure for Getting Protection

Patent protection is obtained by demonstrating in an application filed with the U.S. Patent and Trademark Office that the invention meets the stringent standards for grant of a patent. The patent application process is expensive and time-consuming (it generally takes at least two years). Although you can file a patent application yourself, the application process is very complex. You should consider using an experienced patent attorney or patent agent (a nonlawyer who has passed the special patent bar exam given by the U.S. Patent and Trademark Office).

## Exclusive Rights

A patent owner has the right to exclude others from making, using, or selling the patented invention or design in the United States during the term of the patent. Anyone who makes, uses, or sells a patented invention or design within the United States during the term of the patent without permission from the patent owner is an infringer—even if he or she did not copy the patented invention or design or even know about it.

*Developer's staff members, working on their own, developed a software program for manipulating images in Developer's multimedia works. Although Developer's staff didn't know it, Inventor has a patent on that method of image manipulation. Developer's use of the software program infringes Inventor's patent.*

## Duration

Utility patents are granted for a period of 17 years. Design patents are granted for a period of 14 years. Once the patent on an invention or design has expired, anyone is free to make, use, or sell the invention or design.

## Limitations on the Exclusive Rights

There are two major limitations on the patent owner's exclusive rights. They are discussed in this section.

### *Functionally Equivalent Products*

A patent owner can exclude others from making, using, or selling products or using processes that do substantially the same work as the patented invention in substantially the same manner. However, a patent does not protect the patent owner from competition from functionally equivalent products or processes that work in different ways.

> *Microco owns a patent covering a laser printer. While Microco can prevent others from making, using, or selling laser printers that work in substantially the same manner as Microco's printer, it cannot prevent others from making, using, or selling laser printers that operate in a different manner.*

### Invalidation

The validity of an issued patent is subject to challenge in an infringement proceeding. Defendants in infringement suits usually raise the defense of patent invalidity, asserting that the invention covered by the patent was not novel or nonobvious. It is not unusual for a patent infringement suit to result in a determination that the U.S. Patent and Trademark Office made a mistake in granting the patent.

# Trademark Law

Trademarks and service marks are words, names, symbols, or devices used by manufacturers of goods and providers of services to identify their goods and services, and to distinguish their goods and services from goods manufactured and sold by others.

> *The trademark Wordperfect is used by the Wordperfect Corporation to identify that company's word processing software and distinguish that software from other vendors' word processing software.*

For ease of expression, we will use "trademark" in this book to refer to both trademarks (used on goods) and service marks (used for services).

For trademarks used in commerce, federal trademark protection is available under the federal trademark statute, the Lanham Act. (We will refer to this statute as the Lanham Act in this book.) Many states have trademark registration statutes that resemble the Lanham Act, and all states protect unregistered trademarks under the common (nonstatutory) law of trademarks.

## Types of Works Protected

Examples of words used as trademarks are *Kodak* for cameras and *Burger King* for restaurant services. Examples of slogans used as trademarks are *Fly the Friendly Skies of United* for airline services and *Get a Piece of the Rock* for insurance services. Examples of characters used as trademarks are *Pillsbury Dough Boy* for baked goods and *Aunt Jemima* for breakfast foods.

Sounds can be used as trademarks, such as the jingle used by National Public Radio. Product shapes and configurations, such as the distinctively shaped bottle used for Coca-Cola, can also serve as trademarks.

## Standards

Trademark protection is available for words, names, symbols, or devices that are capable of distinguishing the owner's goods or services from the goods or services of others. A trademark that merely describes a class of goods rather than distinguishing the trademark owner's goods from goods provided by others is not protectible.

*The word "corn flakes" is not protectible as a trademark for cereal because that term describes a type of cereal that is sold by a number of cereal manufacturers rather than distinguishing one cereal manufacturer's goods.*

A trademark that so resembles a trademark already in use in the U.S. as to be likely to cause confusion or mistake is not protectible. Geographically descriptive marks—"Idaho" for potatoes grown in Idaho—are not protectible trademarks for products that originate in the geographical area (all Idaho potato growers should be able to use "Idaho" to market their potatoes).

## Procedure for Getting Protection

The most effective trademark protection is obtained by filing a trademark registration application in the Patent and Trademark Office. Federal law also protects unregistered trademarks, but such protection is limited to the geographic area in which the mark is actually being used.

### Federal Protection

Federal registration is limited to trademarks used in interstate commerce (or intended for use in interstate commerce). Before November, 1989, a trademark application could be filed only after the trademark's owner had actually used the trademark in commerce. Under current law, a person who has a "bona fide" intention to use a trademark in commerce may apply to register the trademark.

For federally registered marks, the use of notice of federal registration is optional. A federal registrant may give notice that his or her trademark is registered by displaying with the trademark the words "Registered in U.S. Patent and Trademark Office" or the symbol "®".

### State Protection

State trademark protection under common law is obtained simply by adopting a trademark and using it in connection with goods or services. This protection is limited to the geographic area in which the trademark is actually being used.

State statutory protection is obtained by filing an application with the state trademark office. Those relying on state trademark law for protection cannot use the federal trademark registration symbol, but they can use the symbol "™" (or, for a service mark, "℠").

### Exclusive Rights

Trademark law in general, whether federal or state, protects a trademark owner's commercial identity (goodwill, reputation, and investment in advertising) by giving the trademark owner the exclusive right to use the trademark on the type of goods or services for which the owner is using the trademark. Any person who uses a trademark in connection with goods or services in a way that is likely to cause confusion is an infringer. Trademark owners can obtain injunctions against the confusing use of their trademarks by others, and they can collect damages for infringement.

> *Small Multimedia Co. is selling a line of interactive training works under the trademark Personal Tutor. If Giant Multimedia Co. starts selling interactive training works under the trademark Personal Tutor, purchasers may think that Giant's works come from the same source as Small Multimedia's works. Giant is infringing Small's trademark.*

Tips on how to avoid trademark infringement in naming your multimedia products are given in Chapter 15.

One of the most important benefits of federal registration of a trademark is the nationwide nature of the rights obtained. For the registrant, federal registration in effect reserves the right to start using the mark in new areas of the U.S.

> *Small Multimedia Co., a California corporation, obtained a federal trademark registration on the trademark Abra for videogames. Small Multimedia Co. did not begin using the trademark on videogames in New York until two years after it obtained its federal registration. In the meantime, Giant Co. had started using Abra on videogames in New York. Because Small Multimedia Co.'s federal registration gives Small a right to use Abra that is superior to Giant Co.'s right to use Abra, Small Multimedia Co. can stop Giant Co. from using Abra on videogames in New York—even though Giant started using Abra on videogames in New York before Small did.*

For other advantages of federal registration, see "Trademark Protection," Chapter 16.

A trademark owner's rights under state trademark law (and the rights of an unregistered trademark owner under federal law) are generally limited to the geographical area in which the owner has used the trademark.

> *(For this example, we changed just one fact from the previous example.) Small Multimedia Co. did not get a federal trademark registration. Now Giant's right to use Abra on videogames in New York is superior to Small Multimedia Co.'s right to use Abra on videogames in New York, because Giant was the first to actually use the trademark on videogames in New York.*

### Duration

A certificate of federal trademark registration remains in effect for 10 years, provided that an affidavit of continued use is filed in the sixth year. A federal registration may be renewed for any number of successive 10-year terms so long as the mark is still in use in commerce. The duration of state registrations varies from state to state. Common law rights endure so long as use of the trademark continues.

### Limitations of the Exclusive Rights

Trademark law does not give protection against use of the trademark that is unlikely to cause confusion, mistake, or deception among consumers, but dilution laws may provide such protection (see "Dilution," Chapter 15).

*Western Software has a federal registration for the use of Flash on multimedia development tool software. If Giant Co. starts using Flash on desktop publishing software, Giant Co. may be infringing Western Software's trademarks because consumers may think the desktop publishing software and the multimedia development tool software come from the same source. If Giant Co. starts using Flash on fire extinguishers, though, Giant Co. is probably not infringing Western's trademark. Consumers are unlikely to think that the Flash software and the Flash fire extinguishers come from the same source.*

## Trade Secret Law

A trade secret is information of any sort that is valuable to its owner, not generally known, and that has been kept secret by the owner. Trade secrets are protected only under state law. The Uniform Trade Secrets Act, in effect in a number of states, defines trade secrets as "information, including a formula, pattern, compilation, program, device, method, technique, or process that derives independent economic value from not being generally known and not being readily ascertainable and is subject to reasonable efforts to maintain secrecy."

### Types of Works Protected

The following types of technical and business information are examples of material that can be protected by trade secret law:

- Customer lists.
- Designs.
- Instructional methods.
- Manufacturing processes and product formulas.
- Document-tracking processes.

Inventions and processes that are not patentable can be protected under trade secret law. Patent applicants generally rely on trade secret law to protect their inventions while the patent applications are pending.

### Standards

Six factors are generally used to determine whether material is a trade secret:

- The extent to which the information is known outside the claimant's business.
- The extent to which the information is known by the claimant's employees.
- The extent of measures taken by the claimant to guard the secrecy of the information.
- The value of the information to the claimant and the claimant's competitors.
- The amount of effort or money expended by the claimant in developing the information.
- The ease with which the information could be acquired by others.

Information has value if it gives rise to actual or potential commercial advantage for the owner of the information. Although a trade secret need not be unique in the patent law sense, information that is generally known is not protected under trade secrets law.

### Procedure for Getting Protection

Trade secret protection attaches automatically when information of value to the owner is kept secret by the owner.

### Exclusive Rights

A trade secret owner has the right to keep others from misappropriating and using the trade secret. Sometimes the misappropriation is a result of industrial espionage. Many trade secret cases involve people who have taken their former employers' trade secrets for use in new businesses or for new employers.

Trade secret protection endures so long as the requirements for protection—generally, value to the owner and secrecy—continue to be met. The protection is lost if the owner fails to take reasonable steps to keep the information secret.

*After Sam discovered a new method for manipulating images in multimedia works, he demonstrated his new method to a number of other developers at a multimedia conference. Sam lost his trade secret protection for the image manipulation method because he failed to keep his method secret.*

### Limitations on the Exclusive Rights

Trade secret owners have recourse only against misappropriation. Discovery of protected information through independent research or reverse engineering (taking a product apart to see how it works) is not misappropriation.

## International Protection

To obtain patent, trademark, and trade secret protection in another country, you must comply with that country's requirements for obtaining protection. For these intellectual property rights, there are no international conventions that provide automatic protection for U.S. rights owners.

# 4

## Ownership of Copyrights

This chapter covers the Copyright Act's ownership rules, and, in less detail, the ownership rules for patents, trademarks, and trade secrets. Ownership rules discussed here apply only in the United States (other countries have their own rules of intellectual property ownership).

Ownership issues that arise in specific types of relationships are covered in Chapters 6, 7, 8, 18, and 19.

### Understanding the Copyright Act

If you are a multimedia developer or publisher, you should become familiar with the Copyright Act's ownership rules. Multimedia works and many of their components—music, graphics, text, software, and video, film, and television show clips—are protected by copyright. If you fail to deal with ownership issues while creating a multimedia work, you may not have clear title to the work and all its components. If there is uncertainty concerning your title to the work, it may complicate distribution of the work.

*April hired Don, a freelance software designer, on a contract basis to develop the software for April's multimedia work. April and Don did not discuss who would own the copyright in the software. According to the Copyright Act's "default" rule for works created on commission by independent contractors, Don owns the copyright in the software.*

The Copyright Act's default rules on ownership apply if the parties—employer and employee, employer and independent contractor, developer and client, or developer and publisher—do not reach their own agreement on ownership. Those rules are discussed in "Initial Ownership" and "The Work Made for Hire Rule" in this chapter.

### Initial Ownership

Ownership of copyright initially belongs to the author or authors of the work.

*Sarah, a photographer, took a photograph of the Lincoln Memorial. Sarah is the author of the photograph and the initial owner of the copyright in the photograph.*

The "author" is generally the individual who created the work, but there is an exception for "works made for hire." This exception is discussed in the next section.

## The Work Made for Hire Rule

The "author" of a work made for hire is the employer or hiring party for whom the work was prepared. This default ownership rule is known as the work made for hire rule. Unless the parties have agreed otherwise in a signed written document, the employer or hiring party owns the copyright of a work made for hire.

There are actually two branches to the work made for hire rule: one covering works made by employees, and one covering specially commissioned works. We discuss these in this section.

### Works Made by Employees

A work created by an employee within the scope of his or her employment is a work made for hire. The employer for whom the work is made is the "author" of the work for copyright purposes and is the owner of the work's copyright (unless the employee and employer have agreed otherwise).

*As part of his job, John, an employee of Big Co.'s training division, created a training film using Big Co.'s facilities. Even though John created the film, Big Co. is the author for copyright purposes. Big Co. owns the copyright in the film (unless John and Big Co. have agreed in a signed contract that John owns the copyright).*

The work made for hire rule does not give employers ownership of works made by employees outside the scope of their employment.

*Darryl, an engineer at Productions, Inc., wrote the script for Productions' newest multimedia work on his own initiative on weekends. Because Darryl did not write the script within the scope of his employment, the work made for hire rule does not apply. If Productions wants ownership of the copyright in the script, it must get an "assignment" (discussed in "Assignments," later in this chapter) from Darryl.*

### Specially Commissioned Works

The second category of works made for hire is limited to eight types of specially ordered or commissioned works. These are works commissioned for use as:

- A contribution to a collective work.

- Part of a motion picture or other audiovisual work.

- A translation.

- A supplementary work.

- A compilation.

- An instructional text.

- A test or answer material for a test.

- An atlas.

For these types of works, if the hiring party and independent contractor creating the work agree in writing to designate the work as a work made for hire, the work is a work made for hire. If the parties do not have an agreement to treat the independent contractor's work as a work made for hire, it's not a work made for hire.

- *April hired Don, a software developer, to design the software for April's multimedia work.*
- *April and Don did not agree in writing to consider the software a work made for hire, so the software is not a work made for hire. Don owns the copyright in the software.*

Even if the hiring party and independent contractor agree in writing to consider the independent contractor's work a work made for hire, the work is not a work made for hire unless it falls into one of the eight special categories listed in the first paragraph of this subsection.

- *Sarah commissioned John, a freelance painter, to do an oil painting of Sarah's home.*
- *Although Sarah and John agreed in writing that the painting would be considered a work made for hire, the written agreement does not make the painting a work made for hire because the painting is not in one of the eight categories of works that can be specially commissioned works made for hire.*

The rules governing ownership of copyrights in works created before January 1, 1978 (the effective date of the Copyright Act of 1976), were different from the rules described in this chapter. The 1909 Copyright Act did not distinguish between employees and independent contractors (works created by both independent contractors and employees were automatically owned by the employer or hiring party unless the parties agreed otherwise). In a 1989 case, *Community for Creative Non-Violence v. Reid*, the U.S. Supreme Court made it clear that the current Copyright Act does distinguish between employees and independent contractors.

The issue in Reid was who owned the copyright in a sculpture created by the artist Reid for the Community for Creative Non-Violence (CCNV). The Court concluded that the work made for hire rule did not apply for two reasons: Reid was not an employee of CCNV, and the sculpture was not one of the eight types of works that could be designated a work made for hire by written agreement of the parties.

### Foreign Copyright Law

The work made for hire rule discussed in this chapter and in other chapters of this book applies to copyrights in the United States. Other countries have different rules on copyright ownership. Although many countries have rules similar to the first branch of the Copyright Act's rule (works made by employees), the second branch (specially commissioned works) is not covered by most countries' work made for hire rules.

To obtain international copyright ownership for works that fall within the second branch of the Copyright Act's work made for hire rule, parties that commission works should obtain "assignments" of copyrights (see "Assignments," later in this chapter) from independent contractors. Ownership of independent contractors' works is discussed in "Copyright Ownership," Chapter 8.

## Joint Authorship and Ownership

According to the Copyright Act, the authors of a joint work jointly own the copyright in the work they create. A joint work is defined in Section 101 of the Copyright Act as "a work prepared by two or more authors with the intention that their contributions be merged into inseparable or interdependent parts of a unitary whole."

- *Ann and Bruce worked together to create a multimedia work, with Ann developing the software and user interface and Bruce developing the content. The work is a joint work, and Ann and Bruce jointly own the copyright.*

You do not become the author of a joint work merely by contributing ideas or supervision to a work. You do so by contributing material that meets the standards for copyright protection (see "Standards," Chapter 2).

- *Susan suggested that John write a book on how to beat the stock market, and John did so. Susan is not a joint author of John's book.*

When the copyright in a work is jointly owned, each joint owner can use or license the work in the United States without the consent of the other owner, provided that the use does not destroy the value of the work and the parties do not have an agreement requiring the consent of each owner for use or licensing. A joint owner who licenses a work must share any royalties he or she receives with the other owners.

The issue of joint ownership has arisen in a dispute about the ownership of the copyright in the *Spaceship Warlock* product. In a lawsuit filed in San Francisco, Joe Sparks, who worked on *Spaceship Warlock*, claims he is joint owner of the copyright in the product. However,

Michael Saenz of Reactor, Inc. claims that Sparks was an employee of Reactor. If Sparks was an employee and his work on the project was within the scope of his employment, Reactor would be the owner of the copyright in *Spaceship Warlock* (see "The Work Made for Hire Rule," this chapter, and "Works Made by Employees," Chapter 7). If Sparks was not an employee, he could be a joint owner of the copyright, entitled to 50 percent of the profits from the sale of this product.

Many foreign countries (Germany and France, for example) require that all joint owners consent to the grant of a license. Generally, joint ownership is not recommended because of the complications it adds to licensing worldwide rights. In addition, it is unclear what effect the filing of bankruptcy by one joint owner would have on co-owners.

## Community Property

In nine states (Arizona, California, Idaho, Louisiana, Nevada, New Mexico, Texas, Washington, and Wisconsin), any property acquired during a marriage is jointly owned by the husband and wife. Several years ago, a court in California held that the copyrights in several books created by a man during his marriage were jointly owned by the man and his wife. The court's reasoning—that the copyrights were community property because they were the result of one spouse's expenditure of time, effort, and skill during the marriage—could apply to patents, trademarks, and trade secrets as well.

## Assignments

A transfer of copyright ownership is known as an assignment. When a copyright is assigned, the assignee (individual or company to whom it is assigned) becomes the owner of the exclusive rights of copyright in the protected work. (These rights are discussed in "The Exclusive Rights," Chapter 2.)

*Tom, an individual working on his own, created multimedia software and then assigned the copyright in the software to Developer. After the assignment, Developer has the exclusive right to reproduce and publicly distribute the software. If Tom starts selling the software, he will be infringing the Developer's rights as copyright owner.*

The ownership of copyright may be transferred in whole or in part. Examples of partial transfers are an assignment of the copyright for a term of 10 years (time limitation) and an assignment limited to California (geographic limitation). In addition, the individual exclusive rights (reproduction, modification, and so forth) can be transferred.

Assignments are common in many industries—for example, music composers often assign copyrights in their compositions to music publishers.

An assignment is not valid unless it is in writing and is signed by the owner of the rights conveyed or the owner's authorized agent.

An assignment can be recorded in the Copyright Office to give others "constructive notice" of the assignment. Constructive notice is a legal term that means you are presumed to know a fact (because it is a matter of public record) even if you have no actual knowledge of the fact. (Constructive notice is discussed in more detail in "Obtaining a License," Chapter 10.)

Recording an assignment in the Copyright Office to give constructive notice protects the assignee from future conflicting transfers. An assignment that is recorded properly within one month after its signing prevails over a later assignment. If the assignment is signed outside the U.S., the assignee has two months to record it. (The benefits of recording are discussed in more detail in "Determining Who Owns the Copyright," Chapter 10.)

> *Songwriter assigned the copyright in her song to Music Publishing Co. in Boston on August 1, 1993. On August 15th of the same year, Songwriter assigned the copyright in the same song to Media Enterprises. So long as Music Publishing Co. recorded its assignment properly in the Copyright Office by September 1, Music Publishing Co. owns the copyright because its assignment prevails over Songwriter's later assignment to Media Enterprises.*

A properly recorded assignment even prevails over an earlier assignment that was not recorded if the later assignment meets two criteria:

- The later assignment was taken in good faith and without notice of the earlier assignment.

- The assignee paid money or something of value for the assignment or made a promise to pay royalties.

> *Author assigned the copyright in his novel to Publishing, Inc. on November 1, 1993. Publishing, Inc. did not record the assignment. On January 15, 1994, Author assigned the copyright in the same novel to Media, Inc. for $10,000. Media, Inc. recorded its assignment in the Copyright Office. So long as Media, Inc. acted in good faith and did not know or have reason to know about Author's 1993 assignment to Publishing, Inc., Media, Inc. owns the copyright. The assignment to Media, Inc. prevails over Author's earlier assignment to Publishing, Inc.*

## Licenses

A license is a copyright owner's grant of permission to use a copyrighted work in a way that would otherwise be copyright infringement. A copyright owner who grants a license is known as a licensor. A party receiving a license is known as a licensee.

Implied in every license is a promise by the licensor to refrain from suing the licensee for infringement based on activities within the scope of the license.

A copyright license can be exclusive or nonexclusive. An exclusive license is a license that does not overlap another grant of rights.

*Author granted Publisher the exclusive right to sell Author's novel in the United States. She granted Movie Developer the exclusive right to create and distribute a movie version of the novel. Both Publisher and Developer have exclusive licenses. There is no overlap between the two licenses.*

Under copyright law, an exclusive license is considered a transfer of copyright ownership. An exclusive license, like an assignment, is not valid unless it is in writing and signed by the owner of the rights conveyed. A nonexclusive license is valid even if it is not in writing.

An exclusive license, like an assignment, can be recorded in the Copyright Office to give constructive notice. Recording the exclusive license protects the license against unrecorded earlier transfers of copyright ownership and against later transfers. (See "Assignments," earlier in this chapter.)

Licensing is discussed in detail in Chapter 10.

## Termination Right

The author of a work other than a work made for hire has the right to terminate any license or assignment granted on or after January 1, 1978 during a five-year period that starts 35 years after the grant was made. If the grant involves the right to distribute the work to the public, the termination period begins 35 years after distribution begins or 40 years after the grant was made, whichever is earlier. For works published before January 1, 1978, the five-year termination period begins 56 years after the work was first published.

The termination right cannot be waived in advance. If the author dies before the termination period begins, the termination right can be exercised by the author's widow or widower, children, and grandchildren.

## Owning a Copy of a Work

Copyright law distinguishes the ownership of a copy of a protected work (a print of a photograph, a compact disc, a book, a diskette) from ownership of the intangible copyright rights. The transfer of a copy of a work does not transfer any rights in the copyright. Thus, purchasing a book (a copy of a literary work, in copyright terminology) does not give you permission to make copies of the book and sell those copies.

There are two exceptions to the preceding paragraph's first sentence. If you buy a copy of a work, you have a right to resell (distribute) that copy. This exception is known as the "first sale doctrine." You also have the right to display your copy publicly, "either directly or by the projection of no more than one image at a time, to viewers present at the place where the copy is located." These two exceptions do not give you any right to exercise the copyright owner's reproduction, modification, or public performance rights. (The five exclusive rights are discussed in "The Exclusive Rights," Chapter 2).

*Don bought a copy of Publisher's multimedia work. Don can resell his copy of the work. The "first sale doctrine" gives him that right. If he makes copies of the work, though, he will be infringing Publisher's copyright.*

## Patents, Trademarks, and Trade Secrets

Patent law does not have a work made for hire rule. Patentable inventions created by employees within the scope of their employment are owned by the employee. However, the employee may have a legal obligation to transfer ownership to the employer under patent law's "hired to invent" doctrine. This doctrine provides that when an employee is hired to perform research or solve a specific problem, the employer is entitled to get an assignment of a patent received by the employee on the results of the research.

Generally, as a condition of employment, employers require employees to agree to assign their interests in patentable inventions to the employer. The Patent Act implicitly recognizes the validity of such agreements, providing that a patent may be granted to the assignee of the inventor.

A trademark is owned by the first party to use it in connection with goods or services or the first to apply to register it. A trademark can be owned by an individual, company, or any other legal entity. Trademark rights are discussed extensively in Chapter 15.

An employer or hiring party generally owns trade secrets developed by employees and by independent contractors who are hired to invent.

Ownership of patents, trade secrets, and trademarks, like the ownership of copyrights, can be assigned. As with copyrights, owners of these types of intellectual property frequently grant licenses authorizing others to do things that would otherwise violate the owner's exclusive rights.

# 5

## Contracts Law

Multimedia developers enter into business relationships with both individuals and businesses to help them create and distribute multimedia works. Most of these relationships result in "contracts" with legal consequences. Most contracts don't have to be in writing to be enforceable.

The purpose of this chapter—one of the "building block" chapters—is to provide an overview of the basic principles of contracts law.

In later chapters, we discuss special types of contracts: Development agreements are discussed in Chapter 6, contracts with employees are discussed in Chapter 7, contracts with independent contractors are discussed in Chapter 8, and distribution agreements are discussed in Chapters 18 and 19. The special legal rules that apply to contracts for the sale of goods are discussed in Chapter 17.

### What Is a Contract?

A contract is a legally enforceable agreement between two or more parties. The core of most contracts is a set of mutual promises (in legal terminology, "consideration"). The promises made by the parties define the rights and obligations of the parties.

Contracts are enforceable in the courts. If one party meets its contractual obligations and the other party doesn't ("breaches the contract"), the nonbreaching party is entitled to receive relief through the courts.

*Developer promised to pay Graphic Designer $5000 for creating certain promotional materials for Developer's multimedia work. Graphic Designer created the materials and delivered them to Developer, as required in the contract. Developer admits that the materials meet the contract specifications. If Developer does not pay Graphic Designer, Graphic Designer can go to court and get a judgment against Developer for breach of contract.*

Generally, the nonbreaching party's remedy for breach of contract is money damages that will put the nonbreaching party in the position it would have enjoyed if the contract had been performed. Under special circumstances, a court will order the breaching party to perform its contractual obligations.

Because contracts are enforceable, parties who enter into contracts can rely on contracts in structuring their business relationships.

> *Developer entered into a contract with Composer, promising to pay Composer $4000 for composing a brief composition for Developer's multimedia work. Shortly after Composer started work on the piece for Developer—before Developer paid Composer any money— Composer got an offer from a movie studio to compose all the music for a movie and abandoned Developer's project. Developer had to pay another composer $6000 to do the work that Composer had contracted to do. Developer can sue Composer and obtain a judgment against Composer for $2000 (the amount that will result in Developer's obtaining the music for a net cost of $4000, the contract price).*

In this country and most others, businesses have significant flexibility in setting the terms of their contracts. Contracts are, in a sense, private law created by the agreement of the parties. The rights and obligations of the parties are determined by the contract's terms, subject to limits imposed by relevant statutes.

> *Developer promised to pay Composer $5000 to create music for Developer's multimedia training work. Composer created the music and delivered it to Developer, as required in the contract. Developer did not pay Composer, so Composer sued Developer for breach of contract. Developer's defense was "Composer did what she promised to do, but I never should have agreed to pay her $5000 for that work. $2000 is a fair price." The court will enforce Developer's promise to pay Composer $5000.*

## Written Contracts

A deal done on a handshake—"You do X for me, and I'll pay you Y"—is a contract, because it is a legally enforceable agreement involving an exchange of promises. Most contracts are enforceable whether they are oral or written. Nonetheless, you should always have written contracts for all your business relationships.

There are several reasons why written contracts are better than oral contracts:

- The process of writing down the contract's terms and signing the contract forces both parties to think about—and be precise about—the obligations they are undertaking. With an oral contract, it is too easy for both parties to say "yes" and then have second thoughts.

- When the terms of a contract are written down, the parties are likely to create a more complete and thorough agreement than they would by oral agreement. A hastily made oral agreement is likely to have gaps that will have to be resolved later—when the relationship may have deteriorated.

- With an oral contact, the parties may have different recollections of what they agreed on (just as two witnesses to a car accident will disagree over what happened). A written agreement eliminates disputes over who promised what.

- Some types of contracts must be in writing to be enforced. The Copyright Act requires a copyright assignment or exclusive license to be in writing (see "Assignments" and "Licenses," Chapter 4). State law requirements vary from state to state, but in most states, a contract for the sale of goods for $500 or more must be in writing (see "Important Provisions of Article Two," Chapter 17).

- If you have to go to court to enforce a contract or get damages, a written contract will mean less dispute about the contract's terms.

## Who Can Enter Into a Contract?

Minors and the mentally incompetent lack the legal capacity to enter into contracts. All others are generally assumed to have full power to bind themselves by entering into contracts. In most states, the legal age for entering into contracts is 18. The test for mental capacity is whether the party understood the nature and consequences of the transaction in question.

Corporations have the power to enter into contracts. They make contracts through the acts of their agents, officers, and employees. Whether a particular employee has the power to bind the corporation to a contract is determined by an area of law called agency law or corporate law. If you doubt whether an individual with whom you are dealing has authority to enter into a contract with you, insist that the contract be reviewed and signed by the corporation's president.

A corporation has a separate legal existence from its founders, officers, and employees. Generally, the individuals associated with a corporation are not themselves responsible for the corporation's debts or liabilities, including liability for breach of contract.

## Offer and Acceptance

A contract is formed when one party (the "offeror") makes an offer which is accepted by the other party (the "offeree"). An offer—a proposal to form a contract—can be as simple as the words, "I'll wash your car for you for $5." An acceptance—the offeree's assent to the terms of the offer—can be as simple as, "You've got a deal." Sometimes acceptance can be shown by conduct rather than by words.

When an offer has been made, no contract is formed until the offeree accepts the offer. When you make an offer, never assume that the offeree will accept the offer. Contractual liability is based on consent.

> *Developer offered to pay Photographer $500 to use Photographer's photo in Developer's multimedia work. Photographer said, "Let me think about it." Developer, assuming that Photographer would accept the offer, went ahead and used the photo. Photographer then rejected Developer's offer. Developer has infringed Photographer's copyright by reproducing the photograph for use in the multimedia work. Developer must now either remove the photo from the multimedia work before distributing the work (or showing the work to others) or reach an agreement with Photographer.*

When you are an offeree, do not assume that an offer will remain open indefinitely. In general, an offeror is free to revoke the offer at any time before acceptance by the offeree. Once the offeror terminates the offer, the offeree no longer has the legal power to accept the offer and form a contract.

> *Animator offered his services to Developer, who said, "I'll get back to you." Developer then contracted with Client to quickly produce a multimedia work involving animation (making the assumption that Animator was still available to do the animation work). Before Developer could tell Animator that he accepted Animator's offer, Animator sent Developer a fax that said, "Leaving for Mexico. I'll call when I get back." Developer and Animator did not have a contract. Developer should not have assumed, in entering into the contract with Client, that Animator was still available.*

When you are the offeree, do not start contract performance before notifying the offeror of your acceptance. Prior to your acceptance, there is no contract. An offer can be accepted by starting performance if the offer itself invites such acceptance, but this type of offer is rare.

> *Big Co. offered to pay Developer $5000 to create a corporate presentation multimedia work for Big Co. Before Developer's president notified Big Co. that Developer accepted the offer, Big Co. sent Developer a fax that said, "We've changed our minds. Due to budget cuts at Big Co., we can't afford to do the multimedia project." In the meantime, Developer's staff had begun preliminary work on the project. Developer and Big Co. did not have a contract, so Developer has no legal recourse against Big Co. for loss of the deal or for the costs of the preliminary work.*

Until an offer is accepted, the offeror is free—unless it has promised to hold the offer open—to revoke the offer.

> *On June 1, Big Co. offered to hire Developer to create an interactive training work for Big Co. On June 4 (before acceptance by Developer), Big Co. notified Developer that it was giving the contract to Developer's competitor. Big Co. terminated the offer to Developer. Developer has no legal recourse against Big Co.*

If you need time to make up your mind before accepting an offer, get the offeror to give you a written promise to hold the offer open for a few days. That will give you time to decide whether to accept.

Don't reject an offer and then try to accept it. Once an offeree rejects an offer, the offer dies and the offeree's legal power to accept the offer and form a contract terminates.

> *Publisher offered to buy all rights in Developer's multimedia work for $100,000. Developer, hoping for a better offer, said no. Then Developer realized that Publisher's offer was the best Developer could do. Developer called Publisher and said, "I accept your offer." Because the offer was no longer open, Developer cannot form a contract by trying to accept the offer.*

Except for the simplest deals, it generally takes more than one round of negotiations to form a contract. Often, the offeree responds to the initial offer with a counter-offer. A counter-offer is an offer made by an offeree on the same subject matter as the original offer, but proposing a different bargain than the original offer. A counter-offer, like an outright rejection, terminates the offeree's legal power of acceptance.

> *Publisher offered to buy all rights in Developer's multimedia work for $100,000. Developer responded by saying, "I'll give you the right to distribute the work in the U.S. for $100,000." Developer's response to the offer was a counter-offer. Developer no longer has the legal power to form a contract based on Publisher's offer to purchase all rights in the work.*

## Consideration

Consideration, in legal terminology, is what one party to a contract will get from the other party in return for performing contract obligations.

> *Developer promised to pay Artist $500 if Artist would let Developer use one of Artist's drawings in Developer's multimedia work. The consideration for Developer's promise to pay Artist $500 is Artist's promise to let Developer use the drawing. The consideration for Artist's promise to let Developer use the drawing is Developer's promise to pay Artist $500.*

According to traditional legal doctrine, if one party makes a promise and the other party offers nothing in exchange for that promise, the promise is unenforceable. Such a promise is known as a "gratuitous promise." Gratuitous promises are said to be "unenforceable for lack of consideration."

> *John told Sam, "When I buy a new car, I'll give you my truck." John bought a new car but did not give Sam the truck. According to traditional legal doctrine, John's promise to give Sam the truck is an unenforceable gratuitous promise. Sam gave nothing to John in exchange for John's promise to give Sam the truck.*

In some states, a gratuitous promise can be enforced if the party to whom the promise was made relied on the promise. Other states no longer require consideration for certain types of promises.

Lack of consideration is rarely a problem for promises made in the context of business relationships. In most business contracts, there is consideration for both parties ("mutual consideration," in legal terminology).

The lack of consideration problem can arise in the context of amendments to contracts. Also, in some states, a promise to hold an offer open (see "Offer and Acceptance," earlier in of this chapter) is unenforceable unless the offeree gives the offeror consideration (pays the offeror money) to keep the offer open.

A special application of the problem of lack of consideration in contracts with employees is discussed in "Using the Employment Agreement," Chapter 7.

## Typical Contract Provisions

Many contracts include special types of provisions. We'll discuss these common types of provisions in the next subsections.

### Duties and Obligations

The duties and obligations section of a contract is a detailed description of the duties and obligations of the parties and the deadlines for performance. If one party's obligation is to create a multimedia work, software, or content for a multimedia work, detailed specifications should be stated.

### Representations and Warranties

A warranty is a legal promise that certain facts are true. Typical representations or warranties in contracts concern such matters as ownership of the contract's subject matter (for example, real estate) and the right to sell or assign the subject matter. In multimedia industry contracts, warranties of ownership of intellectual property rights and noninfringement of third parties' intellectual property rights are common. These warranties are discussed in "The Contract," Chapter 6, in "Contracts with Independent Contractors," Chapter 8, in "Obtaining a License," Chapter 10, in "Warranties," Chapter 18, and in "Due Diligence," Chapter 19.

For contracts involving the sale of goods, certain warranties are implied under state law unless they are specifically disclaimed by the parties (see "Important Provisions of Article Two," Chapter 17).

### Termination Clauses

These clauses ensure that either or both parties have the right to terminate the contract under certain circumstances. Generally, termination clauses describe breach of contract events that trigger the right to terminate the contract (for example, nonpayment of royalties). Termination clauses also describe the methods of giving notice of exercise of the termination right, and whether the breaching party must be given an opportunity to cure the breach before the other party can terminate the contract.

### Remedy Clauses

These clauses state what rights the nonbreaching party has if the other party breaches the contract. In contracts for the sale of goods, remedy clauses are usually designed to limit the seller's liability for damages (see "Important Provisions of Article Two," Chapter 17).

### Arbitration Clauses

An arbitration clause states that disputes arising under the contract must be settled through arbitration rather than through court litigation. Such clauses generally include the name of the organization that will conduct the arbitration (the American Arbitration Association, for example), the city in which the arbitration will be held, and the method for selecting arbitrators. Arbitration is discussed in "Arbitration," Chapter 1.

### Merger Clauses

Merger clauses state that the written document contains the entire understanding of the parties. The purpose of merger clauses is to ensure that evidence outside the written document will not be admissible in court to contradict or supplement the terms of the written agreement.

## Tips for Contracts

The contract formation process varies widely, from contracts formed quickly in face-to-face meetings to contracts formed after teams of attorneys have spent months in negotiations. Contracts covering specific multimedia industry relationships are covered elsewhere in this book: Development agreements are covered in Chapter 6, contracts with employees are covered in Chapter 7, contracts with independent contractors are covered in Chapter 8, and distribution agreements are covered in Chapter 18. (The publisher's perspective on distribution agreements is covered in Chapter 19.)

Here are some general tips for all types of contracts:

- *Write it down.* All contracts should take the form of a written document signed by both parties. You do not have to hire an attorney to create a written contract. If you reach an agreement over the phone or in a meeting, write the agreement as soon as possible and have the other party sign the written memorandum. If you are making a written offer, you may want to make your offer in the form of a letter, with a space at the end for the offeree to indicate acceptance by signing.

- *Make sure you are comfortable with your obligations.* If a term—for example, a deadline—makes you uneasy, make a counter-offer that substitutes a term with which you are more comfortable. Do not assume that the other party will excuse you from strict compliance and do not rely on the other party's oral assurances that it will not insist on strict compliance.

- *Remember Murphy's Law.* Before you sign a contract, consider what could go wrong or what could make performance of your obligations difficult or expensive. If the actual performance is more difficult or expensive than you anticipated, that is not a valid excuse for not performing. Enter into a contract only if you believe that you can meet your obligations.

- *Don't leave anything out.* Accurately cover all aspects of your understanding with the other party. If the other party wrote the agreement based on an oral understanding reached earlier, make certain that the written terms match the terms of your oral agreement. Don't leave points out of the written document, even if the other party says, "We don't need to put that in writing."

- *Cover all options.* Cover all options, consequences, and possibilities. You should not fail to address an issue because it is "sensitive." Deal with the sensitive issue during the negotiations. Make sure that your contract includes a merger clause (see "Typical Contract Provisions," earlier in this chapter) to avoid disputes about whether proposals made during negotiations but not included in the final written agreement are part of your contract.

- *Don't use unclear language or try to sound like a lawyer.* If you don't understand exactly what the other party is expecting you to do, don't try to camouflage the lack of understanding by using vague language. Vague language leads to misunderstandings, disputes, and lawsuits. Use simple language that accurately expresses your agreement with the other party. Don't try to sound like a lawyer, and don't complicate things unnecessarily.

- *Define any ambiguous terms.* There's a classic contracts case in which one party contracted to sell chickens to the other party. The seller thought "chicken" meant chicken of any age, including old and tough chickens. The buyer assumed "chicken" meant tender young chickens suitable for frying. The seller shipped old chickens, and the buyer screamed "breach." To avoid such misunderstandings, define any terms that may be ambiguous.

- *Be careful using "terms of art."* Terms of art are words with specific meaning in the law. "Assignment," for example, has a number of meanings in the English language. In intellectual property law, "assignment" means a transfer of ownership of intellectual property (see "Assignments," Chapter 4). Use "assignment" in your contracts when you mean transfer of ownership of intellectual property. Don't use the word in its other meanings or you will create confusion. A number of terms of art are defined throughout this book.

- *Use terms consistently.* When you write contracts, you are creating your own "law." Legal writing is not creative writing. Don't use "royalty" in one paragraph, "license fee" in a second paragraph, and "use fee" in a third paragraph to refer to the same concept. Pick one term and stay with it throughout the contract.

# 2

## Production Relationships

# 6

## Development Agreements

This chapter covers the special legal issues that a developer should consider when asked by a client to create a multimedia work. Most of these issues are equally applicable to development agreements between a developer and a publisher. Joint development projects are covered at the end of the chapter.

### Proposals and Bids

Don't spend a lot of time and effort on a proposal for a potential client without first qualifying the client. Make sure that the client is seriously considering the project and has the ability to pay for the work.

Make certain that the person with whom you are dealing has the authority to approve the project. If that person does not have the authority, find out as soon as possible whether the person with authority is really interested in doing the project.

Don't start work on the project until the client has signed a written contract. Your proposal to a client is an offer. Until your client accepts the offer, there is no contract (see "Offer and Acceptance," Chapter 5).

Some companies send requests for proposals (RFPs) to several multimedia developers. Responding to an RFP takes considerable time and effort. If you respond with a bid but do not get the contract, you will have no legal basis for getting reimbursement for your costs from the company that sent out the RFP.

Any proposal that you send to a potential client is protected by copyright. However, copyright protection does not cover the ideas used in the bid (see "Limitations on the Exclusive Rights," Chapter 2). If the recipient of a proposal photocopies all or part of your proposal, that's copyright infringement. If the recipient hires another multimedia developer to create a multimedia work based on the ideas used in your proposal, that's not copyright infringement. You may be able to get some protection for a proposal containing novel ideas by getting your potential client to sign a nondisclosure agreement (Form 1 in Appendix B).

Make your proposals in writing. Oral proposals are rarely complete (it is difficult in a phone conversation or face-to-face meeting to remember everything that you need to tell the client). If you make an oral proposal and it is accepted, you still should have the client sign a written contract (see "Written Contracts," Chapter 5). If the written contract contains terms that you did not mention in your oral proposal, the client may think that you are trying to change the deal.

Some multimedia developers have a standard proposal format that they use with all clients. This saves time and eliminates the possibility that a key provision will be left out of a particular proposal.

If your bid is accepted, you will be bound by the price and terms of your bid. If you discover that you made a mistake in calculating the bid price—you forgot to add in the cost of hiring a music composer, for example—you will probably still have to do the work at the bid price and absorb the added cost yourself (and that will lower your profit). It is difficult to cancel contracts made through the bid process.

## The Contract

An agreement between a developer and a client should always take the form of a written contract signed by both parties (see "Written Contracts," Chapter 5). If your written proposal to a client is complete, you and your client can form a contract by having the client sign the proposal to indicate acceptance. You may want to finish your proposals with acceptance instructions, such as, "If you wish to accept this proposal and form a contract on the terms stated in this proposal, please sign below and return this proposal to me." It's permissible for you and your client to make handwritten changes to the proposal or mark provisions out, but both parties should initial any changes or deletions to avoid disputes later.

The balance of this section discusses the issues you should cover in your contract to create a multimedia work for a client.

### Deliverables

In both the formal proposal and the contract, be as specific as possible about what you are to create for the client. Vagueness in the proposal and in the contract can camouflage misunderstanding that will come to light when you deliver the finished work to the client.

The inclusion of a detailed statement of deliverables will help you and your client make certain that you agree on the nature, content, quality, and uses of the work you are promising to create. Some deliverables that are frequently found in development agreements are:

- Statements of technical issues (delivery platforms, choice of programming language, authoring environment, graphic resolution, and so forth).

- Elements (script, storyboards, graphics/design, audio, video, "talent").

- Prototype.

- Beta version.

- Packaging.

- "Gold disk" (final CD-ROM version).

### Content

You should discuss the range of content options with the client before you enter into a contract. If the client is expecting you to use expensive content—an excerpt of Michael Jackson singing *Bad*, for example—the contract should state that requirement (and you should raise your price or get the client to reimburse you for the costly license fees). Be careful not to commit yourself to obtaining rights in specific works, because those works may not be available for licensing. If the client requests specific works, make sure that you have the right to substitute different works if the requested works are not available.

Licensing costs for obtaining permission to use content owned by third parties can be substantial (the licensing process is described in Chapter 10). It may be possible to obtain suitable material relatively inexpensively from stock houses and libraries (see "Stock Houses and Libraries," Chapter 10). A resource list appears in Appendix D.

### Deadlines and Delivery Schedule

The contract should state when you must deliver the finished project to the client. In setting deadlines, remember that it will probably take more time than you expect to clear the rights to any third-party content that is used and to make certain that the components fit together. (Clearing rights is discussed extensively in Chapter 10.)

Make certain that the deadlines are realistic. Serious delay on your part can be grounds for termination by the client—especially if the contract states that "time is of the essence" for performance of contract obligations. If the client is entitled to terminate the contract because of your failure to deliver the project on time, you may have to absorb the costs that went into the project before the termination. Normally, the client will have no obligation to reimburse you for those costs.

The contract should include deadlines for the client's decisions and approvals. Such deadlines will protect you, if the project is finished late because of client delay. In addition, the contract should include an acceptance clause that requires the client to "sign off" on the whole project by a certain date. (See "Acceptance Clause," later in this chapter.)

## Payment

The contract should state the amount and form of your payment—whether it is on a time-and-costs basis, a fixed-price basis, royalty, or other basis—and when payment is due. Some contracts provide for installment payments (for example, one-third upon execution, one-third at the delivery of the gold disk, and one-third when the final product is accepted by the client).

## Acceptance Clause

For your protection, the proposal and contract should provide a procedure for objections to any deliverables. It's a good idea to require that objections be made in writing. There should also be a deadline for objections to the finished project. You need to know that after a certain period of time passes, it will be too late for the client to say, "I won't accept this. Do it again."

## Ownership of Copyright

One of the most important issues to address in the contract is who will own the copyright. By addressing this issue in the written agreement, you will eliminate future legal disputes over ownership. We'll discuss the two ownership options in "Client Ownership" and "Developer Ownership."

### *Client Ownership*

Your client does not obtain ownership of the copyright by paying for its development. For copyright purposes, when you create a multimedia work for a client, you work as an independent contractor, not as the client's employee. (The term "independent contractor" is discussed in "Who is an Independent Contractor?," Chapter 8.) A work created by an independent contractor for a client is generally owned by the independent contractor unless the client obtains an assignment of the copyright (see "Copyright Ownership," Chapter 8).

A work can be automatically owned by the client only in very limited circumstances: if the agreement describes the work as a "work made for hire" and if the work is a one of eight special types of works listed in the Copyright Act's definition of specially commissioned works made for hire (see "The Work Made for Hire Rule," Chapter 4, and "Copyright Ownership," Chapter 8). These rules apply only in the United States.

*Assigning the Copyright*   If the client is to own the rights in the multimedia work, the contract should provide for an assignment of these rights to the client (see "Assignments," Chapter 4). You should be prepared to sign a separate "short form" copyright assignment (Form 2 in Appendix B) for filing with the Copyright Office. Your client may want you to grant it a power of attorney authorizing the client to execute and file assignment documents. If you are married, live in a community property state, and work as an individual, your client may ask that you get your spouse to sign a statement acknowledging that he or she does not claim any ownership interest in the work's copyright (the reason for this is explained in the "Community Property," Chapter 4). This sort of statement is known as a "quitclaim." A quitclaim form is included in Appendix B (Form 3).

***Legal Effect of Assignments***    If you agree to assign the copyright in the multimedia work to the client, you will not be able to sell copies of that work to other clients. Unless you retain the modification right (see "The Exclusive Rights," Chapter 2) or have the client grant you a license to modify the work to create new works (see "Licenses," Chapter 4), you will not be able to modify the work for sale to other clients. Once you assign the copyright, the client will have the exclusive rights to reproduce the work, distribute it, publicly perform it, publicly display it, and modify it for use in derivative works. However, you will still be able to reuse ideas that you used in the work.

***Retaining Ownership of Components***    If you are creating a multimedia work to fill a client's special needs, you may not object to giving the client ownership of the copyright. You may, however, want to retain ownership of components—for example, a software engine—that you created for the work, or at least reserve the right to use the components in future projects. Unless you retain ownership of the components or get a license from your client to reuse them, your use of the components in future projects will infringe the client's copyright. (See "Assignments," Chapter 4.)

> *Developer created an interactive training program that used a software engine for manipulating game images. Developer assigned the copyright in the work to Big Co. If Developer uses the software engine in a new multimedia project without getting a license from Big Co., Developer will be infringing Big Co.'s copyright.*

***Third-Party Components***    Assigning the copyright to the client does not give the client ownership of components owned by third parties. You cannot assign rights that you do not own.

> *The interactive training program that Developer created for Big Co. contained an excerpt of a song written by Joe Composer. Since Developer did not own the copyright in Joe's song, Developer's assignment of its copyright in the program to Big Co. did not give Big Co. ownership of the copyright in Joe's song.*

***Demo Rights and Credits***    If the copyright is to be owned by the client, you may want to include a clause in the contract authorizing you to retain a copy of the work to show to future clients. Such demonstrations are "public performances" of the work. (The term "public performance" is defined in "The Exclusive Rights," Chapter 2.) You may also want to specify how your credit should appear in the client's copies of the multimedia work.

### *Developer Ownership*

If you are to retain the copyright in the multimedia work, the contract should state that you retain copyright ownership. If the contract says nothing about ownership of the copyright, you, as an independent contractor, will automatically own the copyright in the work (see "Copyright Ownership," Chapter 8). However, including a statement to that effect in your contract will help you avoid misunderstandings with clients who think that ordering and paying for a work gets them ownership of the copyright.

If the client contributes "copyrightable" material to the work (see "Standards," Chapter 2), the client may be a joint author and thus a joint owner of the copyright. (Joint ownership is discussed in "Joint Authorship and Ownership," Chapter 4.) Stating in the contract that you will own the copyright in the entire work may help you avoid joint ownership claims by clients.

### Reimbursement of License Fees and Costs

The contract should state whether any license fees, union reuse fees (see "Reuse Provisions," Chapter 14), and other costs you incur in creating the multimedia work will be reimbursed by the client.

### Warranties and Indemnities

The client will probably insist that the contract include representations and warranties from you. Typical warranties in development agreements are as follows:

- You have the right to enter into the agreement.
- You have title to the multimedia work and all intellectual property rights in the work.
- You have the right to grant the client the assignment of copyright or to license the work.
- The work does not infringe third parties' intellectual property rights.

Warranty clauses typically include an indemnity provision in which the developer promises to indemnify and hold the client harmless for the breach of any of the warranties (in other words, pay for all costs arising out of the breach of the warranties).

### *Reason for Warranties*

Clients have good reason for asking for warranties and indemnities. If you infringe any third-party intellectual property rights in making a multimedia work, your client will become an infringer by using the work (even though innocent of intent to infringe).

*Developer created a kiosk-type multimedia work called Cheese Expert for client, owner of a gourmet grocery. Cheese Expert contains pictures of Minnie Mouse and Mickey Mouse. Developer did not obtain permission from Disney to use Minnie and Mickey. Client's "public performance" of Cheese Expert in the grocery store infringes Disney's copyright and trademark rights.*

### Levels of Warranties

There are three levels of intellectual property warranties:

- *The "absolute" warranty.* "The work does not infringe any third-party intellectual property rights."

- *The "know or should know" warranty.* "To the best of my knowledge, the work does not infringe any third-party intellectual property rights."

- *The "actual knowledge" warranty.* "To my actual knowledge, the work does not infringe any third-party intellectual property rights."

As a developer, you should try to negotiate for the "know or should know" warranty or "actual knowledge" warranty rather than the unlimited "absolute" warranty. Although you should do everything possible to ensure that your multimedia work does not infringe third parties' intellectual property rights (see "When You Need a License," Chapter 9), you can never be certain that a work composed of many components does not infringe others' copyrights. For example:

- The employee who created the software code for your work may have reused code that is owned by a former employer (see "Rights of Former Employers," Chapter 7).

- An independent contractor that you hired to create a component may have copied someone else's work.

- A composer who granted you a license to use his music throughout the world may turn out to not be the owner of the copyright in the music in all countries.

You should try to get "absolute" warranties from all your independent contractors and licensors (see "Contracts With Independent Contractors," Chapter 8, and "Obtaining Licenses," Chapter 10).

### Duration of Warranties

The contract should state whether the warranties continue during the term of the contract or are limited to the date on which the final product is delivered to the client.

### *Patent Warranties*

Consider whether you want to warrant that your work does not infringe any patents. Patent applications in the United States are secret, so there is no way you can find out what patents might be granted during the term of your agreement. If you give a warranty that your work does not infringe any patents, you may be liable for infringing a later-issued patent that you did not know about. You may want to limit your exposure. One way to do that is to warrant only that, to the best of your knowledge, the multimedia work does not infringe any patents in effect on the date the finished product is delivered to the client.

## Other Important Provisions

The contract should also contain several other provisions, as explained in the next sub-sections.

### *Modifications*

The contract should state who is responsible for correcting performance errors in the multimedia work. It should state whether the client has any right to require you to make changes to the multimedia work after it is delivered, and if the client must pay for modifications.

If you are retaining ownership of the copyright, the contract should state whether the client has the right to modify the work to correct errors. If the client does not have that right, modification by the client may infringe your modification right (see "The Exclusive Rights," Chapter 2). If the contract provides that the client will own the copyright, the client as owner of the modification right will automatically have the right to make changes.

Many development contracts provide that the developer will make changes to correct performance errors for free during a "warranty period" and will provide maintenance for an annual fee after the warranty period ends.

### *Merger Clause*

The contract should include a merger clause (see "Typical Contract Provisions," Chapter 5) to help eliminate claims that the "real deal" is something other than what is stated in the contract (for example, an earlier proposal that was modified during negotiations).

### *Termination Clause*

The parties may wish to provide that the contract can be terminated for cause (which should be defined) or even at will. Termination clauses are discussed in "Typical Contract Provisions," Chapter 5.

The termination provision should state how notice of breach that justifies termination should be given. The provision should include a "cure period" during which the breaching party has a right to cure the breach and avoid termination of the contract.

### Nondisclosure Agreement

If the client will be giving you access to proprietary or confidential information or trade secrets, you may be asked to include a nondisclosure agreement in the contract (see Form 4 of Appendix B). If you will be disclosing trade secrets and other proprietary information to your client as well, you and your client should both sign a mutual nondisclosure agreement (Form 5 in Appendix B).

The nondisclosure agreement should state what information is to be considered confidential information, and how confidential information must be treated (for example, whether the receiving party can disclose the information to all employees or only to certain employees or to consultants). It should also state the duration of the obligation to keep the information confidential.

Generally, confidential information is defined in one of these two ways:

- Information marked confidential by its owner.

- Information that the receiving party knows or should know is confidential.

If you use the first definition, you need to include a method for identifying confidential information disclosed orally or by exhibition.

The following types of information are generally specifically excluded from the definition of confidential information:

- Information that is in the public domain at the time it is disclosed to the receiving party.

- Information that later enters the public domain (but not through the fault of the receiving party).

- Information that is required to be disclosed by a court or government.

- Information that is received from a third party without restrictions on disclosure.

Another exception, which is more controversial, is "independent development." This is information that is independently developed by the receiving party. Some agreements require the party claiming that information is not confidential under this exception to bear the burden of proving that it independently developed the information.

### *Disclaimer of Implied Warranties*

When goods are sold, according to the law of every state except Louisiana, certain warranties are implied as part of the transaction unless they are disclaimed. Because a contract for the development of a multimedia work could be considered a contract for the sale of goods, implied warranties may apply to a development agreement unless they are disclaimed. Disclaimer of the implied warranties is covered in "Important Provisions of Article Two," Chapter 17.

### *Remedies*

You may want to limit the remedies available to the client should you breach the contract. Limitation of remedies is discussed in "Important Provisions of Article Two," Chapter 17.

## "Battle of the Forms"

In the business world, contracts are often created based on an exchange of forms. The offeror sends a proposal to the offeree, and the offeree accepts by sending back a purchase order form. While the purchase order normally contains a number of terms that match the proposal's terms (price and delivery date, for example), it will generally include additional or contradictory terms as well.

The legal rules for determining what terms are included in a contract created this way are complex (attorneys call the process the "battle of the forms"). These rules are discussed in "Important Provisions of Article Two," Chapter 17. To avoid the"battle of the forms," don't create a contract with a client by exchanging documents containing inconsistent terms. Make every effort to get the client to sign your proposal or negotiate a separate contract. If the client must use a purchase order, read it carefully, including its fine print, as soon as you receive it. If the purchase order form contains terms that are unacceptable to you, notify the client of your objection as soon as possible.

## Joint Development Agreements

Individuals or companies that plan to work together on multimedia projects should enter into written joint development agreements documenting the terms of the relationship.

A joint development agreement should state who will do what, when each party's performance is due, and how much time each party will devote to the project (particularly if the parties have other jobs or other projects).

In the United States, the Copyright Act provides that joint authors of a work have equal undivided interests in the work's copyright. (See "Joint Authorship and Ownership," Chapter 4.)

However, the parties to a joint development agreement can provide that royalties and profits from a work will be divided in a manner other than fifty-fifty—and one party can assign its interest in the copyright to the other.

According to U.S. copyright law, each single joint owner can, without getting the consent of the owners, grant nonexclusive licenses to third parties to use the work in "nondestructive" ways. Nondestructive use is a use that does not diminish the value of the work. A joint owner who grants a license must share any royalties received with the other owners. Joint owners can provide by contract that the consent of all owners is required for granting licenses.

The rules for joint ownership of copyright vary from country to country. In many countries in Europe (Germany and France, for example), the consent of all joint owners of a copyright is necessary to obtain an enforceable license. This rule applies even if the work was created in the United States by U.S. citizens. This issue is very complex. You should try to avoid joint ownership if the work will be distributed overseas.

One risk that joint development agreements pose is that it is sometimes difficult to draw the line between a joint development agreement and a general partnership. Partners in a general partnership are all liable for the debts of a partnership. To avoid this problem, many joint development agreements state that the parties are not forming a general partnership. The purpose is to protect each developer from liability for general debts of the co-developers (debts arising out of ventures or projects other than the joint development project).

# 7.
# Employees

If you are a multimedia developer with employees, you should take proper steps to ensure that you own your employees' contributions to your multimedia works. This chapter focuses on practical applications of the Copyright Act's "work made for hire" rule, on the limitations of the rule, and on strategies for overcoming those limitations.

The rights of publicity and privacy are addressed in Chapter 13. Union issues are addressed in Chapter 14. Other employment issues—for example, employment law and labor law issues—are beyond the scope of this book.

## Works Made by Employees

According to the Copyright Act's work made for hire rule, an employer is the "author" and copyright owner of a work made for hire unless the parties agree otherwise. A work made for hire is a work created by an employee within the scope of his or her employment. Certain types of specially commissioned works can also be works made for hire, as discussed in "The Work Made for Hire Rule," Chapter 4, and in "Copyright Ownership," Chapter 8.

The work made for hire rule reverses the Copyright Act's general rule on copyright ownership, which states that the individual who creates a work owns the copyright in that work. This rule is discussed in "Initial Ownership," Chapter 4.

The Copyright Act's general ownership rule and the work made for hire rule apply only in the United States. Other countries have their own copyright ownership rules. Most have something similar to the "employee branch" of the Copyright Act's work made for hire rule.

The work made for hire rule applies only to works created by employees within the scope of their employment. It does not apply to works created by employees on their own, nor does it apply to works created by independent contractors for hiring parties. (See "The Work Made for Hire Rule," Chapter 4.)

## Who Is an Employee?

The Copyright Act does not define the term "employee." The Supreme Court has held that 13 factors must be considered to determine whether a worker is an employee or an independent contractor. No one factor is determinative. The factors are:

- Whether the hiring party had a right to control the manner and means by which the product is accomplished.

- The level of skill required.

- Whether the instruments and tools used were provided by the hiring party or the hired party.

- Whether the hired party worked at the hiring party's place of business or the hired party's place of business.

- The duration of the relationship between the two parties.

- Whether the hiring party had the right to assign additional projects to the hired party.

- The extent of the hired party's discretion over when and how long to work.

- The method of payment.

- Whether the hired party had a role in hiring and paying assistants.

- Whether the work was part of the regular business of the hiring party.

- Whether the hiring party was in business at all.

- Whether employee benefits were provided by the hiring party for the hired party.

- How the hiring party treated the hired party for tax purposes.

Whether your employee creates a short tune for your multimedia project or handles the entire project, you, the employer, own the copyright in the employee's work so long as the employee's work is done within the scope of employment. An employee—although the actual author—is not considered the author a work made for hire for copyright purposes. Of course, you and your employee can agree that the employee will own the copyright, as discussed in "Giving Ownership to an Employee," later in this chapter.

*Writer, employed by Developer to write text for multimedia works, wrote all the text for Developer's new medical training work during normal working hours as part of Writer's job. The text is a work made for hire. The copyright law considers Developer the author of Writer's text. Unless Writer and Developer have agreed otherwise, Developer owns the copyright in the text.*

Because you, the employer, are deemed the author and copyright owner of works made for hire, you can use works made for hire without obtaining permission from the employees who created them. Any employee who exercises the copyright owner's exclusive rights in a work made for hire infringes the employer's copyright.

> *Writer in the previous example quit working for Developer and formed his own multimedia production company. Writer has informed Developer that Developer no longer has Writer's permission to use the text created by Writer. In his first project for the new company, Writer used a modified version of the text Writer had written for Developer's medical training work. Because Developer owns the copyright in the text, Developer does not need Writer's permission to continue to use the text. Writer's modification of the text infringes Developer's modification right (discussed in "The Exclusive Rights," Chapter 2).*

The work made for hire rule applies whether the employer is an individual, partnership, or corporation. For corporate employers, the rule applies to works created by officers and managers as well as to works created by rank and file employees.

> *John, the co-founder and president of ABC Multimedia Co., a California corporation, created the retail kiosk work Cheese Expert within the scope of his employment with ABC. The copyright in Cheese Expert belongs to ABC Multimedia, not to John. Although John may think of ABC as his company, the corporation is a separate legal entity. If John has a falling out with his co-founder and leaves ABC, ownership of the copyright in Cheese Expert remains with ABC.*

## Using the Employment Agreement

Don't rely solely on the Copyright Act's work made for hire rule as a means of obtaining ownership of works made by your employees. Supplement the work made for hire rule by getting all employees to sign an "Employee Nondisclosure and Assignment Agreement" (Form 6 in Appendix B). In the rest of this chapter, we'll refer to this agreement as the "Employment Agreement."

The Employment Agreement protects you against employee claims that works were created outside the scope of an employee's employment. It gives the employer an assignment of intellectual property rights in:

- Works conceived or developed during the period of the employment.

- Works that relate at the time of conception or development to the employer's business or research.

- Works that were developed on the employer's time or with the use of its equipment, supplies, facilities, or trade secret information.

- Works that resulted from work performed for the employer.

### Limitations on the Work Made for Hire Rule

There are four limitations on the work made for hire rule that make it prudent for you to use the Employment Agreement with all employees as a back-up to the work made for hire rule. They are discussed in this section.

#### *International Ownership*

In other countries, ownership of employee-made works will be determined by applying local law rather than U.S. law. Although many countries have rules similar to the work made for hire rule, some do not. The assignment provision of the Employment Agreement (see Article 3 of Form 6 in Appendix B) is designed to give you ownership rights in employee-made works that will be recognized throughout the world.

#### *Works Outside the Scope of Employment*

The rule does not give employers ownership of works created by employees outside the scope of their employment. In new fields such as multimedia development, job descriptions are sometimes vague or nonexistent, and employees frequently wear many hats or take on responsibilities beyond those contemplated at hiring time. These factors could provide a basis for an employee's claim that you, the employer, do not own the copyright in a particular work because the work was created outside the scope of the employee's employment.

*Multimedia Co. hired Sue to do graphic design work. In her free time, Sue began to assist the animator, eventually taking over many of the animator's duties. Animation work done by Sue could be deemed outside the scope of Sue's employment. That would mean that Sue—not Multimedia Co.—owns the copyrights in her animation work.*

#### *Employee or Independent Contractor?*

The rule applies only to works created by employees, not to works created by independent contractors. It is sometimes difficult to tell, using the factors discussed in "Who is an Employee?," earlier in this chapter, whether a worker is an employee or an independent contractor.

*Media Co. hired Mark, an animator, to do the animation work for Media's new work City Tour. Three factors in Mark's relationship with Media indicate that Mark is an independent contractor: Mark worked at home, Media had no right to assign him more work, and*

*Media did not give him employee benefits. However, three factors indicate that Mark is an employee of Media Co.: Media provided the tools for the job, Media provided detailed instructions for the work, and Media required Mark to work normal working hours. In this situation, it is difficult to tell whether Mark is an independent contractor or Media's employee.*

Should one of your employees someday maintain that he or she worked for you as an independent contractor rather than as an employee, and that therefore you can't rely on the work made for hire rule for ownership of copyrights in works he or she created, you can say, "It doesn't matter whether you were an employee or an independent contractor. You assigned me those copyrights when you signed the Employment Agreement."

### *Patents, Trademarks, and Trade Secrets*

The work made for hire rule does not apply to patents, trademarks, trade secrets, or other forms of intellectual property. The assignment provision of the Employment Agreement (Article 3 of Form 6, Appendix B) gives you, the employer, ownership of these other forms of intellectual property. That means you don't have to worry about these other laws' ownership rules for works created by your employees.

## Provisions of the Employment Agreement

The Employment Agreement contains three important provisions, discussed in the next three subsections.

### *The Confidentiality Provision*

The confidentiality provision of the Employment Agreement (Article 2 of Form 6) is a necessary part of your trade secrets protection program. (See "Trade Secret Protection," Chapter 16.) "Confidential information" is defined as any information not generally known in the relevant trade or industry that is either obtained from the employer, or learned or developed by the employee in the scope of the employment.

### *The Assignment Provision*

The assignment provision of the Employment Agreement (Article 3 in Form 6) is broad enough to give you ownership of trade secrets, trademarks, and patent rights arising out of an employee's work for you.

The "power of attorney" aspect of the Agreement (Section 7.2) gives you the authority to execute and file copyright assignment documents on behalf of the employee to secure and record your ownership rights in intellectual property created by the employee. The power of attorney does not give you authority to act for the employee in other ways.

If you are located in California, you should be aware of Section 2870 of the California Labor Code. It states that any employment agreement provision that requires an employee to assign to the employer any inventions the employee developed entirely on his or her own time without using the employer's equipment, supplies, facilities, or trade secret information is unenforceable and against public policy. The statute makes an exception for inventions that relate to the employer's business, research, or development, or that result from work performed by the employee for the employer. The Employment Agreement's assignment provision does not give you ownership of inventions that are nonassignable under Section 2870. (See the "Limited Exclusion Notification" at the end of Form 6.)

### *List of Employee Inventions*

The Employment Agreement does not give you ownership of intellectual property already owned by an employee when he or she started work for you (see Section 3.2(b) in Form 6). If the employee owns copyrights or other intellectual property at the time the employment begins, they should be listed in Exhibit A to the Agreement, "Prior Work Products." If you want to use listed inventions, you will have to negotiate with the employee to obtain a separate license or an assignment (see "Assignments" and "Licenses," Chapter 4, and "Obtaining a License," Chapter 10).

## When Employees Should Sign

Each employee should sign a copy of the Employment Agreement before he or she begins work or on the first day of work. That way, the job will be the consideration that you give the employee in exchange for the employee's signing the Employment Agreement. An Employment Agreement that is signed later may be unenforceable for lack of consideration, although in some states, continued employment may count as consideration for "at will" employees (those without employment contracts). Consideration and the problem of lack of consideration are discussed in "Consideration," Chapter 5.

## Delayed Signing

Getting an Employment Agreement signed by an employee after the employee has started work is better than not getting the Agreement signed at all. It is a good idea to offer some consideration—money or a promotion—to a late signer in order to avoid a "lack of consideration" defense (see "Consideration," Chapter 5). The Employment Agreement, in that case, should state what consideration you gave the employee in exchange for the employee's signing the Agreement.

If you are concerned that the work done by a former employee was not covered by the work made for hire rule because it might have been done outside the scope of employment, or because the individual could have been an independent contractor rather than an employee, consider asking the individual for an assignment. (See Forms 9 and 10 in Appendix B.) If he or she agrees to execute an assignment, provide some consideration for the assignment. Asking for an assignment, of course, will alert the individual to the fact that you think there may be some defect in your title to the work. The former employee may refuse to give you the assignment.

### Independent Contractors

Do not use the Employment Agreement with individuals who work as independent contractors. Instead, use the Independent Contractor Agreement (Form 7 in Appendix B), which is discussed in "Copyright Ownership," Chapter 8.

Determining whether an individual is an employee or an independent contractor can be very complex (see "Who is an Employee?," earlier in this chapter). You should consider consulting an experienced attorney in close cases. As a practical matter, it will probably be difficult for you to convince a court that an individual whom you did not treat as an employee for tax or employment-benefit purposes should be treated as an employee for copyright ownership purposes.

## Giving Ownership to an Employee

If you want to give a key employee ownership of a work created within the scope of employment, it is easy to do so. You and the employee simply have to sign a written agreement stating that the employee owns all copyright rights in the work. An oral agreement is not sufficient to give an employee ownership of works made for hire.

If you sign an agreement giving copyright ownership in a work to an employee, you as the employer will still be considered the "author" of the work for copyright purposes, but the employee will be the copyright owner. If you give an employee copyright ownership, you should consider having the employee grant you an irrevocable, nonexclusive, royalty-free, worldwide license to use the work in existing multimedia projects and to modify the work for use in future multimedia projects. License provisions are discussed in "Obtaining a License," Chapter 10.

## Joint Ownership

An employee is not a joint owner of a work made for hire unless the employer assigns an ownership interest to the employee. An employee's contributions to a work made for hire do not make the employee a joint author or a joint copyright owner.

*Dan hired Janet to help develop a multimedia work, Restaurant Guide. Janet helped Dan with all aspects of the development of Restaurant Guide. If Janet was Dan's employee and Janet's contributions to Restaurant Guide were made within the scope of Janet's employment, Dan, as the employer, owns the entire copyright in Restaurant Guide.*

## Rights of Former Employers

Respect the intellectual property rights of your employees' former employers. If one of your employees created a copyrighted work within the scope of employment with a former employer, the former employer owns the copyright (unless the employee and former employer agreed otherwise). Trade secrets developed for a former employer are also normally the property of the former employer.

While employees are free to reuse ideas that they used for a former employer and to draw on their general knowledge and job skills, do not permit your employees to use copyrighted material or trade secrets belonging to former employers without getting licenses.

# 8.

## Contractors and Consultants

Many multimedia developers use freelancers and consultants to create content, develop software and user interfaces, and even to supervise production. Most freelancers and consultants are considered "independent contractors" for copyright law purposes. According to copyright law, when an independent contractor creates a work for a hiring party, the copyright is owned by the independent contractor unless the hiring party takes steps to secure ownership.

This chapter deals with legal issues arising out of a developer's use of independent contractors, including the steps that a developer should take to get ownership of copyrights in works created by independent contractors such as graphic artists, writers, content specialists, and software designers.

### Who Is an Independent Contractor?

The Copyright Act does not define "independent contractor" or "employee." Instead, according to the Supreme Court, whether a worker is an employee or an independent contractor must be determined by weighing 13 factors. (These are the same 13 factors listed in "Who is an Employee?," Chapter 7.)

No one factor is determinative. The factors are as follows:

- Whether the hiring party had a right to control the manner and means by which the product is accomplished.

- The level of skill required.

- Whether the instruments and tools used were provided by the hiring party or the hired party.

- Whether the hired party worked at the hiring party's place of business or the hired party's place of business.

- The duration of the relationship between the two parties.

- Whether the hiring party had the right to assign additional projects to the hired party.

- The extent of the hired party's discretion over when and how long to work.

- The method of payment.
- Whether the hired party had a role in hiring and paying assistants.
- Whether the work was part of the regular business of the hiring party.
- Whether the hiring party was in business at all.
- Whether employee benefits were provided by the hiring party for the hired party.
- How the hiring party treated the hired party for tax purposes.

Much of the work that is done on multimedia projects is done by freelance professionals who work on a project basis. A worker who is hired on a project basis—whether for a lump-sum fee or at an hourly rate—is probably an independent contractor rather than an employee, especially if the worker provides his or her own workplace and tools, and works without day-to-day supervision. Partnerships and corporations can also be hired on an independent contractor basis.

Unless you have good reason to believe (based on the 13-factor test) that a particular worker hired on a project basis is an employee, you should assume that such a worker is an independent contractor. As a practical matter, it will probably be difficult for you to convince a court that an individual whom you did not treat as an employee for tax or employment-benefit purposes should be treated as an employee for copyright ownership purposes.

## Copyright Ownership

When a hiring party and an independent contractor fail to address the issue of ownership of copyrights in works created by the independent contractor, the copyrights are owned by the independent contractor. This "default rule" is the opposite of the default rule for works created by employees (discussed in "The Work Made for Hire Rule," Chapter 4, and in "Works Made by Employees," Chapter 7).

You should try to obtain ownership of copyrights in all works created for you by independent contractors. There are two ways to obtain ownership:

- *Assignment.* For all types of works created for you by independent contractors, you can obtain ownership of copyrights by including an assignment provision in your contract with the independent contractor.
- *Work made for hire agreement.* For contributions to audiovisual works and seven other types of works (listed in "Work Made for Hire Agreements," later in this chapter), you can obtain ownership of copyrights by including a "work made for hire" agreement in your contract with the independent contractor. This approach makes use of the second branch

(specially commissioned works) of the Copyright Act's work made for hire rule (see "The Work Made for Hire Rule," Chapter 4).

These two options for obtaining ownership are discussed in the next two subsections, "Assignments" and "Work Made for Hire Agreements." Unless you use one of these two options, the copyrights in works done for you by independent contractors will be owned by the contractors—even though you ordered and paid for the works.

*Developer hired Software Design House on a project basis to create the software for Developer's multimedia work. Developer did not get Software Design House to sign a work made for hire agreement, nor did it get an assignment of the copyright in the software from Software Design House. Software Design House owns the copyright in the software that it created for Developer's multimedia work.*

### Assignments

If you get an assignment of copyright from an independent contractor who creates material for your multimedia work, you will own the copyright in the contractor's work. (See "Assignments," Chapter 4.)

The independent contractors who give you assignments will have the right to terminate the assignments in 35 years (see "Termination Right," Chapter 4). There is nothing you can do about this situation.

For an example of an assignment provision that you can use in contracts with independent contractors, see Section 4.4 of the Independent Contractor Agreement (Form 7 in Appendix B). This assignment provision states that:

- Inventions resulting from the contractor's work under the Independent Contractor Agreement, and copyrightable works developed within the scope of the contractor's work for the hiring party, are the exclusive property of the hiring party.

- The contractor assigns all intellectual property rights in those inventions and copyrightable works to the hiring party.

This assignment provision includes a power of attorney. (Power of attorney provisions are discussed in "Using the Employment Agreement," Chapter 7.) Other aspects of the Independent Contractor Agreement are discussed in "Contracts With Independent Contractors," later in this chapter.

If you are in a community property state, you may want to get the spouses of married independent contractors to sign quitclaims (see "Community Property," Chapter 4).

### Work Made for Hire Agreements

For certain types of works, you can obtain ownership of works created by independent contractors by using a work made for hire agreement (Form 8 in Appendix B). This method of obtaining ownership makes use of the second branch of the Copyright Act's work made for hire rule (discussed in "The Work Made for Hire Rule," Chapter 4).

Both you and the independent contractor must sign the work made for hire agreement in order to make the contractor's works into works made for hire.

#### *Limitations*

If you are going to use a work made for hire agreement rather than get an assignment, make sure you understand the limitations of work made for hire agreements. They are discussed in this subsection.

***Types of Works***   A work made for hire agreement is only effective for eight types of specially commissioned works:

- Contributions to collective works.

- Part of a motion picture or other audiovisual work (many multimedia works are audiovisual works).

- Translations.

- Supplementary works (works prepared as adjuncts to other works).

- Compilations.

- Instructional texts.

- Tests or answer material for tests.

- Atlases.

These are the same eight types of works listed in "The Work Made for Hire Rule," Chapter 4, in the discussion of the "specially commissioned works" branch of the rule.

While some books of legal forms—particularly older ones—give you the impression that you can make any type of specially commissioned work a work made for hire by getting a work made for hire agreement from the independent contractor, that is not true.

*John hired Writer, a freelancer, to write John's biography. John got Writer to sign an agreement stating that the work was to be considered a work made for hire. The agreement was worthless. Biography is not one of the types of specially commissioned works that can become a work made for hire based on agreement of the parties. Unless John got an assignment from Writer, Writer owns the copyright in the biography.*

*Unsolicited Works*    You can't use a work made for hire agreement to obtain ownership rights in works that "came in over the transom"—that is, unsolicited work. To obtain ownership rights in works that you did not commission, you need an assignment.

*Foreign Rights*    A work made for hire agreement probably won't get you foreign rights in the commissioned works because most countries' rules do not have anything comparable to the "specially commissioned works" branch of the Copyright Act's work made for hire rule. To protect your ownership abroad, you should obtain assignments from independent contractors.

### Timing

Several courts have recently held that a work made for hire agreement for a specially commissioned work is valid only if the agreement is signed before the work is begun. You should make every effort to get your independent contractors to sign work made for hire agreements before they start work on your projects.

If you discover that an independent contractor has started work without signing the work made for hire agreement, you should try to get the contractor to sign an assignment. (See Forms 9 and 10 in Appendix B.)

If the contractor refuses to give you an assignment, try to get a broad written license from the contractor. If the contractor refuses to grant a written license, you will have to either rely on an implied license (discussed in "Implied Licenses," later in this chapter), or remove the contractor's work from your multimedia project.

You can claim copyright for the multimedia work as a whole even though an independent contractor owns the copyright in a component. (For details on registering copyrights, see "How to Fill Out Form PA," Chapter 16.)

### California Labor Code

A provision of the California Labor Code states that a person who commissions a work made for hire is the employer of the hired party for purposes of worker's compensation, unemployment insurance, and unemployment disability insurance laws. No one is certain exactly what the provision means. If you are located in California, you may want to acquire ownership of copyrights in works made by independent contractors by assignment rather than using work made for hire agreements.

## Implied Licenses

If you order and pay for a work created by an independent contractor and fail to get an assignment or a work made for hire agreement, you may have an implied license to use the contractor's work as intended by you and the contractor. An implied license to use the work is much less valuable than owning the copyright in the work.

If you own a work created by a independent contractor, you can exercise all of the copyright owner's exclusive rights in the work—in other words, you can make copies of the work, modify the work, distribute the work, and publicly perform and display the work (see "The Exclusive Rights," Chapter 2). If you merely have an implied license to use the work, you can only do those things that are within the scope of the license (and you and the contractor may not agree on the scope of the license).

*Developer hired Composer to create music for a multimedia work commissioned by a client. The music is so good that Developer would like to modify it for use in other multimedia works. If Developer owns the copyright in the music, Developer can modify and reuse the music. If Developer just has an implied license to use the music, the implied license probably only authorizes Developer to use the music in the original client's project.*

License scope is discussed in "Determining What Rights You Need," Chapter 10.

## Contracts with Independent Contractors

You should have written contracts with all of your independent contractors for the reasons stated in "Written Contracts," Chapter 5.

### Contract Provisions

The contract with an independent contractor should include, in addition to an assignment or a work made for hire agreement (see "Copyright Ownership," earlier in this chapter), the following provisions:

- Deliverables or services, described as specifically as possible.
- Deadlines.
- Payment and payment schedules.
- Responsibility for expenses.

Such provisions are discussed in "The Contract," Chapter 6.

### Services of Individuals

If you enter into a contract with a corporation and expect to get the services of particular individuals employed by the corporation, your contract should state that the work can be done only by the named individuals. Otherwise, the corporation will be free to use any of its employees to do the job.

### Warranties

You should get warranties and an indemnity from each independent contractor. For sample provisions, see Sections 4.6 and 4.8 of the Independent Contractor Agreement (Form 7 in Appendix B).

Warranty and indemnity provisions are designed to give you legal recourse against a contractor who uses works belonging to others. If a contractor gives you material that infringes a third party's copyright, incorporating that material into your multimedia work will make you liable for infringement of the third party's copyright.

*Developer hired Graphic Artist to create original graphics for Developer's multimedia work Downtown Tonight. Graphic Artist copied some designs from a design book and delivered them to Developer to fulfill her contract with Developer. When Developer incorporated the designs into Downtown Tonight, Developer infringed the copyright owner's reproduction and modification rights (see "The Exclusive Rights," Chapter 2).*

Warranty provisions are discussed in more detail in the section "The Contract," Chapter 6.

Of course, these provisions are not worth much if the contractor does not have the resources to pay the damages. You may want to consider obtaining insurance to cover that risk.

### Nondisclosure Provisions

The contract should contain a nondisclosure provision. Such provisions are part of a trade secrets protection program (see "Trade Secret Protection," Chapter 16). For an example, see Section 4.2 of the Independent Contractor Agreement (Form 7 in Appendix B).

### Miscellaneous Issues

If you will be using an independent contractor's voice, image, or face in a multimedia work, your contract should include a release authorizing that use to avoid violations of the laws of publicity and privacy (see Chapter 13).

If you will be hiring independent contractors who belong to entertainment industry unions, read about union issues in Chapter 14.

### Standard Agreements

Independent contractors in many fields have professional associations that have developed and distributed standard agreements. The Graphic Artists Guild, for example, has standard contracts for use by graphic designers and illustrators with clients.

If a contractor insists on using a standard form, read the form carefully, particularly the ownership of rights provision, and be prepared to negotiate over deleting unacceptable provisions and adding your own provisions.

## Employment Law Risks

If federal or state authorities conclude that an individual that you have treated as an independent contractor is an employee, you could have a number of problems. They could include:

- Federal tax liability for failure to withhold payroll taxes for the individual.

- Liability for workers' compensation awards paid to the individual.

- Liability for violation of state and federal wage and hours laws.

- Liability for violation of wrongful discharge laws.

You should be aware that the distinction between employees and independent contractors has importance in areas of the law other than copyright law. An individual who is an independent contractor for copyright law purposes may not be an independent contractor for employment law purposes.

# 3

## Other Production Issues

# 9.

## Using Preexisting Works

Every time you use a copyrighted work owned by a third party, you must determine whether it is necessary to obtain a license from the owner. For most uses, a license should be obtained.

The first two sections of this chapter discuss when you do and don't need a license to use a copyrighted work. The third section covers the use of public domain works. The fourth section covers the use of works that you own.

### When You Need a License

You need a license to use a third party's copyrighted work if your intended use of the work would, without a license, infringe any of the copyright owner's exclusive rights (discussed in "The Exclusive Rights," Chapter 2). To use material from a copyrighted work owned by a third party, you will copy the work and possibly modify it. Therefore, you need a license unless "fair use" or one of the other exceptions to the owner's rights applies. (Exceptions are discussed in "When You Don't Need a License," later in this Chapter.)

### Myths

There are a number of myths out there concerning the necessity of getting a license. Don't make the mistake of believing them:

**Myth #1**  *"I don't need a license because I'm using only a small amount of the copyrighted work."*

It is true that *de minimis* copying (copying a small amount) is not copyright infringement. Unfortunately, it is rarely possible to tell where *de minimis* copying ends and copyright infringement begins. There are no "bright line" rules.

Copying a small amount of a copyrighted work is infringement if what is copied is a qualitatively substantial portion of the copied work. In one case, a magazine article that used 300 words from a 200,000-word autobiography written by President Gerald Ford was found to infringe the copyright on the autobiography. Even though the copied material was only a small part of the autobiography, the copied portions were among the most powerful passages in the autobiography.

Copying any part of a copyrighted work is risky. If what you copy is truly a tiny and non-memorable part of the work, you may get away with it (the work's owner may not be able to tell that your work incorporates an excerpt from the owner's work). However, you run the risk of having to defend your use in expensive litigation. If what you are copying is tiny, but recognizable as coming from the protected work, it is better to get a license (unless fair use or one of the other exceptions discussed in "When You Don't Need a License," later in this chapter, applies). You cannot escape liability for infringement by showing how much of the protected work you did not take.

**Myth #2**   *"I paid for the tape (compact disc, videotape) that I'm going to copy, so I already have the permission I need."*

Copyright law distinguishes between ownership of the copyright in a work and ownership of a copy of the work. Purchasing a copy of a work (a tape, compact disc, videotape, book, photographic print) does not give you permission to exercise the exclusive rights of copyright. You can resell your copy, but that's all. (See "Owning a Copy of a Work," Chapter 4.)

**Myth #3**   *"I didn't know I needed a license. Because my infringement was innocent rather than intentional, I'm not liable for infringement damages."*

Lack of intent to infringe is not a defense to infringement—nor is ignorance of the copyright law.

In a recent case involving innocent infringement, a federal appellate court refused to dismiss a case brought against Sara Lee Corporation for unauthorized distribution of books by Sara Lee. Sara Lee Corporation thought it was getting its copies of the book from an authorized distributor. Between the copyright owner and an innocent infringer, the court reasoned, the innocent infringer rather than the copyright owner should suffer.

**Myth #4**   *"I don't need a license because my multimedia work will only be used in-house by my client. It will never be shown or marketed to the public."*

Technically, you need a license to copy even if you are the only one who will ever use your multimedia work. The Copyright Act does not permit copying for "private use" other than under the "fair use" doctrine.

*Marty's multimedia work, The Country and Western Music Treasury, includes scanned photographs of a number of singers. Even if Marty created the work entirely for his own private use, he has infringed the reproduction right for each photograph. Unless his use is fair use, he should have gotten licenses from each copyright owner. He should also have gotten releases from each singer (see "The Rights of Publicity and Privacy," Chapter 13).*

How a work will be shown or used is relevant in determining whether you need permission to exercise the public performance right (see "Determining What Rights You Need," Chapter 10). Even if you don't need a license for public performance, you need a license to copy a third party's copyrighted work into your multimedia work and to "distribute" to a client a copy of the multimedia work that contains the third party's work.

**Myth #5** *"I don't need a license because I'm making this multimedia work for a nonprofit group."*

Copying for educational or public service use *may* be fair use but is not necessarily fair use. Type of use is one of the factors that determines whether a use is fair or unfair. Other factors must be considered. (Fair use is discussed in "When You Don't Need a License," later in this chapter.) Even if you are creating a multimedia work for an educational or public service group, you should get a license. Maybe you can get the copyright owners whose works you use to waive the licensing fee to help a good cause.

**Myth #6** *"I don't need a license because no one will ever have to pay a fee to see my multimedia work."*

Whether a fee is charged for public performances of a work is relevant for determining whether a public performance license is needed (see "Determining What Rights You Need," Chapter 10). It is irrelevant in determining whether a license is needed for copying. Even if it's true that no one will ever pay to see your work, you need a license to copy if you use a third party's copyrighted work (unless fair use or one of the other exceptions in "When You Don't Need a License," later in this chapter, applies).

**Myth #7** *"My multimedia work will be a wonderful showcase for the copyright owner's song, so I'm sure the owner will not object to my use of the song."*

Don't assume that a copyright owner will be happy to have you use his or her work. Even if the owner is willing to let you use the work, the owner will probably want to charge you a license fee.

**Myth #8** *"The work I want to use doesn't have a copyright notice on it, so it's not copyrighted. I'm free to use it."*

For works published on or after March 1, 1989, the use of copyright notice is optional. The fact that a work doesn't have a copyright notice doesn't mean that the work is not protected by copyright. Unless you have good reason to believe a work is in the public domain (see "Public Domain Works," later in this chapter), assume that it is protected by copyright and get a license.

**Myth #9** *"The developer who created the work I want to use never bothered to file a copyright registration application, so the work is uncopyrighted. I'm free to use it."*

Copyright protection arises automatically when an original work of authorship is fixed in a tangible medium of expression. Registration is optional. Checking the Copyright Office's registration files (see "Determining Who Owns the Copyright," Chapter 10) is a good way to find out who owns a registered copyright. It's not a good way to determine whether a work is protected by copyright.

**Myth #10** *"Since I'm planning to give credit to all authors whose works I copy, I don't need to get licenses."*

If you give credit to a work's author, you are not a plagiarist (you are not pretending that you authored the copied work). However, attribution is not a defense to copyright infringement.

**Myth #11** *"I don't need a license because I'm going to alter the work I copy."*

You cannot escape liability for copyright infringement by altering or modifying the work you copy. You can use a copyrighted work's unprotected elements, as discussed in "When You Don't Need a License," later in this chapter, but if you copy and modify protected elements of a copyrighted work, you will be infringing the copyright owner's modification right as well as the copying right. If the work is a "work of visual art," you may also be infringing the owner's rights under the Visual Artists Rights Act (discussed in "The Visual Artists Rights Act," Chapter 10).

**Myth #12** *"If I paraphrase the author's words rather than use the author's words verbatim, I won't need a license."*

Paraphrasing can be copyright infringement. Infringement is not limited to word-for-word copying. If the paraphrased version of a protected work copies the work's protected "expression"—which is more than the words alone—the paraphrased version infringes the copyright on the original work.

**Myth #13** *"Rather than just scanning in the copyrighted cartoon character I want to use, I'll hire an illustrator to create my own version of the cartoon character. That way, I won't need a license."*

Using an illustrator's version of a character is copyright infringement if the illustrator copied the protected character. If you tell the illustrator, "Draw me a character that looks like Garfield," the illustrator's character will be a copy of Garfield (assuming the illustrator is competent). If you can't afford a merchandise license (see "Logos and Characters," Chapter 11) to use a protected character, or the owner will not grant you a license, create your own original characters.

**Myth #14**   *"We've used this song (photo, design, and so on) in our productions in the past, so we don't need to get a license to use the work now."*

Don't assume that past use was licensed use. Even if the past use was licensed, the license may not cover your use now because the license may have authorized one-time use only, or may have been limited in duration, or there may have been other restrictions. If use has been licensed in the past, check the license to determine whether it authorizes the use you are planning.

**Myth #15**   *"The author of the work that I want to use lives in England, so the work is not protected by copyright in the United States."*

Do not assume that a work lacks copyright protection in the United States because its author is a foreigner. Foreign authors who live in countries that belong to the Berne Convention or the Universal Copyright Convention automatically obtain copyright protection here. (See "International Protection," Chapter 2.) Most major countries are members of at least one of these conventions.

## When You Don't Need a License

There are several situations in which you can use a copyrighted work without getting a license. We'll discuss them in this section.

### Fair Use

You don't need a license to use a copyrighted work if your use is "fair use." Unfortunately, it is difficult to tell whether a particular use of a work is fair or unfair. Determinations are made on a case-by-case basis by considering four factors:

- *Purpose and character of use.* The courts are most likely to find fair use where the use is for noncommercial purposes. They are least likely to find fair use where the use is commercial. In fact, the Supreme Court has stated that commercial use is presumed not to be fair use. While it is possible to overcome the presumption that a commercial use is unfair, it will be hard to do so.

- *Nature of the copyrighted work.* The courts are most likely to find fair use where the copied work is a factual work or a work that has already been distributed. They are least likely to find fair use where the copied work is creative or fictitious, or the work has never before been published.

- *Amount and substantiality of portion used.* The courts are most likely to find fair use where what is used is a tiny amount of the protected work. They are least likely to find fair use where much of the protected work is used. If what is used is small in amount but substantial in terms of importance—the heart of the copied work—a finding of fair use is unlikely.

- *Effect on the potential market for or value of the protected work.* The courts are most likely to find fair use where the new work is not a substitute for the copyrighted work. They are least likely to find fair use where the new work is a complete substitute for the copyrighted work.

If you are creating a multimedia work for purely noncommercial purposes—for example, for use by the American Red Cross for training—it is possible that you can justify copying small amounts of material as fair use.

If your work is designed for commercial use of any sort—for sale to consumers, for use in retail stores, or even for internal training use in for-profit corporations—it will be hard to succeed on a fair use defense.

If your multimedia work serves traditional "fair use" purposes—criticism, comment, news reporting, teaching, scholarship, and research—you have a better chance of falling within the bounds of fair use than you do if your work is sold to the public for entertainment purposes.

### "Reverse Engineering" of Software

In a dispute between Sega and Accolade over Accolade's "reverse engineering" of the control software for Sega's game player, a federal appellate court recently held that copying software for such purposes is fair use if it is necessary to understand the ideas and processes used in a copyrighted work. ("Reverse engineering" is taking a product apart to see how it works.) The copying must not exceed what is necessary to understand the unprotected elements of the copied work.

An important element of the Sega-Accolade decision was that the Accolade game software did not compete with the copied Sega software. Whether it is permissible to reverse-engineer software to create a competitive product has not yet been decided.

### Home Videotaping

Several years ago, in the so-called *Betamax* case filed against Sony by several motion picture studios, the Supreme Court found that home videotaping of television programs with VCRs was noninfringing fair use. The Court's decision was based on the four-factor analysis discussed in "Fair Use," earlier in this chapter. The Supreme Court emphasized that a study showed that most home VCR users taped television programs for noncommercial, time-shifting purposes (so they could watch the copied programs at a more convenient time).

The *Betamax* case does not say that all videotaping of television programs is fair use. Don't rely on the case to justify videotaping television programs or movies for use in multimedia works.

## Other Noninfringing Uses

You don't need a license to copy facts from a protected work, to copy ideas from a protected work, or to parody a protected work.

### Copying Facts

The copyright on a work does not extend to the work's facts. This is because copyright protection is limited to original works of authorship (see "Standards," Chapter 2), and no one can claim originality or authorship for facts. You are free to copy facts from a copyrighted work.

*Susan spent months and thousands of dollars researching President Kennedy's assassination. She discovered a number of never-before-known facts about Lee Harvey Oswald. She reported her discoveries in a book. The copyright on Susan's book does not protect the facts that Susan discovered.*

### Copying Ideas

Copyright does not protect a work's ideas, processes, or systems. You are free to copy these elements.

*John's copyrighted book explains a new system of bookkeeping created by John. While John's copyright protects his expression in the book (his description of the bookkeeping system), it does not protect the system itself or the ideas that make up the system. Others are free to study John's book, figure out and use the bookkeeping system, and even write their own books describing the system.*

Unfortunately, the line between ideas and "expression" is difficult even for experienced attorneys to draw. Only a few generalizations are possible:

- A work's theme or purpose—for example, training telemarketers or helping consumers pick wine—is an unprotected idea.

- Stock characters and situations are unprotected ideas. Examples of stock characters are the jealous boyfriend, proud grandparents, and starving artist. Examples of stock situations are the conflict between a parent and a teenaged child and the rivalry between two siblings. So-called "distinctively delineated" characters, such as Tarzan, E.T., and Indiana Jones, are protected by copyright and possibly by trademark as well (see "Logos and Characters," Chapter 11).

- A novel's detailed plot is protected expression, even though stock situations within the plot are not protected.

If there is only one way to express an idea (or only a limited number of ways), you can copy the expression as well as the idea. For example, one case permitted the copying of a set of game rules because there were only a limited number of ways to express rules for that type of game. Because this concept, called the "merger" principle, is complex, you should consult an experienced copyright attorney before you rely on it.

### *Parody*

You can copy a protected work for purposes of parodying or satirizing the protected work. Parody is considered fair use if the parody does not replace the copyrighted work in the marketplace, and if no more of the copyrighted work is used than is necessary. Parody is also discussed in "Option #2: Using Preexisting Music," Chapter 12.

## Public Domain Works

You don't need a license to use a public domain work. Public domain works—works not protected by copyright—can be used by anyone. Because these works are not copyrighted, no one can claim the exclusive rights of copyright for such works.

The rules regarding what works are in the public domain vary from country to country. A work in the public domain in the United States may be protected by copyright in Canada or other countries.

There are several ways in which works fall into the public domain in the United States:

- *Expiration of the copyright.* A copyright that was in existence before January 1, 1978, and was renewed, has a term of 75 years. All copyright terms run to the end of the calendar year in which they expire. Consequently, in 1994, all works first "published" before January 1, 1919, are in the public domain in the United States.

- *Failure of the copyright owner to renew the copyright.* Under the 1909 Copyright Act, copyright protection lasted 28 years. A copyright owner could obtain an additional term, known as a "renewal term," by filing an application to renew in the 28th year. The Copyright Renewal Amendment of 1992 eliminated the requirement of filing a renewal application for works published between 1964 and 1977, inclusive. Renewal is not required for works created after 1977. However, before 1992, a number of works entered the public domain because the copyright owner failed to file a renewal application. For works to which the renewal requirement applies, you can find out whether the owner renewed the copyright by ordering a Copyright Office renewal search. (See "Determining Who Owns the Copyright," Chapter 10.) The provisions on renewal are complex, and you should get an experienced attorney or rights clearance agent to help you determine how those rules apply to a particular work.

- *Failure to use copyright notice on publicly distributed copies of a work (for works published before March 1, 1989).* Under prior law, the distribution of copies without copyright notice resulted in the forfeiture of copyright protection. For works distributed before January 1, 1978, forfeiture was automatic. For works publicly distributed after that date, the copyright law provided ways around the defect created by distribution without notice. A court recently found that most of the UNIX operating system is in the public domain because copies were publicly distributed without notice.

### Finding Public Domain Works

The Copyright Office does not maintain a list of public domain works, nor does it publish annual lists of copyrights that will expire at the end of the year. You have to find these works yourself.

If the copyright notice on a work is dated more than 75 years ago, the work is in the public domain. It will be harder to determine expiration dates for works covered by the current Copyright Act: Except for works made for hire, the duration of copyright is 50 years beyond the life of the author rather than a set number of years.

If you are interested in using a work to which the 1909 Copyright Act's renewal requirement applies, you can order a Copyright Office renewal search to find out whether the copyright was renewed. (Searches are discussed in "Determining Who Owns the Copyright," Chapter 10.)

Unless you know that a work was distributed without copyright notice, you will only learn about it if the issue has been raised in a reported court decision.

The Copyright Office does not keep copies of works whose registrations have expired. Some content providers sell copies of public domain works, such as WPA photographs (see Appendix D). The Library of Congress has copies of some of these works.

### Complications

Derivative works (works based on preexisting works) are often created from public domain works. New material in a derivative work is protected by copyright. You cannot copy the new material in a new version of a public domain work unless you obtain a license from the owner of the copyright in the derivative work, but you can use the elements that came from the public domain work.

> *The movie Coast is based on a public domain novel. If Developer wants to use a clip from the movie in a multimedia work, Developer must get a license from the owner of the copyright in the movie. Developer is free to use an excerpt from the underlying novel.*

Sometimes the derivative work is in the public domain because the owner didn't renew the copyright, but the underlying work is still protected by copyright.

> *The movie Dream is based on a novel of the same name. Both the movie and the novel are pre-1978 works to which the 1909 Copyright Act's renewal requirement applied. The owner of the copyright in the novel filed a renewal application at the appropriate time in 1980, but the owner of the motion picture copyright did not renew its copyright. The underlying work, the novel, is protected by copyright. The derivative work, the movie, is not protected.*

If the underlying work is protected but the derivative work is not, and you want to use an excerpt of the derivative work, you will generally need permission from the underlying work's copyright owner. This topic is discussed in "Determining Who Owns the Copyright," Chapter 10.

If a public domain work incorporates another work, the incorporated work may still be protected by copyright. If the incorporated work is protected by copyright, you must get a license from the owner of that copyright if you want to use an excerpt of the public domain work that incorporates the protected work.

> *The movie Mountains is in the public domain because the renewal requirement applies to the movie and the copyright owner did not renew the copyright. Mountains contains a song that is still protected by copyright. If Developer wants to use a clip of Mountains that contains the song, Developer needs a license from the owner of the copyright in the song.*

## Using Works That You Own

You can use works that you own without worrying about obtaining licenses.

### Existing Works

If you own the copyrights in all preexisting works that you will be using in your multimedia works, you don't need to obtain licenses.

If you are an employer, you own the copyrights in the United States in works created for you by employees acting within the scope of their employment (see "The Work Made for Hire Rule," Chapter 4, and "Works Made by Employees," Chapter 7). You may not own those rights in other countries. However, you do not own even the U.S. rights in works created for you by independent contractors unless you obtained assignments from them or the works had the status of "specially commissioned works made for hire." (See "Copyright Ownership," Chapter 8.)

If you created a work for a past employer within the scope of your employment, you do not own the copyright in that work. (See "The Work Made for Hire Rule," Chapter 4.) You cannot use the work without obtaining a license.

If you created the work as an independent contractor, you own the copyright unless you assigned the copyright to the hiring party or you signed a valid work made for hire agreement. (See "Copyright Ownership," Chapter 8.)

### New Works

You can avoid obtaining licenses to use third-party content if you create your own content. If works will be created by employees or independent contractors, be sure you follow the strategies described in earlier chapters to ensure that you obtain copyright ownership in the United States and throughout the world. (These strategies are described in the "Using the Employment Agreement," Chapter 7, and in "Copyright Ownership," Chapter 8.)

Special rules apply if you plan to modify a "work of visual art" even if you own the work. A work of visual art, for copyright purposes, is a limited edition painting, drawing, print, sculpture, or a photograph produced for exhibition purposes. The rules apply if the work was created by an artist after the effective date of the Visual Artists Rights Act of 1990. This law is discussed in "The Visual Artists Rights Act," Chapter 10.

# 10 · ·.
## Clearing Rights
## and Obtaining Licenses

Most of this chapter is devoted to the licensing process and its three steps:

- Determining who owns the copyrights in the works you want to use.

- Determining what rights you need.

- Obtaining licenses from the copyright owners.

At the end of this chapter, we'll discuss how to use a rights clearance agency—a convenient aid for developers who will be licensing a large number of works—and how to use stock houses and media libraries to avoid many of the difficulties involved in licensing. We'll also discuss copyright assignments, an alternative to licensing, and the Visual Artists Rights Act, which imposes restrictions on modifying certain types of works.

The industries that generate the types of works that you are likely to want to license are described in Chapter 11. Music licensing is discussed in Chapter 12.

## The Licensing Process

Whether you handle the licensing process yourself or use a rights clearance agency, the process will take time. Make certain that such time is built into your development schedule.

Multimedia is still very new, and many "content" owners may be reluctant to license their works. This is either because they do not understand what multimedia is or because they are concerned that digitization of their works will result in their losing control over their works.

## Determining Who Owns the Copyright

The first step in the licensing process is determining who owns the copyright in the work you want to use.

If the work you want to use contains a copyright notice (many works do, although use of copyright notice is now optional), the name on the notice is your starting point. It is the name of the copyright owner at the time your copy of the work was published—but not necessarily the work's creator or the current copyright owner.

The copyright owner named in the notice may have assigned the copyright to someone else after your copy was published. (Assignments are discussed in "Assignments," Chapter 4.) You need to trace the work's "chain of title" (just like in real estate) to find the current owner, because your license must come from the current copyright owner.

> *John, a freelance writer, assigned the copyright in his book to Mega Books, Inc. If Developer wants to use excerpts from John's book, Developer must get permission from Mega Books, not from John.*

The rest of this section tells you how to check a work's chain of title and how to find the party who has authority to grant you a license to use a work.

### Is the Work Registered?

The chain of title for a registered work can be checked by obtaining an "assignment search" of the Copyright Office's files (discussed in "Checking the Chain of Title," later in this section). There are four ways to find out whether a work's copyright has been registered:

- Check the *Catalog of Copyright Entries*, which lists registered works by title. This catalog is published by the Copyright Office. Some libraries have copies of it. The catalog divides works into eight categories (literary works, performing arts, motion pictures and filmstrips, sound recordings, serials and periodicals, visual arts, maps, and renewals). It does not report registrations made in the year before the publication date.

- Order a Copyright Office registration search from the Copyright Office's Reference and Bibliography Section by filling out a copy of a Search Request Form (Form 1 in Appendix G), and sending it to the Copyright Office. Check the "Registration" box at the top and provide as much of the requested information on the work as you can. The Copyright Office will charge you $20 per hour for a search.

- Hire a copyright search firm to conduct a Copyright Office registration search for you. A list of search firms appears in Appendix C. Using a search firm will cost more than a Copyright Office search done by the Copyright Office Reference and Bibliography Section staff, but you will get the results faster.

- Do a Copyright Office search yourself, if you live in the Washington, D.C. area, using microfilm and automated registration records in the Copyright Office.

### Checking the Chain of Title

How you check a work's chain of title depends on whether the copyright has been registered or not.

### Registered Copyrights

If the copyright in the work has been registered with the Copyright Office, you trace the work's chain of title by obtaining a Copyright Office assignment search. The Copyright Act permits assignees to record their assignments with the Copyright Office to give others constructive notice of the assignment, just as purchasers of real estate do in recording their purchases in county records (recording is discussed in "Assignments," Chapter 4). A Copyright Office assignment search will reveal whether any assignments of the work's copyright have been recorded.

An assignment search, like a registration search, can be obtained by sending a filled-out Search Request Form (check the "assignment" box) to the Copyright Office's Reference and Bibliography Section, by hiring a copyright search firm, or by checking the Copyright Office's files yourself. These options are described in "Is the Work Registered?," earlier in this section. If the work was published before January 1, 1978, you may want to request a renewal search as well as an assignment search, to see if the copyright was renewed. (See "Public Domain Works," Chapter 9.)

The *Catalog of Copyright Entries* does not include entries of assignments, so it cannot be used to check the chain of title. However, it does contain information on renewals.

An assignment search will *only* reveal assignments of registered copyrights that have been recorded in the Copyright Office. It will not reveal recent assignments that have not yet been cataloged. The Copyright Office is frequently six months behind in recording assignments.

### Unregistered Copyrights

If the copyright has not been registered, a Copyright Office search will not help you. The only way to check the chain of title for an unregistered work is to contact the copyright owner named in the copyright notice and ask whether the copyright has been assigned.

## Secret Assignments

If you obtain a license from the person or company that you think is the current copyright owner (because that's what the Copyright Office's assignment records indicate) and later learn that your assignor had actually assigned the copyright to someone else before giving you a license, your license will still be valid if it meets three criteria:

- You didn't know of the unrecorded assignment at the time you entered into the license agreement.

- The license is nonexclusive. (An exclusive license is one that does not overlap another grant of rights. See "Licenses," Chapter 4.)

- The license is in writing.

According to the Copyright Act, a nonexclusive written license prevails over a conflicting earlier copyright assignment if the license was taken in good faith before the copyright assignment was recorded, and without notice of the copyright assignment.

> *According to the Copyright Office's records, songwriter Ben assigned the copyright in Ben's song, Foggy Day, to Rotten Music in 1988. In January, 1993, Rotten assigned the copyright in Foggy Day to First State Bank. Bank did not record its assignment. In November, 1993, Rotten gave Developer a written nonexclusive license to use Foggy Day in a multimedia encyclopedia (Rotten didn't tell Developer it had assigned the copyright to Bank, and Developer had no reason to know about the assignment). Developer's license from Rotten is valid because it is in writing and nonexclusive and Developer got it in good faith and without notice of Rotten's assignment to Bank. Bank should have protected its interests by recording its assignment. (Recording is discussed in "Assignments," Chapter 4.)*

If your license is exclusive, you have to record it in the Copyright Office to obtain protection against a conflicting earlier transfer (see "Obtaining a License," later in this chapter).

### Later Assignments

If you get a license from the copyright owner and the copyright owner later assigns the copyright to someone else, the new owner cannot revoke your license if it is nonexclusive and in writing. A nonexclusive, written license prevails over a later assignment.

> *On May 1, 1993, Big Music granted Developer a written, nonexclusive license to use the song Rainy Day. On June 1, 1993, Big Music assigned the copyright in Rainy Day to Theme Music. Big Music cannot require Developer to get a new license from Big.*

### Multiple Assignments

If the copyright has been assigned several times, you need to get your license from the current owner of the copyright—the most recent assignee.

> *Composer assigned the copyright in her song to Small Music, which recorded the assignment. Small Music later assigned the copyright to Big Music, which recorded the assignment. If Developer wants to use the song written by Composer, Developer should get a license from Big Music.*

### Existing Licenses

Both exclusive licenses and nonexclusive licenses can be recorded in the Copyright Office. (Details are discussed in "Obtaining a License," later in this chapter.) Your Copyright Office search report will tell you what kind of existing exclusive licenses there are on a work. Most nonexclusive licensees do not record their licenses.

Unless you want an exclusive license, you don't need to worry about preexisting nonexclusive licenses. An existing nonexclusive licensee has no grounds for complaint if you are granted permission to use the same work on a nonexclusive basis.

Exclusive licenses are a potential problem, though. A copyright owner cannot give you a license that conflicts with an existing exclusive license.

*Developer wants to use excerpts of Publisher's reference book in a multimedia work. Publisher has already granted Massive Multimedia an exclusive license to use the reference book in multimedia works. Publisher cannot give Developer an exclusive or nonexclusive license to use the reference book.*

According to U.S. copyright law, an exclusive licensee can grant sublicenses unless the license agreement states otherwise (an exclusive licensee is considered an "owner" of an interest in copyright). In the previous example, Developer should find out whether Massive Multimedia has the right to sublicense. If it does, Developer should ask Massive for a nonexclusive license to use excerpts of the reference book.

### Finding the Owner

If you have obtained a Copyright Office search for the work you want to use, the search report will give you the copyright owner's address.

If the work is unregistered and a Copyright Office search is not possible, the work's copyright notice page may give the copyright owner's address. For books, the publisher may act as the author's licensing agent, even if the publisher does not own the copyright (or at least the publisher may be able to contact the author for you).

### Jointly Owned Works

For jointly owned works, a single co-owner can give you a nonexclusive license to use the work in the United States unless the co-owners have a contract requiring the consent of all co-owners (see "Joint Authorship and Ownership," Chapter 4). It's safer to contact all co-owners.

### Complications

Determining who owns the copyright in the work you want to use can be complicated by a number of factors. We discuss three such factors in this subsection.

### Copyrighted Components

If the work you want to use incorporates several different copyrightable works, you may need more than one license.

- *Developer wants to use a film clip in a multimedia work that will be shown at trade shows. The film clip contains part of a song. The film's copyright owner does not own the copyright in the song (the film's producer got a nonexclusive license to use the song in the movie). Developer needs to obtain two licenses—one from the owner of the film copyright and one from the owner of the music copyright. The owner of the film copyright cannot authorize Developer to use the music component of the film clip in Developer's work.*

If you only want to use a separately owned component of a larger work, you do not need to get a license from the owner of the copyright in the larger work.

- *Developer wants to use a photograph that was used in a brochure produced by Graphic Artist. The photograph was created by Photographer, who gave Graphic Artist a nonexclusive license to use it in the brochure. Developer does not need to get a license from Graphic Artist. She does need to get a license from Photographer.*

### Derivative Works

If the work you want to use is a derivative work (a work based on a preexisting work) created and owned by someone other than the owner of the underlying work, you will probably need a license from the owner of the underlying work as well as a license from owner of the derivative work.

- *Developer wants to use a clip from the movie Rainy Day, which is based on Jim Brown's novel by the same name. The movie was made by Movieco, which got an exclusive license to make and distribute a movie version of the book. Developer needs licenses from both Movieco and Brown. The license from Movieco will authorize Developer to use the clip of Movieco's film. The license from Jim Brown will authorize Developer to use the book upon which the movie was based.*

If the excerpt from the derivative work that you want to use was created entirely by the creator of the derivative work and is not based on the underlying work, you do not need a license to use the underlying work.

- *The film clip that Developer wants to use (see the previous example) shows a scene that was in no way derived from Jim Brown's book (it was added by the screenwriter to give "sex appeal" to the movie). Developer does not need to get a license from Brown, just from Movieco.*

### Split Rights

Copyright rights for certain types of work—books and music, for example—are often split among several parties through the grant of a number of exclusive licenses or assignments of individual copyright rights. If the copyright owner has split the rights geographically, you will have to get licenses from all the exclusive licensees to obtain worldwide rights.

In some industries, rights are split by market segment or medium as well as by geographic territory.

> *Author granted Book Publisher an exclusive license to publish Author's novel in book form. Author also granted Book Publisher the exclusive right to license the novel to others for book club and condensed-book publication. Author granted Developer the exclusive right to make a motion picture version of the novel. Author retained all other rights in the novel. The copyright rights in the novel have been split by market segment and medium.*

If your Copyright Office search reveals that the rights in a work have been split among several exclusive licensees, you need to get a license from the assignee or exclusive licensee who owns the particular rights that you need.

> *Author granted Book Publisher an exclusive license to publish Author's book in book form, retaining all other rights. If Developer wants to use excerpts of Author's book in Developer's multimedia work, Developer needs to obtain a license from Author (but Developer should carefully review the preexisting license's grant of rights language).*

If the rights have been split, it can be difficult to determine which assignee or licensee owns the rights you need.

> *Developer wants to use an excerpt from Author's book in a multimedia work. The Copyright Office search shows that Author granted Movieco "all audiovisual rights" in Author's book. Author retained all other rights. Although Developer's multimedia work is an audiovisual work as defined by the Copyright Act (see "Types of Works Protected by Copyright," Chapter 2), it is unclear whether the term "audiovisual rights" as used in Author's grant to Movieco gives Movieco the right to grant licenses for use of the book in multimedia works. To be safe, Developer may have to obtain licenses from both Author and Movieco.*

> *Developer wants to use an excerpt from Author's book in a multimedia work. Author assigned the copyright in his book to Publisher. Publisher granted exclusive "electronic publishing rights" in the book to Electro Publishing and exclusive "audiovisual rights" to Movieco. It is unclear whether Publisher, Electro Publishing, or Movieco owns the rights that Developer wants to license.*

It will be several years before we know whether an exclusive license or assignment using special industry terms—granting a movie developer exclusive audiovisual rights in a book, for example—gives the licensee the right to authorize use in multimedia projects. (In the cases being litigated now, the issue is whether a grant of "motion picture rights" or "television rights" includes the right to distribute a film in videocassette form for home use.) If, after reviewing the Copyright Office search report for a work, you are not sure who owns the rights you need, get help from an experienced copyright attorney or find another work to license.

## Determining What Rights You Need

The second step in the licensing process is determining what rights you need to license from the copyright owner.

### Scope of the License

To shield you from an infringement suit, your license must authorize every type of use that you will be making of the licensed work. Consequently, you need to determine how you will be using the work and what rights you need before you seek your license. A license is no protection for uses not authorized in the license.

> *Developer obtained a license to reproduce Photographer's photograph of the Golden Gate bridge in Developer's multimedia work. Although the license did not authorize Developer to alter the photograph, Developer manipulated the image to eliminate cars and pedestrians and create an uncluttered image of the bridge. If Photographer sued Developer for unauthorized exercise of the modification right, Developer's license would be no defense.*

Using a licensed work in ways not authorized in the license may be material breach of the license agreement. If it is, the licensor can terminate the license. In the previous example, Developer's alteration of the photograph is probably a material breach of Developer's license agreement with Photographer. If Photographer terminates the license, Developer will no longer have even the right granted to Developer in the license (the right to use the original photograph in Developer's multimedia work).

If you want the right to use the licensed work in more than one multimedia project, the license must explicitly give you that right.

> *Developer obtained a license to use a five-second clip of Movieco's movie in Developer's work, City Tour. Developer later used the same film clip in another multimedia work, Downtown. Developer's second use of the film clip is copyright infringement.*

### Disclosure

Before you are quoted a license fee, you will need to disclose to the copyright owner (or the rights clearance agency) all uses you are planning to make of the work, and provide detailed information about your planned use of the work. Copyright owners use this information in determining the license fee.

You may have to explain the nature of multimedia works in general. In negotiating licensing fees, it may be helpful to explain to copyright owners that the market for multimedia works is still small and that your budget is small. Otherwise, the owner may be basing the license fee on unrealistic assumptions about the money to be made in multimedia. If you will be licensing a large number of works, explain that to the copyright owner so that the owner will understand that you cannot afford to pay a large fee for permission to use the owner's work.

### What Rights?

You may need permission to exercise some or all of the copyright owner's exclusive rights. (These are defined in "The Exclusive Rights," Chapter 2.) This subsection discusses which of these rights you will need for different types of multimedia works.

***Reproduction Right***   You need permission to reproduce (that is, copy) the licensed work for use in your multimedia project, whatever the nature of your project. Scanning and digitizing a work is a form of copying.

***Modification Right***   If you plan to alter or modify the licensed work, you need permission to exercise the modification right.

***Distribution Right***   Unless your multimedia project is solely for your own personal use, you need permission to distribute the licensed work as contained in your multimedia project. This is true whether you are planning to "distribute" your multimedia work to a single client or to hundreds of customers.

***Public Performance Right and Public Display Right***   Whether you need permission for public performance and public display depends on how your multimedia work will be used. You don't need such a license if your work will be used only by consumers in their own homes. You do need these rights if the work will be used in one of the following three ways (unless one of the exceptions covered in "Exceptions," later in this section, applies):

- If it will be shown at a place open to the public.

- If it will be shown at a place where a substantial number of persons outside a normal circle of family and social acquaintances gathers.

- If it will be transmitted to the public or to a public place by means of a device or process, whether the audience is in the same place or in separate places.

For example, multimedia works that will be used at information kiosks in places such as convention centers, train stations, and tourist attractions, will be publicly performed and displayed because they will be shown at a place open to the public. Works used for corporate training or presentations will be publicly performed and displayed because they will be shown at a place where a substantial number of persons outside a normal circle of family and friends gathers. Works that will be transmitted over interactive TV or to hotel rooms will be publicly performed and displayed because they are transmitted to the public by means of a device.

Videogames distributed for home use do not require a public performance and display license, but videogames used in arcades do.

***Exceptions***   A public performance license is not required for the following uses of a copyrighted work:

- Classroom performance or display of a work by instructors or pupils of a nonprofit educational institution.

- Certain performances by government and religious groups.

- Live performance without any purpose of commercial advantage or payment of fees to performers, if there is no admission charge or the proceeds are used exclusively for educational, religious, or charitable purposes.

Details of these very limited exceptions to the public performance right are stated in Section 110 of the Copyright Act. Even if the intended use of your multimedia works falls within these exceptions, you will still need a license of the reproduction right to include a copyrighted work in your multimedia work. Section 110's exceptions apply only to the public performance and public display rights.

## Obtaining a License

The third step in the licensing process is obtaining a license from the copyright owner. A sample content license is included in Appendix B (Form 11).

### Terms

The terms of the license should cover the following seven points:

- *Definition of the multimedia product or products in which the licensed work can be used (by title or by description or both)*. Pay careful attention to the definition of the multimedia product or products covered by the license. If you want to be able to use the licensed work in future versions of your work or in sequels, include the future versions or sequels in the license's definition of the multimedia product. If your current project involves one medium

(CD-ROM, for example), but you might want to shift it to another medium in the future (interactive television, for example), make certain the license does not limit your right to just the current version's medium. Given the rapid advances in technology, you should try to avoid limiting the product definition to a particular format or configuration.

- *Whether the license is exclusive or nonexclusive (see "Licenses," Chapter 4, for definitions).* Obtaining a very limited exclusive license to use a "hot" property—for example, an exclusive license to use characters from a popular movie in videogames—can be very valuable for marketing the work.

- *Specific authorized uses, such as reproduction, modification, distribution, public performance, and public display.* Any limitations on the amount of the work that can be copied and used should be stated. For example, if authorization to use a photograph is limited to use of the photograph on a single branch of the multimedia work, the license should state this.

- *License fee, whether royalties or one-time fee.*

- *Term (duration) of the license.*

- *Territory limitations, if any.* You probably want a worldwide license, but the licensor (the U.S. copyright owner with whom you are dealing) may not own the worldwide rights.

- *Warranties of ownership and noninfringement.* You should try to get the licensor to warrant three things: That it is the sole and exclusive owner of all rights in the licensed material, that it has the right to grant you the license, and that the licensed material does not infringe any third-party intellectual property rights or other proprietary rights. If you are licensing a film or television show clip or a master recording of music, your license should also include a warranty that any applicable union reuse fees have been paid. (See "Reuse Provisions," Chapter 14.)

You should try to get the licensor to indemnify you and your distributors for damages arising out of breach of these warranties. Warranty and indemnity provisions are discussed in more detail in "The Contract," Chapter 6.

It's possible that you will not be able to obtain these warranties and indemnities, or that the licensor will only give you limited versions. In that case, you must decide if using the work is worth the legal risk involved.

### Formalities

There are certain formalities to attend to in getting a license. They are different for exclusive licenses and nonexclusive licenses.

### *Exclusive Licenses*

Exclusive copyright licenses must be signed and be in writing to be valid. It is a good idea to get exclusive copyright licenses notarized. Notarization is legal evidence of the signing of the license.

If you are obtaining an exclusive license, record it in the Copyright Office. If you record it "in the manner required to give constructive notice" (this term is defined in the fourth paragraph of this subsection), your license will take priority over a conflicting assignment or exclusive license, as explained in "Licenses," Chapter 4.

There is no official Copyright Office form for recording assignments or licenses, so you have to create your own document. You can record the license itself, but most people make up a "short form" license (see Form 12 in Exhibit B) for recording. The Copyright Office has a cover sheet for submitting the document for recording (Form 2 in Appendix G).

To record "in the manner required to give constructive notice," the document you record must give the title or copyright registration number of the work being licensed. If the copyright in that work has not been registered with the Copyright Office, recording your license will not give constructive notice. If the copyright of the work you are licensing has not been registered, insist that the licensor register the copyright by sending a completed registration application to the Copyright Office (see "How to Fill Out Form PA," Chapter 16).

### *Nonexclusive Licenses*

Oral nonexclusive licenses can be enforced—if you can prove their existence. However, you should always get a written license so that you will have proof of the license and its terms. Getting the license in writing will give you protection against conflicting earlier and later transfers, as discussed in "Determining Who Owns the Copyright," earlier in this chapter.

You can, if you wish, record a nonexclusive license in the Copyright Office and get the license notarized. The Copyright Act doesn't say that there is any advantage to doing these things for nonexclusive licenses.

## Termination Right

The Copyright Act gives the author of a work other than a "work made for hire" the right to terminate any license or assignment granted on or after January 1, 1978, during a five-year period that starts 35 years after the grant was made. For works that were first published before 1978, the termination period begins 56 years after the work was first published. This right is discussed "Termination Right," Chapter 4.

Except for licenses to use works made for hire, all licenses are subject to this termination right. The termination right is likely to be of importance only for a small percentage of multimedia works. For such multimedia works, the effect of the termination right will be mitigated by the termination right's derivative works exception, which states that a derivative work prepared before termination of the license may continue to be used after termination.

> *In 1990, Developer got a license to use Author's photograph in Developer's multimedia works, Cityscape and New Town. Developer created Cityscape but did not get around to creating New Town. If Author or Author's heirs terminate Developer's license in 2026, Developer can continue to use the photograph in Cityscape but cannot use the photograph in New Town or in a new version of Cityscape.*

## Possible Licensor's Title Defect

If your license is for a work first distributed to the public between 1966 and 1977, and if the licensed work was not a work made for hire when created, and if your licensor is someone other than the original copyright owner, your licensor's title to the work has a potential defect. This defect arises from the renewal provisions of the 1909 Copyright Act that were carried forward in "transition" provisions of the 1976 Copyright Act. The Supreme Court has interpreted those provisions as giving the heirs of a copyright owner the right to terminate an assignee's or licensee's right to use the licensed work beyond the original 28-year copyright term.

> *In 1993, Publisher granted Developer a license to use an excerpt from a book written by Author, an individual. The book was first published in 1966. Publisher was assigned the copyright and the renewal term rights by Author in 1970. Author died in 1977, long before the renewal period would start (in the 28th year, 1994). Author left a widow and one child. If Author's widow and child apply in 1994 to register a claim to the renewal term, they will be able to terminate Publisher's assignment. That will take away Publisher's right to license the book for the renewal term (1995 through 2041) and the basis for Developer's right to use the book. If Developer wants to use the excerpt of the book beyond 1994—even in a multimedia work that Developer created before 1994 ended—Developer must obtain a new license from Author's widow and child.*

This defect exists only for works that are not works made for hire as defined under the 1909 Copyright Act. The 1909 Copyright Act applied a broader definition of the term than the present Copyright Act does. (See "The Work Made for Hire Rule," Chapter 4.) Because the right to cut off licenses and assignments applies only to the author's heirs and not to the author, evaluating the risk means guessing whether the author is likely to die prior to the beginning of the renewal period (the 28th year of the original term).

If you are considering licensing a work that was first distributed between 1966 and 1977 (inclusive), you should be aware of the potential defect in the licensor's title. As each calendar year ends, works published 28 years earlier, by authors still living, become free of this risk. For example, in 1994, the risk exists for works first published between 1966 and 1977 (inclusive). In 1995, the risk exists for works first published between 1967 and 1977. In 1996, the risk exists for works first published between 1968 and 1977.

If you must license a work for which this risk exists, be aware that you may have to obtain a new license from the author's heirs. While you could get a "back-up" license from the author's spouse and children now to protect you from the risk of having your license terminated in the future, this strategy is not foolproof. The spouse and children could predecease the author. Then the right to claim the renewal term would pass to those designated in the author's will (or the author could change spouses before dying).

## Rights Clearance Agencies

To obtain the licenses that you need, you may want to use a rights clearance agency. These agencies are also known as rights and permissions agencies and copyright clearance agencies. There is a list of such agencies in Appendix C.

A rights clearance agency will find out who owns the rights you need and negotiate licenses for you. (You should still read the first four sections of this chapter and become familiar with licensing issues so that you'll understand the process.) Because these agencies perform rights clearance and licensing as their business, they can probably obtain licenses for you in far less time than it would take you to obtain them yourself.

These agencies are just beginning to handle licensing for multimedia use. They primarily handle rights clearance for movie and television production companies, ad agencies, and corporate video departments. If you use an agency, your agent needs to know exactly how you plan to use the licensed works in your multimedia project. Your intended use of licensed works will probably be different from that of the agent's usual clients.

Most rights clearance agencies charge by the hour. An initial consultation is generally free (but you should ask). You should first determine whether the works you want to use are likely to be available (and for what fee) and whether the agent can suggest alternatives to unavailable or expensive material. Sometimes an agent can give you ideas if you need suggestions for works you might license and use.

These agencies frequently handle right of publicity releases for photographs of celebrities (see "The Rights of Publicity and Privacy," Chapter 13) as well as copyright licensing.

## Stock Houses and Libraries

You can obtain film and video clips, photographs, illustrations, music, and sound effects from stock houses and from music and media libraries. A list of stock houses and media libraries appears in Appendix D.

Stock houses and libraries frequently own the copyrights in works that they license (or they provide material that is in the public domain, such as WPA photographs). They will, for a separate fee, do research for you to help you find suitable material (or you can hire your own content specialist).

As with other content licenses, you should make sure that licenses issued to you by stock houses or libraries cover all of the rights needed for your intended uses of the licensed works (see "Determining What Rights You Need," earlier in this chapter).

## Copyright Assignment

If you find a work that is owned by a single owner and is suitable for repeated use in multimedia works, a copyright assignment may be preferable to a license. With a copyright assignment, you will be able modify the work and use it in many multimedia projects (subject to Visual Artists Rights Act and moral rights limitations, discussed in the last section of this chapter). Because an assignment gives you all of the copyright owner's exclusive rights in the work (see "Assignments," Chapter 4), you won't have to predict in advance what rights you will later need.

If you get an assignment, the assignor will have the right to terminate the assignment in 35 years (or, for works published before January 1, 1978, fifty-six years after the work was first published.) Termination is discussed in "Termination Right," Chapter 4. However, you will still be able to use the assigned work in multimedia works prepared before termination. (See the discussion of the termination right in "Obtaining a License," earlier in this chapter.)

To be valid, a copyright assignment must be in writing and be signed by the copyright owner. You should obtain warranties of title and noninfringement and an indemnity from the assignor. (See the discussion of warranties and indemnities in "Obtaining a License," earlier in this chapter.)

Within one month of getting the copyright assignment, you should record a notarized, short-form assignment (Form 13 in Appendix B) in the Copyright Office "in the manner required to give constructive notice" (see the discussion of this phrase in "Obtaining a License," earlier in this chapter). Use the cover sheet shown in Form 2 in Appendix G. Recording the assignment will protect it against conflicting assignments (see "Assignments," Chapter 4).

## The Visual Artists Rights Act

If you are planning on modifying a third-party work, you should consider whether modification will violate the author's rights under the Visual Artists Rights Act (VARA) or his or her moral rights.

### VARA Rights

VARA gives the owner of a "work of visual art" created on or after June 1, 1991, the right to claim authorship of the work and the right to prevent four things:

- Any intentional distortion, mutilation, or other modification of the work that would be prejudicial to the artist's honor or reputation.
- Destruction of a work of recognized stature.
- Use of the artist's name as the author of a work that the author did not create.
- Use of the artist's name as the author of a work that has been modified in such a way as to be prejudicial to the artist's honor or reputation.

Artists who created works of visual art before June 1, 1991, also have these rights if the artist did not transfer the copyright in the work before that date.

### Definition of Works of Visual Art

According to VARA, works of visual art are limited to the following categories of works (in single copy form or as signed and numbered limited editions of no more than 200 copies):

- Paintings.
- Drawings.
- Prints.
- Sculptures.
- Photographs produced for exhibition purposes.

### Excluded Works

Works made for hire are not works of visual art, nor are the following types of works:

- Posters.
- Maps, globes, and charts.
- Technical drawings.
- Diagrams.
- Models.

- Works of applied art.

- Motion pictures and other audiovisual works.

- Books, magazines, newspapers, and periodicals.

- Data bases.

- Electronic information services and electronic publications.

- Merchandising items.

- Advertising material and packaging material.

### Duration of Rights

The artist who creates a work that is protected under VARA owns the VARA rights in the work even if he or she has assigned the copyright in the work to someone else. The VARA rights endure for the artist's lifetime. If the work was created prior to June, 1991, and is covered by VARA because the artist retained the copyright, the VARA rights endure for the life of the artist plus 50 years.

### Waiver

The VARA rights cannot be transferred, but they can be waived through a written document signed by the artist. If you intend to use a work of visual art in your multimedia project in a way that might violate the author's VARA rights, you should obtain a waiver of those rights. This advice applies even if you own the copyright in the work or have obtained a license from the current copyright owner to use the work of visual art.

### Moral Rights

VARA was passed shortly after the United States joined the Berne Convention. Signatories to the Berne Convention are obligated to protect authors' rights of attribution and integrity. These are known as "moral rights." Most other countries have long recognized moral rights for many types of copyrightable works, not just for works of visual art.

If you will be selling your multimedia work in other countries and are planning on modifying existing copyrightable works, you should find out whether you will be violating the artist's moral rights in the countries in which you will be selling, even if you own the copyrights in the existing works.

Several states—New York and California, for example—have statutes that give limited moral rights to certain types of artistic works. In addition, artists sometimes include moral rights provisions in contracts and assignments with parties who buy their works. Some motion picture directors have contract-based rights to control the alteration of their films.

# 11

## Licensing Content: Industry by Industry

Multimedia developers and publishers use several types of works for "content":

- Books, magazines, and newspapers.

- Motion pictures, television programs, and video.

- Photographs.

- Graphics.

- Clip art.

- Software.

Each of these content industries has its own licensing issues. Those issues are described in this chapter.

Music licensing is covered in Chapter 12.

## Books

The book publishing industry has two general categories of books—trade and nontrade.

### Trade Books

The term "trade books" means books of general interest (fiction, nonfiction, and poetry). Trade books are generally written by authors who are not employees of publishing companies. The individual author either assigns his or her entire copyright to the publisher or grants the publisher rights that fall short of total assignment—for example, "the right to publish in book form." (Assignments and licenses are discussed in "Assignments" and "Licenses," Chapter 4.)

In the past, the "all rights" assignment (assignment of the entire copyright) was common. The current trend is for writers to try to retain certain rights for licensing to other parties. Nonetheless, if you want permission to use part of a book, the permissions department of the book's publisher is a good place to start. Even if the publisher doesn't own the copyright, the publisher may be the owner's licensing agent. If not, the publisher's permissions department should be able to put you in contact with the copyright owner or the owner's agent. You should request Copyright Office registration and assignment searches to confirm what the permissions department tells you about ownership of rights. (Copyright Office searches are discussed in "Determining Who Owns the Copyright," Chapter 10).

In book publishing, split rights situations (discussed in "Determining Who Owns the Copyright," Chapter 10) are common, with either the author or the publisher splitting "subsidiary rights" among a number of exclusive licenses. Subsidiary rights are rights to exploit a work in forms other than first-publication book form.

· *Author granted Publisher "the exclusive right to publish Author's book in book form" and granted Movieco "all motion picture, television and allied rights" in the book.*

The current trend is to negotiate and grant exclusive licenses by market or media segment. Some common rights categories are the first publication right, the reprint right, the audiocassette right, the audiovisual or motion picture right, the translation right, and the electronic version right. If the rights are split up, it may be difficult to tell who has the authority to grant you a license.

### Nontrade Books

Nontrade books—reference and educational books—are often written by the publisher's employees and are works made for hire. (The term "work made for hire" is discussed in "The Work Made for Hire Rule," Chapter 4.) If you want to use excerpts from a nontrade book, you should contact the publisher. However, if the publisher has already granted exclusive licenses, it may be difficult to determine whether the publisher or one of its licensees has the authority to issue you a license.

· *Developer wants to use excerpts from a reference book owned by ED Publishing in his CD-ROM reference work. ED Publishing has already granted "electronic rights" in the book to Electronic Publishing. It is unclear whether ED or Electronic Publishing has the authority to license Developer to use the excerpts.*

## Newspapers, Magazines, and Journals

If you wish to use factual material from newspapers, magazines, and journals, review it to make sure that you need a license. You do not need a license to use facts. A work's copyright does not cover its facts, only its expression. (The reason is discussed in "When You Don't Need a License," Chapter 9).

### Newspapers

Newspaper articles are generally works made for hire written by newspaper employees. However, they may not be employees of the newspaper in which you read the article. Many newspapers are now licensing articles from major newspapers such as *The New York Times* or the *Washington Post*, or from syndicates or news services. Special features are often specially commissioned works made for hire (see "The Work Made for Hire Rule," Chapter 4). Copyrights in syndicated columns (*Dear Abby*, for example) are generally owned by the syndicator.

### Magazines

Many magazine articles are written by employees or by freelancers as specially commissioned works made for hire. Some articles are written by freelancers who retain their copyrights. The copyright on an issue of a magazine does not cover preexisting material used in the magazine unless the preexisting material has been assigned to the publisher or is a work made for hire.

In the past, many magazines obtained from freelance authors only one-time publication rights or North American serial rights (that is, the exclusive right to publish the article in newspapers, magazines, and other serials in North America for the copyright term). The freelance author retained all other rights. Now, an increasing number of magazines require that a freelance author assign all rights to the magazine.

### Journals

Articles in technical and scholarly journals are written primarily by freelancers. Many are written as specially commissioned works made for hire (see "The Work Made for Hire Rule," Chapter 4). Other articles are written by freelancers and licensed or assigned to the journal.

## Motion Pictures and Television

To lawfully use a film or television clip, depending on the situation, you may have to obtain licenses or releases from a number of parties:

- The owner of the copyright in the underlying work (novel, short story, or play) on which the work you want to use was based.

- The owner of the copyright in the motion picture, television series or mini-series, or documentary you want to use.

- The performers (and possibly other contributors).

You will also have to pay applicable union reuse fees. If the film clip contains music or choreography, you may also have to obtain separate licenses for those.

These issues are discussed in the rest of the this section.

### The Underlying Work's Copyright

Many movies, television series, and mini-series are derivative works based on original plays, short stories, or novels. If you want to use a clip from a work that was based on a play, short story, or novel, you should obtain Copyright Office registration and assignment searches to find out who owns the copyright in the underlying work, if it is not in the public domain. (Copyright Office searches are discussed in "Determining Who Owns the Copyright," Chapter 10.) Unless the studio or producer acquired all rights in the underlying work, you will probably need a license from the owner of the underlying work. (The reason is discussed in "Determining Who Owns the Copyright," Chapter 10).

### The Desired Work's Copyright

You should request Copyright Office registration and assignment searches to find out who owns the copyright in the motion picture, television series, mini-series, or documentary you want to use. In recent years, many movie production companies and studios have assigned the copyrights in their entire libraries of copyrighted motion pictures, so you cannot assume that the company named in the copyright notice is the current owner of the motion picture's copyright.

Most prime-time television series, mini-series, and documentaries are not owned by the television networks that broadcast these programs. They are licensed by the networks from independent producers. However, networks sometimes acquire audiovisual rights in series or documentaries. This situation may change as the rules regarding network ownership change.

### Performers and Contributors

Find out whether those who worked on the film, series, mini-series, or documentary—writer, writer-producer, director, and performers—have an ownership interest in the copyright. Generally they do not, because their contributions are works made for hire, but you should ask your licensor about this.

#### *The Writer*

The script is usually a specially commissioned work made for hire owned by the studio or producer. Sometimes, though, a motion picture, television series, mini-series, or documentary is made based on an original script created by a writer "on spec" (without a contract). In that situation, the producer usually gets an assignment of the script's copyright and registers the assignment in the Copyright Office.

However, if the script was subject to the Writers Guild Basic Agreement, the writer may have retained certain rights in the script. Thus, either the producer or the writer may own the rights you need. (See "Reuse Provisions," Chapter 14.)

### *The Director*

Contracts between producers and directors generally provide that the director's contribution to a motion picture is a work made for hire that belongs to the producer. However, directors sometimes include in these contracts a clause requiring that the director's consent be obtained if the work is to be altered. Under the Directors Guild Basic Agreement, a director must be consulted if a theatrical motion picture is edited for certain other uses. (See "Reuse Provisions," Chapter 14.)

### *Performers*

Contracts between producers and performers generally provide that a performer's contribution to a motion picture, television series, mini-series, or documentary is a work made for hire owned by the producer, so you probably don't need to get copyright licenses from performers shown in the clip (although you do need a license from the clip's copyright owner). You will probably need to obtain releases from all performers shown or heard in the clip before using the clip in your multimedia work, if the producer didn't get broad releases from them. (This topic is discussed in "The Rights of Publicity and Privacy," Chapter 13.)

If the performers belong to the Screen Actor's Guild or AFTRA (American Federation of Television and Radio Artists), in most instances union rules require that performers' consent be obtained and that reuse fees be negotiated or paid before a clip containing photography or sound track of the performer is used in another work. (This topic is discussed in "Reuse Provisions," Chapter 14.)

## Union Reuse Fees

Directors, actors, and screenwriters generally belong to unions. The unions have collective bargaining agreements with studios and developers requiring the payment of reuse fees when a clip is used in a medium other than the medium for which the film or program was originally intended. If you use a clip in a multimedia project, the current owner of the work's copyright will require you to get the necessary consents and pay reuse fees (or give the owner the money to pay the fees). Union reuse fees are discussed in "Reuse Provisions," Chapter 14.

### Music or Choreography

If the clip contains music or choreography, you may have to obtain a separate license authorizing you to use it. If the music or choreography was created and recorded as a work made for hire for the producer, the owner of the clip's copyright owns the rights to the music or choreography and can authorize you to use the music. However, if the music or choreography was not created as a work made for hire and is still protected by copyright, the clip's copyright owner usually will not have authority to grant you a license to use the music or choreography as contained in the clip. In that case, obtain Copyright Office registration and assignment searches to determine who owns the music or choreography copyright. (Copyright Office searches are discussed in "Determining Who Owns the Copyright," Chapter 10, and music licensing is discussed in "Option #2: Using Preexisting Music," Chapter 12.)

If the music was recorded from a record company's "master recording," you may also need a separate license from the owner of the "master recording" copyright. (See "Option #2: Using Preexisting Music," Chapter 12.)

## Video Footage

If you are obtaining video footage from an independent producer or a video library, make certain that the producer obtained the releases required under the laws of publicity and privacy (see "The Rights of Publicity and Privacy," Chapter 13). Media libraries are discussed in "Stock Houses and Libraries," Chapter 10.

If you will be using a video clip that contains copyrighted music or choreography owned by someone other than the producer, get separate licenses to use the music or choreography. Even if you have good reason to believe that a producer has the right to grant you a license to use the music or choreography in your multimedia work, your use will infringe the music or choreography copyright if the producer does not have that right. If the clip shows copyrighted objects—sculptures or paintings, for example—you need a license to use the images of those objects (see "Permits," Chapter 13), as well as a license from the clip's copyright owner.

## Logos and Characters

If you want to use a title logo or character from a motion picture, television series, fiction series, or cartoon strip in your multimedia work, you need to obtain a "merchandise license" from the owner of the character. So-called "distinctively delineated" characters are protected under both copyright law and trademark law (trademark law protects the owner's right to use the character in connection with goods or services).

*Developer wants to use a drawing of a famous cartoon character in her multimedia work and on the packaging in which her work will be distributed. The cartoon character is protected by the copyright in the cartoon strip in which the character appears. The name and image of the cartoon character are also protected under trademark law. If Developer uses a drawing of the cartoon character without obtaining a merchandise license, she will be infringing third-party copyright and trademark rights.*

A typical merchandise license authorizes the licensee to use the licensed character or title in artwork preapproved by the licensor in connection with the manufacture, sale, and distribution of specified products.

## Photographs

Copyrights in photographs made by employees—a newspaper photographer or employee of a corporation's communications department, for example—are owned by the employer.

Many photographers work as independent contractors. Copyrights in photographs created by a photographer for a client ("on assignment") are owned by the photographer unless:

- The client got an assignment of the copyright; or

- The photograph was made as a specially commissioned work made for hire. (This topic is discussed in "Copyright Ownership," Chapter 8.)

### Who Owns It?

Determining who owns the copyright in a photograph made by a freelance photographer can be difficult. If the photograph was created by a freelance photographer for a client and the copyright is not registered, the only way to determine who owns the copyright is to ask the photographer or the client. Either or both of these parties may have misconceptions about the rules of copyright ownership or the application of the rules to the particular photograph. For example:

- The client may think that because it has a print of the photograph, it owns the copyright and has the right to authorize use of the photograph. This ignores the distinction copyright law makes between ownership of a copy and ownership of copyright rights (discussed in "Owning a Copy of a Work," Chapter 4).

- The client may think that because it ordered and paid for making the photograph, it owns the copyright. This ignores the ownership rules for works created by independent contractors (discussed in "Copyright Ownership," Chapter 8).

- The photographer may not remember giving an assignment or signing a work made for hire agreement, or may not understand the legal significance of those agreements.

The problem of determining copyright ownership for photographs is further complicated because photographs are often incorporated in other works—ads, brochures, and magazine articles, for example. Frequently, the only copyright notice in these works is the one for the owner of the copyright in the larger work. To determine who owns the copyright in the photograph, you have to contact the owner of the copyright in the larger work.

You can avoid "who owns it" problems by using stock photography from stock houses or media libraries, discussed in "Stock Houses and Libraries," Chapter 10.

### Photographers' Concerns

Once a photograph has been digitized, it can easily be copied, distributed, and altered. Some photographers may be reluctant to grant you a license to use their photographs in your multimedia work. This may be because they are concerned that the digitized version that you create will be redistributed to others and that you and others will alter the image without permission. With digital editing software, photographs can be altered to the point where it would be difficult to prove infringement (because it is difficult to prove that a derivative version came from the original photograph). If you plan to alter the image, make sure your license gives you the right to do so.

### Miscellaneous Issues

If you want to use a photograph of a copyrighted work—a piece of sculpture, for example—you need a license from the owner of the copyright in the sculpture and from the owner of the copyright in the photograph. (This topic is discussed in "Permits," Chapter 13.)

If you want to use a photograph of a living person, you should get a release of publicity and privacy rights from the person. In some states, you should not use a photograph of a deceased person unless you get a release from that person's heirs. (See "The Rights of Publicity and Privacy," Chapter 13.)

## Graphics and Illustrations

Graphics and illustrations created by employees—for example, a magazine cover by an employee of a magazine publisher—are owned by the employer as works made for hire.

If the graphics or illustrations appear in a work created for another party, the other party may own the copyright.

*Ed, an employee of Ad Agency, created an ad for Client. The copyright in the ad belongs to Client if Client got an assignment of the copyright. Otherwise, Ad Agency owns the copyright in the ad.*

In the United States, much of the graphic design and illustration work is done by independent contractors. Designs and illustrations made by independent contractors may be owned by the hiring parties through assignment or as specially created works made for hire. (See "Copyright Ownership," Chapter 8.) However, the standard contracts put out by the graphic arts trade associations generally provide that the artist owns the copyright.

If you are negotiating with a graphic artist or illustrator for permission to use his or her work, he or she will probably want to know how you plan to use the work. You should be prepared to discuss your potential use in detail, because many graphic designers are concerned about how their works will look when incorporated into larger works. For example, the latest version of the Graphic Artists Guild standard contract states that "any electronic alteration of original art (color shift, mirroring, flopping, combination cut and paste, deletion) is prohibited without the express permission of the artist." If you do not get an assignment of the copyright in the work done for you by a graphic artist, make sure your license gives you the right to use the work as you plan to use it. (See "Obtaining a License," Chapter 10.)

## Clip Art and Multimedia Tools

In your multimedia projects, you can generally use clip art and stock content from multimedia development tools without obtaining licenses. However, you should carefully review the written material distributed with these works. In many cases, the material comes with express or implied licenses that restrict use of the collection. Some of these licenses provide only limited permission to use the product—for example, use for noncommercial purposes, use in no more than a stated number of copies, or use only by the purchaser.

The packaging for these products can be deceptive. You may have to read the "read me" file to determine what uses are authorized. One common restriction is a limitation on "public performance" uses. (This term is discussed in "The Exclusive Rights," Chapter 2, and "Determining What Rights You Need," Chapter 10.)

Some stock photo collections require the consent of the original photographer for commercial use. Certain clip art collections may also have this restriction.

If you are planning widespread distribution of your work, discuss these issues with the company that created the clip art or stock content to understand the basis of their rights and the authorized uses of the company's products.

## Works of Fine Art

As with photographs, the ownership of copyrights in works of fine art is subject to significant confusion. Owners of a copy of the work—a painting or a sculpture, for example—often think they own the copyright in the work. However, under current law, unless they employed the artist or obtained an assignment of the copyright from the artist, they don't. (See "Copyright Ownership," Chapter 8.)

If you want to use an image of a work of fine art in your multimedia work, and the owner of the copy doesn't own the copyright, you should find the artist and obtain a license from the artist. (This topic is discussed in "Permits," Chapter 13.)

If you plan to alter a "work of visual art," you should read "The Visual Artists Rights Act," Chapter 10, and you should get any necessary waivers from the artist who created the work (in addition to a copyright license). The Act defines a "work of visual art" as a limited-edition painting, drawing, print, sculpture,
or photograph produced for exhibition purposes. Works made for hire are excluded from the definition.

## Software

If you are using software that is owned by a third party, you should obtain a license from the copyright owner. If your software is developed for you by a software consultant, you should obtain a copyright assignment or license from the consultant. For a sample software component license, see Form 14 in Appendix B.

# 12.

## Using Music

To obtain music for your multimedia works, you can create original music, get permission to use preexisting copyrighted music, find public domain music, or use music from a music library. There are legal issues that must be considered for each of these four options.

## Copyrights in Music

Original musical compositions are protected by copyright as soon as they are fixed in any tangible medium of expression. As with other intellectual property, the owner of a copyrighted musical composition has the exclusive right to:

- Reproduce and distribute the musical composition in sheet music and in phonorecords (defined broadly to include audiotapes and compact discs).

- Modify the composition to create derivative works based on the composition.

- Publicly display the composition.

- Publicly perform the composition.

(These are the same rights discussed in "The Exclusive Rights," Chapter 2.)

In some respects, music copyright law differs from copyright law in general. Special features of music copyright law are discussed in this section.

### Compulsory License Provision

For most types of works, whether to permit third parties to use a copyrighted work is solely up to the copyright owner. However, the Copyright Act has a "compulsory license" provision for music. This provision stipulates that once phonorecords of a musical work have been distributed to the public, any other person may obtain a compulsory license to make and distribute phonorecords of the work to the public for private use (in other words, for home use).

The compulsory licensing provision does not apply to licensing for multimedia works for two reasons:

- Multimedia works are not within the Copyright Act's definition of phonorecords ("material objects in which sounds, *other than those accompanying a motion picture or other audiovisual work*, are fixed by any method now known or later developed").

- Multimedia works require "synchronization" licenses—permission to use music in synchronization with an audiovisual work. Synchronization licenses cannot be obtained under the compulsory license provision. (Synchronization licenses are discussed in "Option #2: Using Preexisting Music," later in this chapter.)

### Sound Recordings

Once musical compositions are recorded, the resulting sound recording is a separate work. It has a copyright that is separate from the copyrights on the musical compositions used in the recording. The copyright on a sound recording covers the original expression added by the record developer in creating the recording—the way the musical composition is sung on the recording, the way it is played, the musical arrangement, the sound engineer's mixing, and so on.

The Copyright Act defines sound recordings as "works that result from the fixation of a series of musical, spoken, or other sounds regardless of the nature of the material objects, such as discs, tapes, or other phonorecords, in which they are embodied." Only original sound recordings fixed and published on or after February 15, 1972, are protected by copyright. Pre-1972 sound recordings are not protected under federal copyright law. However, they may be protected under state law.

In the United States, the owner of a sound recording copyright gives notice of copyright by using the ℗ symbol. If you carefully examine the packaging that comes with a record, tape, or compact disc, you will see that the packaging contains a sound recording copyright—for example, "℗ 1993 Pacific Entertainment." Copyright information for the individual songs usually appears on the liner notes inside the package.

### Licensing

What licenses you need to use preexisting music in your multimedia works depends on whether you will be taping a preexisting sound recording or recording your own version of the musical compositions you use.

- If you will be using musicians to record your own version of a musical composition, you need a license from the owner of the musical composition copyright.

- If you will be taping music from a record, tape, or compact disc, you need two copyright licenses—one from the owner of the copyright in the musical composition and one from the owner of the copyright in the sound recording. The owner of the musical composition copyright generally cannot authorize you to copy the version of the song that is fixed in the sound recording. The owner of the sound recording copyright generally cannot authorize you to use the song. Music licensing is discussed in "Option #2: Using Preexisting Music," later in this chapter.

# Option #1: Creating Original Music

You may think that creating original music for your multimedia work is not practical because you don't know any composers, and you can't afford to pay for original music. Both of these assumptions are incorrect. Full-service music arranging and composing services with reasonable fees can be found in most major cities (check the Yellow Pages under "Music Arrangers and Composers" and video industry directories).

A full-service arranging and composing facility can provide orchestration and production of the finished piece as well as composition. It can also create a sound recording (known in the music industry as a "master recording") of the original music.

## Using an Arranging and Composing Service

Like your other production contracts, your agreement with a music arranging and composing service should take the form of a signed written contract (see "Written Contracts," Chapter 5). The contract should spell out the rights and duties of each party to the agreement. The contract should cover the following points:

- Whether the arranging and composing service is obligated to compose, compose and arrange, or compose, arrange, and produce the master recording.

- Who will own the copyright in the music (and in the master recording, if one is to be made). If you obtain ownership of the copyrights in the music and in the master recording, you can copy the master in the future without worrying about copyright clearance and license fees (see "Using Works That You Own," Chapter 9). To avoid future legal disputes with the arranging and composing service and to provide you with maximum flexibility, the contract should state that you will own all rights, including the copyrights, everywhere in the world and for all time. To ensure that you obtain ownership, your agreement should also contain a copyright assignment or work made for hire provision (as discussed in "Copyright Ownership," Chapter 8).

- How much you will pay for the service's work and when payment is due.

- Who will pay any applicable American Federation of Musicians union fees, if the service is to create the master recording as well as compose and arrange the music. (See "Unions and Multimedia," Chapter 14.)

- Whether the agreement is assignable. If you are expecting the work to be done by particular individuals who are employed by the arranging and composing service, the contract should state that the work must be done by those individuals and that the service cannot assign its contract obligations to another party. (See "Contracts with Independent Contractors," Chapter 8.)

### Warranties

Your contract with the arranging and composing service should include a warranty by the service that the material is original and does not infringe upon third parties' copyrights, trademarks, or other property rights. The contract should also include an indemnity provision. (Warranty and indemnity provisions are discussed in "Contracts with Independent Contractors," Chapter 8.)

## Option #2: Using Preexisting Music

To use preexisting copyrighted music, you must obtain licenses for the chosen musical compositions. To use music you create by copying preexisting recordings, you must obtain master recording licenses from the owners of the sound recordings as well as licenses to use the musical compositions.

Most composers in this country assign their copyrights to a music publishing company in exchange for a percentage of all future royalties generated by licensing the composition. If the composer of the musical composition you want to use has assigned the copyright, you need to obtain a license from the current copyright owner, not from the composer (see "Determining Who Owns the Copyright," Chapter 10).

### Myths About Music Copying

The music industry in this country will not permit copyright infringement and you should not use copyrighted musical compositions or sound recordings without getting licenses—nor should you believe the following myths about music copying:

**Myth #1**     *"Copying a small amount is OK."*

Many people think that it is permissible to use three or four bars of a song without getting permission from the copyright owner. This is not true. Copying a small amount of a work is copyright infringement if what is copied is a qualitatively substantial portion of the copied work—part of the chorus of a song, for example.

In one case, the court held that copying a *six-note phrase* from a work was copyright infringement because the copied phrase, in spite of its brevity, was what caused audiences to listen, applaud, and buy copies of the work.

Whether copying a small amount of a song is infringement or not can only be decided on a case-by-case basis. Given the costs of copyright litigation and the penalties for infringement, you should obtain a license if you plan to use any portion of a song.

**Myth #2**    *"Digital sampling is OK."*

Digital sampling means extracting portions of a prior recording for use in a new recording using a device that can store the copied material in a computer's memory. This process may be copyright infringement of both the sound recording and the copied musical composition.

In 1991, a Federal District Court in New York enjoined all sales of a rap artist's album because the artist had included a digital sample of three words and accompanying music taken from a recording of a Gilbert O'Sullivan song. While some digital sampling may be noninfringing—using a two-note phrase or a single grunt from a background singer, for example—it is difficult to know where to draw the line between infringing and noninfringing sampling. (*De minimus* copying—copying a small amount—is discussed in "Myths," Chapter 9).

Fair use (discussed in "When You Don't Need a License," Chapter 9) is unlikely to be a defense to digital sampling for commercial production of multimedia works. Avoid sampling or obtain a license.

**Myth #3**    *"It's OK to copy a song's melody so long as I don't copy the lyrics."*

Using the melody of a copyrighted song without the lyrics is infringement if you don't obtain a license. The copyright on a song covers both the lyrics and the melody. The fact that you have not copied the entire copyrighted work (lyrics plus melody) does not excuse the copying of the protected melody.

**Myth #4**    *"It's OK to copy a song's melody if I use new words with the melody."*

When you add new words to a song, you are "reproducing" the melody and creating a "derivative work" based on the original song, violating the copyright owner's reproduction and modification rights. (These rights are discussed in "The Exclusive Rights," Chapter 2.) To lawfully use the melody of a copyrighted song with new lyrics, you need a license to modify the work.

**Myth #5**    *"I bought this record, so it's OK for me to copy it."*

The purchase of a copy of a protected work does not give the purchaser permission to exercise the copyright owner's exclusive rights with respect to the work. In copyright law, ownership of a copy of a protected work or of a phonorecord is separate from ownership of the copyright rights. (This topic is discussed in "Owning a Copy of a Work," Chapter 4.)

**Myth #6**    *"It's OK to copy a song to poke fun at it."*

In the past, copyright law has generally viewed parody—copying a portion of a copyrighted work for satirical comment (to poke fun at it)—as a form of fair use. (Parody is discussed in "When You Don't Need a License," Chapter 9.)

However, a federal appellate court recently held that a rap group's version of *Pretty Woman*, created with "blatantly commercial" purpose, was not a parody and not fair use. The case has been appealed to the Supreme Court. Be cautious about relying on a parody defense until this case (*Campbell v. Acuff-Rose*) is decided.

## Methods of Obtaining Licenses

The performing rights organizations—American Society of Composers, Authors, & Publishers (ASCAP) and Broadcast Music Incorporated (BMI)—cannot help you obtain the permission you need to use copyrighted music in a multimedia work. While most songwriters belong to one of these organizations, ASCAP and BMI grant public performance licenses only. To use music in a multimedia work, you need a "synchronization" license (discussed in "What Rights You Need," later in this chapter).

There are two types of agencies that can help you get music licenses: the Harry Fox Agency, which represents a number of music publishers, and rights clearance agencies.

### The Harry Fox Agency

While some music publishers handle their own music licensing, many publishers have authorized the Harry Fox Agency (established by the National Music Publishers Association) as their licensing agent. The agency's phone number is (212) 370-5330.

This agency has been granting multimedia licenses for the last several years, both for works designed for in-house use and for works designed for the consumer market. There is no charge for using the agency's services. Of course, the copyright owner will charge you a license fee for using the composition. The agency's fee is paid by the music publisher on whose behalf the agency acts.

### Rights Clearance Agencies

You can use a rights clearance agency (also known as a rights and permission agency) to obtain the music licenses you need. A rights clearance agency will find out who owns the copyrights and whether licenses are available for your intended use. These agencies will also negotiate license fees and obtain licenses for you. Rights clearance agencies are discussed in "Rights Clearance Agencies," Chapter 10. A list of these agencies is in Appendix C.

Using a rights clearance agency is a good idea if you are planning on using excerpts of many musical compositions in your work (you may go crazy if you don't use one). If you are using excerpts of only a few, decide whether the clearance fee charged by a clearance agency is worth the trouble you will save yourself.

### Getting Started

If you are planning on using copyrighted music in your multimedia work, clear the rights before you put your multimedia work together. Remember, the Copyright Act gives you no legal basis for demanding that a copyright owner give you a license. If you have a record, tape, or compact disc of a song that you want to use, you may find the name of the copyright owner for the song in the liner notes (for example, *Sunny Day*, by Susie Songwriter, Copyright 1992 XYZ Music, Inc.). The company named in the sound recording copyright notice—"Ⓟ"—owns the copyright in the sound recording, not the copyrights in the individual songs. You need permission from the record company only if you are planning on copying the actual recording of the song. (This topic is discussed in "Master Recording Licenses," later in this chapter).

To get started, call the music publisher and ask whether it has its own licensing department or uses the Harry Fox Agency for licensing. If the Harry Fox Agency handles the publisher's licensing, call them and ask for the agent who handles multimedia licenses. If you are using a rights clearance agency, the agency will find out who owns the copyrights in the songs you want to use. Make certain that the agent with whom you are dealing understands what multimedia is and what use you will be making of music in your multimedia work. (See "Determining What Rights You Need," Chapter 10.)If you do not know who owns the copyright in the song you want, call the Harry Fox Agency or the index department of ASCAP or BMI (the phone numbers are in Appendix C) to find out. You can also look the song up by title in the *Catalog of Copyright Entries* to find out who registered the copyright. (This catalog is discussed in "Determining Who Owns the Copyright," Chapter 10.)

If you are planning widespread distribution of your work, you should request Copyright Office registration and assignment searches for each song you want to use—even if you think you have identified the copyright owners. (Searches are discussed in "Determining Who Owns the Copyright," Chapter 10.) While you should try to get a warranty of noninfringement and an indemnity from all copyright owners who grant you licenses (see "Obtaining a License," Chapter 10), music publishers will generally give you only a limited indemnity in which their exposure is limited to the amount of the license fee.

Complete the Copyright Office search early, so that you will be able to substitute other works if there are problems with the work's chain of title. (Chain of title complications are discussed in "Determining Who Owns the Copyright," Chapter 10.)

Music publishers that have not previously granted multimedia licenses may be reluctant to grant licenses for this new medium. The reluctance comes from concern that granting licenses for a new medium will somehow have a negative effect on the value of the musical works. You may have to educate the publisher's licensing agent about multimedia works. Explain the technology, explain what role music will play in your multimedia work, and even send the licensing agent a copy of a sample multimedia work. You might also suggest the name of a commercially marketed multimedia work that the agent can view. Music publishers should be encouraged to view multimedia as a new avenue for the exploitation of music—and a way to increase the public's exposure to their music. Most members of the music publishing business are eager to find new markets for music and for music licenses, and they will work with you to create a good business agreement.

As with other types of works, before you begin negotiating for a license, you should know exactly what use you will make of the licensed music and disclose all your planned uses. (See "Determining What Rights You Need," Chapter 10.) You will need to provide detailed information before you are quoted a license fee (music publishers use the information on your planned uses in determining their fee).

Remember that while a copyright license is a defense to infringement, a license is no protection for uses of the work that are not authorized in the license. (See "Determining What Rights You Need," Chapter 10.)

*Developer obtained a license from Music Publisher to use Music Publisher's copyrighted song, Windy Hill, in Developer's multimedia work. Although the license did not authorize Developer to change the lyrics, Developer changed them. Developer's license is no defense to an infringement suit charging Developer with unauthorized modification of the song. If Developer wanted to change the words, Developer should have obtained "parody authorization" from Music Publisher (permission to modify the lyrics).*

If you want the right to use the music in more than one multimedia work, the license must explicitly give you that right. Consequently, the licensing agent needs to know what you want.

*Developer obtained a license to use a five-second excerpt of Music Publisher's copyrighted song in Developer's work City Tour. Developer later used the same excerpt in another multimedia work, Downtown. Developer's use of the music in Downtown is copyright infringement.*

## What Rights You Need

To use copyrighted music in a multimedia work, you need a license to reproduce the chosen music for use in your multimedia work and to distribute copies of the music as it appears in your finished product. In some cases, you will also need a public performance and public display license. (These rights are discussed in "The Exclusive Rights," Chapter 2, and in "Determining What Rights You Need," Chapter 10). If you plan to modify the music—create new lyrics, for example—you also need a license to do that. The music publisher's contract with the songwriter may require that the songwriter give consent for alterations.

The music industry has its own licensing terminology, and it is helpful to know the terminology when dealing with music publishers:

- *Mechanical license.* A license to copy and distribute a song in the form of records, tapes, or compact discs (audio only) is known as a "mechanical" license. This type license doesn't apply to multimedia works.

- *Synchronization license.* A license to copy and distribute music in synchronization with an audiovisual work is known as a synchronization license (also called a "synch" license). Because multimedia works contain audiovisual features, the synch license is closest—in terms of traditional licensing categories—to what you need to reproduce music in your multimedia work.

- *Parody authorization.* Permission to modify the lyrics to a song is known as parody authorization.

## The License

The license should cover the following points:

- Definition of the multimedia product or products in which the music can be used (by title or by description or both). Pay careful attention to this provision. To be able to use the licensed music in future versions or in sequels, you must include future versions or sequels in the definition of the multimedia product. Given the rapid advances in technology, you should try to avoid limiting the product definition to a particular format or configuration (CD-ROM, for example).

- Authorized uses, including any limitations on the amount of the work that can be copied and used.

- Consideration for the license, whether royalties or one-time fee. (See "Fee Considerations," later in this chapter.)

- Term (duration) of the license.

- Territory limitations, if any. You will probably want a worldwide license, but the United States copyright owner may not own the worldwide rights.

- Whether the license is exclusive or nonexclusive. (These terms are defined in "Licenses," Chapter 4).

- Warranties and indemnity. (These are discussed in "Obtaining a License," Chapter 10.)

Licenses are discussed in more detail in "Obtaining a License," Chapter 10.

The Harry Fox Agency has created a special multimedia license. A copy of it appears as Form 15 in Appendix B. For another example of a multimedia music license, see Form 16 in Appendix B.

### Fee Considerations

If you are planning to use excerpts from a large number of songs in your multimedia work, you may find it useful to bring this to the attention of licensing agents with whom you deal. You cannot afford to pay each music publisher's motion picture rate for hundreds of songs (not to mention other copyrighted works).

If your work is intended for commercial distribution to consumers, tell the licensing agent how many units you expect to sell and what the retail price per unit will be. Otherwise, music publishers and licensing agents are likely to think that the market and the amount of money you will make on your work are much larger than they are likely to be.

In determining license fees, publishers traditionally take into account the importance of the music in the finished work. For example, the fee for using a publisher's song as "theme" music played over a movie's title is generally higher than the fee for using the song as background music. In an interactive multimedia work, the importance of a song or song excerpt will often vary according to how the user interacts with the multimedia work (because the song plays only when a certain segment of the work is accessed, or because the developer made it possible for the user to customize the work). Similarly, length of use (in number of seconds) is generally a factor in determining the license fee. For an interactive multimedia work, the number of seconds a song is actually played during use of the work will vary from one user to the next.

### After You Get a License

Once you have obtained a license, stick to its terms. Do only what you are authorized to do. Be careful to comply with all your license obligations, such as royalty payments. Failure to make royalty payments as required by the license may be material breach of contract. (Breach is discussed in "What is a Contract?," Chapter 5). If you are required by the license to pay royalties every quarter and you have a quarter in which you make nothing and so owe no royalties, tell the licensor that no royalties are due for that quarter.

### Master Recording Licenses

If you decide to copy existing sound recordings, you need licenses from the record companies that own the sound recording copyrights. Licenses to copy sound recordings are known in the music industry as master recording licenses or master licenses. Music licenses from music publishers do not authorize you to copy the copyrighted sound recordings.

Obtaining a master license is likely to be difficult. If you succeed in obtaining a license, the license fee may be high. However, as the record industry becomes more knowledgeable about multimedia works, it is likely that an increasing number of record companies will begin making their works available to multimedia developers.

The record company's contract with the recording artist may require that the record company obtain the artist's permission before granting you a master license. Even if the contract does not require the artist's permission for the grant of master licenses, you should obtain the artist's consent to avoid violating an artist's right of publicity in his or her voice (see "The Rights of Publicity and Privacy," Chapter 13). This is true unless the artist's contract with the record company waives the right of publicity for all uses of the recording. If the recording was made by a vocalist who belongs to AFTRA (the American Federation of Radio and Television Artists), you must also comply with AFTRA's reuse rules (see "Reuse Provisions," Chapter 14.) Many recording artists belong to AFTRA.

You may also need permission from the American Federation of Musicians (AFM) to use the master recording (see "Reuse Provisions," Chapter 14). The master license should contain a warranty that the record company has paid all applicable AFM fees.

A sample sound recording license is shown in Form 16 in Appendix B. This license authorizes the licensee to use the licensor's musical compositions and sound recordings.

Sound recordings fixed and published before February 15, 1972, are not protected by federal copyright law, but they may be protected under common law copyright or under state antipiracy statutes. It is advisable to get record company consent for the use of pre-1972 sound recordings.

### Recording Your Own Version

Given the difficulty and expense of obtaining master licenses from record companies, you may decide to hire your own musicians to record music for your multimedia work (or to use a music production service to do that). Whether you hire musicians or use a production service, you should get a written contract with an appropriate copyright assignment or work made for hire provision. (See "Copyright Ownership," Chapter 8.)

Musicians' union issues are covered in "Signing Collective Bargaining Agreements" and "Unions and Multimedia," Chapter 14. If you are using a production service, your contract with the service should state whether you or the production service are responsible for paying any applicable American Federation of Musicians union fees.

### Sound-Alike Recordings

In 1988, Bette Midler won a $400,000 judgment in federal court in California against an ad agency that used a sound-alike version of her hit, *Do You Want to Dance*. The singer who recorded the sound-alike version—a back-up singer for Ms. Midler—was instructed to sound as much as possible like the Bette Midler record. The court held that the ad agency had appropriated what was not theirs. Because of this case, several similar cases have been filed. You should not create sound-alike recordings for use in your multimedia work without consulting an experienced attorney.

### Public Performance Licenses

If you need a public performance license (see "Determining What Rights You Need," Chapter 10), ASCAP and BMI may be able to help you. This will depend on whether you need a dramatic or nondramatic performance license. A dramatic performance of a composition is a rendition that is woven into and carries forward a plot and its action (for example, an opera). Whether a use is dramatic or nondramatic must be determined on a case-by-case basis.

ASCAP and BMI issue only nondramatic public performance licenses. Copyright owners—music publishers, generally—retain the right to license dramatic performance rights.

If you need a nondramatic performance license because your work will be shown on television or at a public facility that regularly hosts musical entertainment events (a convention center, for example), you may find that you are already covered by a license obtained by the television station or facility. Television stations, nightclubs, concert halls, and even amusement parks generally pay ASCAP and BMI an annual fee for a "blanket license" that permits the licensee to make unlimited nondramatic-performance use of all songs in these organizations' catalogs.

If you need to obtain your own license, you can find out whether ASCAP or BMI handles the songs you want by calling either of those organizations. If you have album liner notes for a recorded version of the song, the liner notes will usually indicate whether ASCAP or BMI handles performance rights for the song—for example, "1989 Massive Music (BMI)."

If you are obtaining a master license to copy a song from an existing recording, your license does not need to include permission for public performance. There is no public performance right in sound recordings.

## Option #3: Public Domain Music

If you can locate appropriate public domain music for your multimedia work, you are free to use it—that is, you are free to record your own version of the public domain song. You cannot lawfully copy a public domain song as recorded on a copyrighted record, tape, or compact disc unless you get a master license from the record company that owns the sound recording copyright (see "Master Recording Licenses," earlier in this chapter).

### Copyrighted Arrangements

While you are free to use a public domain work, you cannot (unless you obtain a license) use a copyrighted *arrangement* of a public domain work. An arrangement of a public domain work is, if sufficiently original, a separate copyrightable work. (See the discussion of derivative works in "Public Domain Works," Chapter 9). If you want to use the public domain elements of a copyrighted arrangement, you may need a musicologist to separate the public domain elements from the arrangement's copyrighted elements.

If you are trying to separate out the public domain elements of a copyrighted arrangement, you may find it helpful to obtain a copy of the arranger's copyright application from the Copyright Office. The application should identify the new matter on which the claim of copyright is based. (See the discussion of copyright registration applications in "How to Fill Out Form PA," Chapter 16.) While the Copyright Office will not send you a copy of someone else's song or other copyrighted work unless litigation is threatened, it will send you a copy of their registration application. To get this, you need the copyright registration number for the arrangement. You can obtain it by looking in the *Catalog of Copyright Entries* or through a Copyright Office registration search. (See "Determining Who Owns the Copyright," Chapter 10.)

### Finding Public Domain Music

You can sometimes find out whether a song is in the public domain by looking at the copyright notice. If the copyright date is greater than 75 years ago, the work is in the public domain. If the composition is less than 75 years old, it could be in the public domain for reasons discussed in "Public Domain Works," Chapter 9.

Every major city has dealers that handle old sheet music. The Lincoln Center Library of the Performing Arts in New York City has an extensive collection of old songs. ASCAP and BMI catalogs—which include many copyrighted arrangements—indicate the public domain status of underlying works for arrangements. The ASCAP booklet, *ASCAP Hit Songs*, is a good source of public domain works. *The Art of Music Licensing*, a book by Al Kohn and Bob Kohn (Prentice Hall Law and Business), has a list of popular songs that are in the public domain.

In searching for public domain works, don't be fooled by a recent copyright notice and date on what is actually an arrangement of a public domain work. For example, if a new arrangement of a public domain folk tune shows a 1993 copyright date, you cannot—without obtaining a license—use the new arrangement, but you can use the public domain version of the song.

If someone else has written lyrics for a public domain tune, you are free to write your own lyrics for that tune. Both of you are creating new derivative works based on a public domain tune. If you use an arranger or lyricist to create the new lyrics, make certain that your contract with the arranger or lyricist includes a copyright assignment or work made for hire provision (see "Copyright Ownership," Chapter 8).

## Option #4: Using Music from Music Libraries

If you don't want to create your own music, deal with rights clearance, or pay license fees, and you can't find suitable public domain music, you may be able to obtain appropriate music from music libraries. A list of music libraries appears in Appendix D.

Music libraries specialize in providing "cleared" music—music in which they own both the musical composition and the master recording copyrights. Many libraries now offer their material in digital audio and MIDI form on CD-ROM.

Make sure that the music library you choose can provide you with all the rights you need. Some music libraries grant only limited licenses to use the works they license. Also be certain that the agent with whom you deal understands how you will be using the licensed music in your multimedia work (see "Option #2: Using Preexisting Music," earlier in this chapter.)

# 13

## The Laws of
## Publicity, Privacy, and Libel

Multimedia developers and publishers must make certain that they don't violate rights of publicity and privacy of individuals appearing in their works. This can usually be accomplished by getting releases from individuals before using illustrations, recordings, photographs, or film or video clips that include those individuals' names, faces, images, or voices.

The law of libel, which protects individuals against the dissemination of falsehoods injurious to their reputation, is generally not a major concern for multimedia developers. Nonetheless, developers and publishers should know enough about libel law to recognize the kind of material that might be libelous.

### The Rights of Publicity and Privacy

Most states in the United States recognize that individuals have a right of privacy. The right of privacy gives an individual a legal claim against someone who intrudes on the individual's physical solitude or seclusion, and against those who publicly disclose private facts. Remedies for invasion of privacy include injunctions against continued intrusion and damages for mental distress.

Almost half the states in the United States recognize that individuals have a right of publicity. The right of publicity gives an individual a legal claim against one who uses the individual's name, face, image, or voice for commercial benefit without obtaining permission. The states recognizing the right are California, Connecticut, Florida, Georgia, Hawaii, Illinois, Kentucky, Massachusetts, Michigan, Minnesota, Missouri, Nebraska, Nevada, New Jersey, New York, Ohio, Oklahoma, Pennsylvania, Rhode Island, Tennessee, Texas, Utah, Virginia, and Wisconsin.

*Developer took a picture of Clint Eastwood standing on a street corner in Carmel. Developer used the picture in a multimedia work that was sold in California. Unless Eastwood gave Developer permission to use Eastwood's image, Developer's use of the image violated Eastwood's right of publicity (even though Developer, as "author" of the photo, owned the copyright in the photo).*

Remedies for misappropriation of the right of publicity include injunctions against continued use of the misappropriated name, face, image, or voice, and damages based on the fair market value of the use or the profits earned by the infringer.

The law of publicity varies from state to state. In some states, the only unauthorized uses that violate the right of publicity are commercial uses (in advertising, for example). Since most multimedia works will be distributed nationwide, you should avoid trying to determine which states' laws you need to worry about. Instead, you should obtain releases (Form 17 in Appendix B) from any person whose name, face, image, or voice is recognizable in your multimedia projects.

Newspapers and news magazines have a "fair use" privilege to publish names or images in connection with reporting a newsworthy event. Multimedia developers are unlikely to be able to rely on fair use. Even if your project has no commercial benefit for you or anyone else—for example, if it's a public service project that you are doing for free—get releases to avoid violating the rights of publicity and privacy.

Experienced performers and models are accustomed to signing these releases. If a person won't sign a release, don't use their name, face, image, or voice in your multimedia project. If you are using a client's employees as actors, models, or narrators, make sure the employees sign releases. If you are using your own employees, make sure they sign releases.

### Photographs and Film Clips

If you want to use a photograph of a living person, get the person to sign a statement authorizing you to use his or her face or image as shown in the photograph. You also need a license authorizing you to use the photograph, unless you own the copyright in it. (See "When You Need a License," Chapter 9.)

Some photographers routinely obtain releases, but don't assume that this is the case. Even if the photographer did obtain a release, the release may not be broad enough to cover your use of the photograph in a multimedia work.

If you want to use a clip from a film or television show, you should obtain releases from all performers shown or heard in the clip. Motion picture producers often require performers to sign releases authorizing the use of the actors' name, face, voice, or image in clips, but the scope of such releases may be too narrow to cover your use (they may cover only the use of clips for publicizing the movie). If the performers shown or heard in the clip belong to SAG or AFTRA, you probably need their consent (see "Reuse Provisions," Chapter 14).

To make the clearance process easier, you may want to eliminate certain individuals from the clip. You'll need the consent of the clip's copyright owner to modify it (see "Determining

What Rights You Need," Chapter 10). For example, one multimedia developer wanted to use a television clip of an interview between Isaac Asimov and Jane Pauley. Rather than negotiate with Ms. Pauley, the developer eliminated her image and voice from the clip.

### Sound Recordings

If you want to use an excerpt from a sound recording, get the consent of anyone whose voice is heard in it. In addition, you should get copyright licenses from the musical composition's copyright owner and the master recording copyright owner (see "Option #2: Using Preexisting Music," Chapter 12), and comply with AFTRA and American Federation of Musicians reuse requirements (see "Reuse Provisions," Chapter 14).

### Deceased Individuals

In some states, an individual's right of publicity terminates when the individual dies. In other states, the right passes to the heirs of the deceased original owner. In California, Oklahoma, and Texas, the right passes on to the heirs only if the person's likeness has acquired some commercial value at the time of death. In Kentucky, the right is passed on to heirs for public figures only.

The right of publicity lasts 20 years beyond the year of death in Virginia, 40 years in Florida, 50 years in California, Kentucky, Nevada, and Texas, and up to 100 years in Oklahoma. In Tennessee, the right lasts as long as it is continuously exploited by the heirs.

As a rule of thumb, don't use the name, voice, face, or image of a celebrity who has been dead less than 50 years—for example, Marilyn Monroe or Martin Luther King, Jr.—without checking applicable state law on descendability. If state law provides for the right of publicity to descend to heirs, get permission from the current owners of the deceased celebrity's right of publicity before using the celebrity's name, voice, face, or image.

## Libel

The law of libel (also known as defamation) protects an individual against the dissemination of falsehoods about the individual. Libel is defined as a false statement about a person, communicated to at least one other person, that injures the defamed person's reputation or subjects the defamed person to hatred, contempt, or ridicule.

To recover damages for libel, a plaintiff must prove that the statement was false and:

- Was communicated to others.
- Was reasonably understood as referring to the plaintiff.
- Injured the plaintiff.

Injury can consist of monetary losses, damage to reputation, or mental anguish. A public figure or official must prove that the publisher or broadcaster made the statement either knowing it was false or entertaining serious doubts about its truth. A private individual only has to prove that the publisher or broadcaster acted negligently in failing to ascertain that the statement was false. The higher burden for public figures and officials flows from the First Amendment.

Here are some tips for avoiding libel:

- *Original material.* If you plan to use any statements in your multimedia work that could injure someone's reputation, make certain that you can prove that the statements are true. There is often a big difference between "knowing" that something is true and being able to prove that it is true. Journalists are taught to be particularly careful about statements concerning arrests and convictions and statements concerning professionals' qualifications and ethics.

- *Photographs.* With digital editing software, it is now very easy to edit and merge photographs. Avoid using an edited image that falsely associates an individual with controversial or unsavory events, places, or people. Using an altered image that puts a person in a "false light"—for example, a photograph created by merging a photograph of an elected official with a photograph of a Mafia figure—will expose you to liability for both libel and breach of privacy.

- *Licensed material.* If licensed materials include potentially libelous material, don't use the material. If you use it, even though the material didn't originate with you, you could have liability for libel.

- *Quotations.* Many people believe that one who merely quotes what someone else said has no liability for libel. This is not true. Don't quote a statement made by someone else if that statement could harm someone's reputation unless you know the statement is true.

- *Opinion.* Many people think that you can escape liability for libel by making it clear that you are only stating your opinion. There is no "opinion" exemption to libel. Don't use a statement of opinion that might harm someone's reputation unless you have a factual basis for the opinion.

- *Statements About Corporations.* Corporations can recover damages for libel. Many executives are zealous about protecting their corporation's reputation. If you make statements that might damage a corporation's reputation, make sure the statements are true.

A truthful statement is not libel, but a truthful statement that discloses private facts about an individual in an objectionable manner may violate the individual's right of privacy.

*Journalist discovered that Sue was abused as a child and reported that fact without Sue's permission in a story on child abuse. Journalist's statement about Sue is not libel, because the statement was true, but Journalist may have violated Sues' right of privacy by publishing the statement.*

## Permits

If you are going to shoot photographs or video on public property, get a permit from the appropriate government authority (usually a local or state film commission).

If you are going to shoot on private property, get a location agreement from the property owner that authorizes you to enter and use the premises for shooting and to show the premises in your work.

If your shots of public or private places will show a work that is protected by copyright—a sculpture, for example—you should obtain a license from the copyright owner authorizing you to use the image. Because ownership of the copyright in a work is distinct from ownership of a copy (see "Owning a Copy of a Work," Chapter 4), the owner of the copy of the work that you film or photograph is probably not the owner of the copyright in that work.

*Mr. Rich has given Developer permission to create a CD-ROM showing Mr. Rich's private art collection. Unless Mr. Rich owns the copyrights in the paintings in the collection, Mr. Rich cannot authorize Developer to use images of the paintings in Developer's multimedia work. If Mr. Rich did not get assignments from the artists who created the paintings, Developer should get permission to use the images of the paintings from the artists (or those to whom the artists assigned the copyrights).*

# 14.

## Union Issues

Many people who work in the entertainment industry are represented by unions. Performers in the movie and television industries are represented by the Screen Actor's Guild (SAG) and the American Federation of Television and Radio Artists (AFTRA). Recording artists are also represented by AFTRA. Film and television directors are represented by the Directors Guild of America. Screenwriters are represented by the Writers Guild of America and musicians by the American Federation of Musicians. In addition, there are unions for technical workers.

The unions have collective bargaining agreements with many entertainment industry employers. A company that signs a collective bargaining agreement with a union must comply with its numerous rules concerning employee pay, benefits, and working conditions.

This chapter deals with two issues:

- Signing collective bargaining agreements.

- Reuse of material created by union members.

## Signing Collective Bargaining Agreements

If you sign a union's collective bargaining agreement, you will be bound for the duration of the agreement (usually several years) to comply with all provisions of the agreement. The collective bargaining agreement's provisions on hiring, contracts, work conditions, and pay will, in effect, be "written in" to your contracts with union members.

Collective bargaining agreement requirements vary from union to union, because each agreement was negotiated separately by union representatives and industry representatives.

### If You Don't Sign

Union members are prohibited from working for those who have not signed the union's collective bargaining agreement. A member of the Writers Guild of America, for example, is prohibited from accepting employment with or selling literary material to a nonsignatory. If you plan to hire screenwriters, performers, directors, or musicians, you may find that the most qualified people in these professions are union members. You will not be able to hire union members unless you sign collective bargaining agreements.

Some unions offer "One Production Only" contracts which permit you to hire union members for the single production covered by the contract. These contracts, also known as "OPOs" (and referred to that way in the rest of this chapter), are discussed in "Unions and Multimedia," later in this chapter.

### If You Sign

If you sign a collective bargaining agreement, you generally will not be permitted to hire nonunion members to do work that is within the scope of the agreement. (This is not true of the Writers Guild. See "Writers Guild," later in this chapter.) For example, if you sign the Directors Guild agreement, you can hire a director who is not a member of the Guild only if that director joins the Guild.

Signing one union's collective bargaining agreement (SAG's, for example) does not mean that you have to use union members for work not covered by the agreement (electrical work, for example).

## Unions and Multimedia

The entertainment industry unions are just beginning to develop collective bargaining agreements for multimedia developers. Those agreements are discussed in the rest of this section.

### SAG and AFTRA

SAG and AFTRA, which represent performers, have already developed collective bargaining agreements for multimedia.

If you will be using performers in your multimedia works, you may want to consider signing collective bargaining agreements with SAG or AFTRA. Traditionally, SAG has represented motion picture performers and AFTRA has represented television performers and recording artists. However, over the years, the jurisdictional lines between the two unions have become blurred. At present, both unions consider the use of performers in the production of new material for new interactive multimedia works an area of shared jurisdiction. That means you can pick the union you want to join. Most professional performers belong to both SAG and AFTRA, and the compensation scales for the two unions are identical. Some companies sign with both unions.

*Developer plans to hire three performers to act in a video production that will be used in Developer's new multimedia work. If Developer wants to join one of the performers' unions (so he will be able to use union performers), he can join either SAG or AFTRA.*

There are exceptions to the "shared jurisdiction" rule:

- *SAG Jurisdiction.* If you are creating a multimedia work that is based 50 percent or more on preexisting material that was originally shot on film, SAG has exclusive jurisdiction. SAG also has exclusive jurisdiction over traditional animation.

- *AFTRA Jurisdiction.* If you are creating a multimedia work that is based 50 percent or more on preexisting material that was originally shot for network television on videotape, AFTRA has exclusive jurisdiction. AFTRA also has exclusive jurisdiction over televised game shows, concerts, and news programs.

AFTRA has exclusive jurisdiction over recording artists. If you want to use an AFTRA recording artist in your multimedia work, you will have to sign an agreement with AFTRA.

### SAG's Agreement

SAG has a collective bargaining agreement for multimedia developers. This agreement is known as the Standard Interactive Media Agreement (referred to as the SAG IMA in this chapter). A copy of the SAG IMA is in Appendix B (Form 18).

This agreement is an interim agreement that will be in effect until June 30, 1995. Michael Prohaska, Senior Administrator for Interactive Media Contracts at SAG, was instrumental in developing the SAG IMA. In developing the agreement, he talked with a number of multimedia developers about the multimedia industry's special needs and unique features. The reason for the relatively short term of the SAG IMA is that Mr. Prohaska and multimedia developers who negotiated the agreement realize that the multimedia industry is still evolving.

The minimum rates of compensation set by the SAG IMA are $485 per eight-hour day for a day performer, off-camera performer (narrator), or performer who provides voice-over for animation. This rate goes up to $504 on July 1, 1994. The rates for extras are $99 per eight-hour day. A developer who employs more than 10 SAG extras a day may employ any number of non-SAG persons to perform crowd work.

A question that came up when the SAG IMA was being negotiated was whether multimedia developers would have to pay performers fees when a work was distributed to consumers, in addition to paying the daily performance rates stated in the previous paragraph (television producers have to pay performers extra fees when they distribute copies of a show to supplemental markets, such as the videocassette market). SAG agreed to not charge multimedia developers separate distribution fees. This point is covered in Paragraph 5 of the SAG IMA, which states that the performance compensation "shall cover the distribution of Interactive Programs for use on home-type television or computer screens." (SAG reserved the right to negotiate this provision in 1995.)

Paragraph 5 does not affect a developer's obligation to pay reuse fees if material made for one multimedia work is reused in another work (these fees are discussed in "Reuse Provisions," later in this chapter). However, if you know that you will want to use material in several multimedia works, you should negotiate with SAG for the right to do so (expect to pay additional compensation to performers for this right).

SAG wants to encourage multimedia developers to sign collective bargaining agreements, and Mr. Prohaska has indicated that he is flexible and willing to modify the SAG IMA as new situations come up—for example, modifying Paragraph 5 for a multimedia developer whose works will be used in retail kiosks rather than on television or computer screens (the devices mentioned in Paragraph 5). He is also willing to discuss modifying the agreement for experimental, government, and pilot multimedia projects. In addition, SAG will, under certain conditions, allow a producer to sign an OPO contract.

If you are interested in signing an agreement with SAG or in finding out more about SAG, you can reach Mr. Prohaska at (213) 549-6847.

### *AFTRA's Agreement*

AFTRA's agreement for multimedia developers is similar to the SAG IMA. The compensation rates are the same as SAG's. According to Karen Stuart, Assistant National Executive Director of Entertainment Programming at AFTRA, AFTRA is working on a new multimedia agreement with a major game producer in the San Francisco area. She hopes this new agreement will become AFTRA's prototype for the multimedia industry.

For multimedia developers who want to join AFTRA for one production, an OPO agreement is available. However, AFTRA prefers that developers sign a regular agreement (one that runs until 1995). If you use the OPO more than two times, you will have to pay regular compensation plus 200 percent to use the OPO again. (This rule is designed to encourage developers to sign a regular agreement.)

If you are interested in signing an agreement with AFTRA or in finding out more about AFTRA, you can reach Karen Stuart at (213) 461-8111 (extension 400).

## Writers Guild of America

The Writers Guild (WGA) is currently using OPOs with multimedia developers as an interim measure while it develops a collective bargaining agreement for this industry. According to Joel Block, Director of Industry Alliances at the WGA, the Writers Guild is in the process of developing a regular agreement for multimedia that recognizes the current economic realities of the multimedia marketplace.

The WGA, according to Mr. Block, is "trying to create a user-friendly environment to encourage multimedia developers to use Writers Guild members." The WGA's Creative Media and Technology Committee has been working with the IICS (International Interactive Communications Society) on topics of mutual interest.

In the meantime, the Writers Guild is using a one-page OPO "letter of adherence" with multimedia developers. The letter of adherence does not set compensation rates. Compensation is to be determined by the multimedia developer and the member of the WGA that the developer hires. The letter of adherence simply requires a multimedia developer who signs the letter to pay 12½ percent of the agreed-upon compensation to the Guild's pension and health plans for the member who is hired. A developer can also hire a non-WGA designer or writer under the letter of adherence, in order to permit the designer or writer to earn membership units toward full WGA membership and become eligible for WGA pension and health benefits.

If you are interested in finding out more about the Writers Guild or in signing a collective bargaining agreement with the WGA, contact the Department of Industry Alliances at (310) 205-2511.

### Directors Guild of America

The Directors Guild (DGA) is dealing with multimedia developers on a case-by-case basis.

According to Warren Adler, Western Executive Secretary for DGA, "Interactive movies are an exciting new business that promises to offer significant additional employment opportunities for DGA members." The DGA recently announced that Digital Pictures, a developer of live-action, interactive video software for consumer CD-ROM platforms, signed an agreement to use DGA members to direct its productions.

The role of directors in multimedia productions is still evolving. The DGA has flexibility in terms of initial compensation for directors, but wants to see directors participate on the back-end through revenue-sharing or royalties. In addition to directors, DGA represents film production managers and assistant directors for film productions, and associate directors and stage managers for videotape productions. Generally, a signatory must hire a full DGA crew if the project involves work for the whole crew. However, the DGA is flexible about scaling down the hiring requirement for smaller productions.

The DGA prefers that multimedia developers sign long-term agreements. It is resistant to OPOs. However, the Guild occasionally does OPOs.

If you are interested in finding out more about the Directors Guild or in signing a collective bargaining agreement with the DGA, contact Mr. Adler at (310) 289-2003.

### American Federation of Musicians

The American Federation of Musicians is currently dealing with multimedia developers on a case-by-case basis. According to Dick Gabriel, Director of the Electronic Media Services Division at the Federation, two compensation patterns are emerging: revenue-sharing and up-front payment. A developer who chooses revenue-sharing agrees to make an initial payment to each Federation musician used on a project, and then to pay the musician a percentage of revenues from the project later. This option is appealing to start-ups. The up-front payment system involves a larger initial payment to the musician but no "back-end" revenue-sharing payments.

If you are interested in finding out more about the American Federation of Musicians or in signing a collective bargaining agreement, contact Mr. Gabriel or Sue Collins at (800) 237-0988.

## Reuse Provisions

Even if you don't sign a union collective bargaining agreement, the reuse provisions of these agreements will affect you if you want to use an excerpt from a movie or television show or from a master recording of music. (Master recordings are discussed in the "Option #2: Using Preexisting Music," Chapter 12.)

Reuse provisions fall into two categories:

- Reuse fees (union fees for using preexisting material).

- Consent requirements.

They are discussed in this section.

### Reuse Fees

The Directors Guild, Writers Guild, and American Federation of Musicians collective bargaining agreements all require that a signatory pay fees to union members involved in creating a work if that work (or a portion of it) is used in a different production.

*Producer, a signatory to the Writers Guild collective bargaining agreement, owns the copyright in Hotdog, a motion picture that is based on a screenplay written by Victor, a member of the Writers Guild. Producer wants to use a portion of Hotdog in a new motion picture. Producer will have to pay Writers Guild reuse fees to Victor (even though Producer has already paid Victor for his work on the Hotdog screenplay).*

These fees are referred to as "reuse fees," "new use fees," or "supplemental market fees." In this book, we'll use the term "reuse fee."

The theory behind the reuse fee provisions is that using existing material takes away jobs that would be available if new material had been created instead. The reuse fees are substantial.

The company for whom the performer did the work is actually responsible for paying the reuse fees. If the copyright has been assigned, the assignee generally assumes this obligation. Your licensor will either require you to pay these fees or add them to your license fee. (Copyright licenses are discussed in Chapter 10.) Your license should include a warranty that any applicable union reuse fees have been paid. (See "Obtaining a License," Chapter 10.)

If you want to use an excerpt from a work that was created before the 1950s, you should call the unions whose members were involved in the work and find out when the union's collective bargaining agreement reuse provisions went into effect. You may find that you can use the material without paying reuse fees, because the reuse provisions were not in effect when the work was made. Always check with the appropriate unions on this issue.

## Consent Requirements

Several of the entertainment industry unions have consent requirements for the reuse of existing material. Those requirements are discussed in this section.

### Performers

The SAG and AFTRA collective bargaining agreements state that no part of the photography or sound track of a performer can be used in a picture or program in any medium other than the picture or program for which the performer was employed without separately bargaining and reaching an agreement with the performer regarding payment for the reuse. The performer is not permitted to consent to reuse at the time of original employment. Either you or the copyright owner will have to negotiate for the consent of performers who are shown or heard in clips you plan to use. The consent agreement does not apply to AFTRA non-network, non-prime time programs, but reuse fees apply to such programs.

To start the consent process, contact the appropriate union. Contact SAG if the material was originally shot on film and contact AFTRA if it was originally shot on videotape. The union will put you in touch with the performers' agents. If the clip you want to use shows a deceased performer, the union will put you in touch with the performer's executor.

### Writers

The Writers Guild's standard contract contains a unique "separation of rights" provision that gives the writer the right to retain certain rights in his or her script. Because of "separation of rights," a Writers Guild member who no longer owns the copyright in a script he or she wrote may own certain rights that you need to license to lawfully use a clip of a movie or television program that is based on that script. Rights retained under the "separation of rights" can include the following rights:

- *Publication right.* This is the right to publish the work in any book or periodical.
- *Sequel right.* This is the right to use the leading character or characters of a work for a different story in a television program or a motion picture.
- *Merchandising right.* This is the right to manufacture and to sell objects first fully described in the literary material.

If you want to use a clip and the writer has retained any of these rights, you should get permission from the writer to use the clip (as well as a license from the copyright owner, as discussed in Chapter 10).

### Directors

According to the Directors Guild Basic Agreement, a director must be consulted if a theatrical motion picture made by the director is edited for network television or syndication, or licensed for videodisc or videocassette distribution. In addition, some directors have a contractual right to approve alterations to works they made.

### Recording Artists

AFTRA represents recording artists as well as performers. If you want to use an excerpt from a master recording that involves the voice of an AFTRA recording artist, contact AFTRA to start the consent process.

### Musicians

The American Federation of Musicians collective bargaining agreements state that use of an existing master recording in a new work requires the union's consent (in addition to the payment of fees for the new use, discussed in "Reuse Fees," earlier in this chapter). If you want to use an existing recording in your multimedia project, contact Colleen Howell at the American Federation of Musicians to get permission for "phono new use." Ms. Howell's telephone number is (800) 237-0988.

## Other Legal Issues

In addition to dealing with union reuse requirements, if you plan to use film or television clips or excerpts of master recordings in your multimedia work, you must obtain copyright licenses from all copyright owners and you must get right of publicity releases from all performers shown or heard in the clip or excerpt. Clearing these rights can be complicated and expensive.

Copyright licenses are discussed in Chapter 10. Music licenses are discussed in "Option #2: Using Preexisting Music," Chapter 12. The right of publicity is discussed in Chapter 13.

If you want to use the leading character from a movie or television series in a multimedia work, you should find out whether the writer has retained the sequel right. (See "Writers," earlier in this chapter.)

# 4

# Post-Production Issues

# 15

## Choosing a Name for Your Product

Trademarks and service marks are words, names, symbols, or devices used by manufacturers of goods and providers of services to identify their goods and services, and to distinguish their goods and services from those sold by others. (For simplicity, the word trademark will serve as a shorthand term in this book for both trademarks and service marks.)

Trademarks can be among your most valuable assets. The value of the *Coca-Cola* trademark has been estimated to be in the billions of dollars.

This chapter covers two main topics:

- Choosing a strong trademark for your product that will qualify for the broadest trademark protection.

- Clearing a trademark (choosing a trademark that does not infringe another company's trademark or tradename).

We'll also discuss the standards for determining "confusing similarity" between trademarks, and the treatment of titles under trademark law.

Three other topics—dilution law, international trademark protection, and using third-party trademarks in your multimedia projects—are covered briefly at the end of the chapter. The basics of trademark law are covered "Trademark Law," Chapter 3. The steps that you must take to protect your trademark rights are discussed in "Trademark Protection," Chapter 16.

### Choosing a Strong Trademark

Trademarks can be word, symbols, slogans, or devices. They take many forms:

- *Word*   *Apple* for computers, *Coca-Cola* for soft drinks.
- *Design*   Prudential's rock for insurance services, Apple's bitten apple for computers.
- *Phrase*   *Fly the friendly skies* for airline services, *The Weiner the World Awaited* for meat.
- *Shape*   The pinched scotch bottle for whiskey, the Coca-Cola bottle shape for soft drinks.
- *Sound*   The roar of the MGM lion for films, the Star Wars theme for films and videotapes.

Such words, symbols, and devices can be grouped into four categories depending on their ability to serve as a trademark: generic, descriptive, suggestive, and arbitrary or fanciful. We'll discuss these four categories in this section. Because arbitrary or fanciful terms receive the strongest protection under trademark law, you should choose a trademark that is arbitrary or fanciful.

### Generic Terms

A generic term can never function as a trademark because it is a commonly used name of a particular type of good or type of product. Examples of generic terms are *386* for microprocessors and *Softsoap* for hand soap.

Do not choose a generic term for your trademark. Such a term will not qualify for trademark protection.

> *Developer chose the trademark Multimedia Software for its software. This trademark is "generic" for this type of software and Developer will not be able to prevent a competitor from using Multimedia Software for the competitor's own product.*

### Descriptive Terms

A descriptive term is one which directly describes the characteristics, functions, or qualities of a product. Examples are *Five Minute* for fast-drying glue and *After Tan* for lotion to be used after sun-bathing. Surnames—for example, *McDonald's* and *Dupont*—are also considered descriptive.

Although "descriptive" words or symbols may serve as trademarks, they qualify for trademark protection only if they have "secondary meaning." Secondary meaning is a term in trademark law that means that the public already associates the trademark with the goods or services of a particular company.

> *A federal appellate court found that the word "Fish-fri" was descriptive when used on fish-coating mixes. Because the trademark had acquired secondary meaning in the geographical area in which it was used, the court found that "Fish-fri" was protectable as a trademark.*

Secondary meaning is achieved through advertising and sales. Market surveys are frequently used to prove secondary meaning. In the case mentioned in the last example, the trademark owner used a market survey that showed that 23 percent of shoppers surveyed identified *Fish-fri* as a product on the market for use in frying fish.

The problem with choosing a descriptive term as your trademark is that until secondary meaning is established, any competitor could adopt the same "descriptive" term for similar goods. You would not be able to prevent the competitor from using the term on his or her goods.

*Developer picked PC Gallery as its trademark for its multimedia software product. This product is a series of pictures of famous paintings with commentary. However, Developer did not have much money and only sold 100 copies of its program over several years. Two years later, Big Co. started distributing its own collection of paintings for personal computers under the trademark PC Gallery. Big Co. is probably not infringing the rights of Developer because PC Gallery is descriptive and Developer has not sold sufficient copies of his program to create "secondary meaning" in the trademark.*

Three varieties of descriptive terms and symbols present particular problems:

- *Laudatory terms.* Terms that are laudatory in general (rather than laudatory about a particular product) are generally not protectable as trademarks until you obtain secondary meaning because such terms need to be used by other companies. Examples are *Best* and *Blue Ribbon*.

- *Geographically descriptive terms.* If a geographic area is well known for a particular type of product, the area's name is not protectable as a trademark for that type of product without secondary meaning. All sellers of that type of product should be able to use that term. Examples are *New England* for clam chowder and *Cambridge Digital* for computers (Cambridge is the home of a number of computer companies whose products are "digital" in nature).

- *Common symbols.* Marks that include commonly used designs and symbols—triangles and squares, for example—will require proof of secondary meaning unless the design is unique.

## Suggestive Terms

A suggestive term infers something about the qualities, functions, or characteristics of the goods without directly describing them. Such terms are protectable under trademark law *without* the necessity of proving secondary meaning. (Secondary meaning is discussed in "Descriptive Terms," earlier in this chapter). Examples of suggestive trademarks are *Rapid Shave* for shaving cream and *7-11* for convenience store services.

The distinction between suggestive and descriptive trademarks is one of the most important ones in trademark law, but it also is very difficult to draw. If a term requires imagination or thought to reach a conclusion as to the nature of the goods or services—for example, *7-11* for convenience store services—it is considered suggestive rather than descriptive.

### Arbitrary and Fanciful Terms

An arbitrary term is a commonly used word that is applied to a product or service with which that term is not normally associated. An example is the word *Apple* for computers. (The term would be generic if used for the fruit.)

A fanciful term is a coined or created word or symbol. *Kodak* for film is an example of a coined term.

If you choose an arbitrary or fanciful term as the trademark for your product, you will receive the broadest possible trademark protection. Because an arbitrary or fanciful term has no relationship to the products or services to which it is applied (unlike generic and descriptive terms), other companies do not need to use such a term on their products. Like suggestive terms, these terms are protectable without proof of secondary meaning, and you receive rights in such trademarks immediately upon use or upon filing a federal intent-to-use application.

## Clearing a Trademark

Trademark rights in the United States arise in three different ways: under common law, through state registration, and through federal registration. The three methods of obtaining trademark protection are discussed in "Trademark Law," Chapter 3.

No matter which method of trademark protection you choose, before adopting a trademark, you should ensure that it is available. Clearance of trademarks is a complex but necessary process. It is much cheaper to ensure that the trademark is available before adopting it than to try to purchase the rights of third parties once the trademark is in use and you have invested in packaging and advertising.

Generally, a trademark is cleared in two steps: a federal registrations search, then a state and common law search.

### Federal Registrations Search

The purpose of the federal search is to determine if there are any federally registered trademarks that are "confusingly similar" to the trademark that you want to adopt. If you adopt a trademark that is confusingly similar to existing trademarks, the owner of the existing trademark will be able to prevent your use and registration of the trademark. The determination of whether a trademark is confusingly similar to an existing trademark is based on an eight-factor test that is discussed in "Scope of Trademark Rights," later in this chapter. You can use the TrademarkScan database through the Dialog database service to do the federal registrations search yourself, or you can hire one of the trademark search firms listed in Appendix C.

The federal registration search does not indicate whether a term is available for your adoption, only that it is not available (because the term is confusingly similar to a federally registered trademark that is still in use). If the search shows a confusingly similar trademark, you should check to see if the trademark is still in use. If the owner of the trademark registration has ceased using the trademark for more than two years and does not intend to use the trademark again, the trademark may be available for your use despite the federal registration. However you may have to purchase or "cancel" the existing registration (an administrative procedure done through the U.S. Patent and Trademark Office) in order to register your trademark.

Even if the search is "clear," just because someone has not federally registered a trademark does not mean that the trademark (or a similar trademark) is available. Your proposed trademark or a similar one may be in use for similar goods by another company that has superior rights based on common law (the other party may also have rights based on a state trademark registration).

Although you can perform a preliminary review of a trademark search report yourself, you should consider having an experienced trademark attorney review the search report because trademark law includes a number of obscure rules that make it difficult for someone not experienced in the area to interpret a search report. For example, according to the doctrine of "foreign equivalents," all foreign words must be translated into English and then compared with existing trademarks.

*Multimedia, Inc. owns a federal trademark registration for the trademark Vert for multimedia products. The word vert is French for "green." Multimedia, Inc. can prevent another company from using Green for multimedia products. Although Vert and Green are very different in appearance and sound, according to the doctrine of "foreign equivalents," Vert and Green are considered the same word.*

### State and Common Law Search

The second step is to search for state trademark registrations and common law uses. The common law search will review both "trademark" use (use on products) and "tradename" use (use for company names). The earlier user of a word or device for a tradename (for example, Multimedia Development Company is a tradename) can prevent the use of a similar word or device as a trademark for similar goods or services. A trademark search firm can do this search for you (see Appendix C). However, these firms do not interpret the results for you. For that, you need a trademark attorney.

The state and common law search generally will produce many more potential problems than the federal registrations search. However, you may discover that many of the trademarks listed in the search report are no longer in use (or the companies that own them are out of business).

A trademark search firm will generally take seven to 10 days to provide you with a complete state and common law search report, although you can pay more to get the search completed faster. "Clearance" at the state and common law level can take several weeks as you try to gather information on the current use of the trademarks shown in your search report. You should consider using an experienced trademark attorney to interpret the search report.

## Titles

Treatment of titles is a special issue in trademark law. The title of a film or book is generally not protectable under trademark law unless it is part of a series or has obtained secondary meaning through extensive use. For example, *Star Wars* is protectable as a trademark because it is part of a series of films (and due to its fame). *Gone With the Wind* is protectable because the film and novel achieved great fame.

This special rule has not yet been applied to computer or multimedia products, but it might be applied in the future. If it is applied to multimedia products, it will make obtaining trademark rights for single products (as opposed to a series) much more difficult.

## Scope of Trademark Rights

Trademark law does not give protection against use of a trademark that is unlikely to cause confusion, mistake, or deception among consumers (but dilution laws, discussed in "Dilution," later in this chapter, may provide protection).

> *Western Software has a federal registration for the use of Flash on multimedia development tool software. If Giant Co. starts using Flash on desktop publishing software, Giant Co. may be infringing Western Software's trademarks because consumers may think the desktop publishing software and the multimedia development tool software come from the same source. If Giant Co. starts using Flash on fire extinguishers, though, Giant Co. is probably not infringing Western's trademark. Consumers are unlikely to think that the Flash software and the Flash fire extinguishers come from the same source.*

A senior party is the first person or company to use the trademark or file a federal "intent to use" application to register the trademark. A junior party is the second (or later) person or company to use the trademark or file a federal "intent to use" application to register the trademark. ("Intent to Use" applications are discussed in "Trademark Law," Chapter 3.) A senior party can prevent a junior party from using the trademark without proving that consumers are actually confused by the junior party's use of the trademark. The senior party need only show that a "likelihood" of confusion exists.

## Determining "Confusing Similarity"

The test for determining whether two trademarks are confusingly similar varies in minor ways in different parts of the country. The test includes multiple factors, but eight of the most common factors are described in the next sections (this test is used in the Ninth Circuit, which interprets the law in the states of Washington, Oregon, California, Arizona, New Mexico and Idaho).

### *Trademark Strength*

Descriptive trademarks generally have the narrowest scope of protection because other companies need to use these terms on their goods. Suggestive trademarks have a narrower scope of protection than either arbitrary or fanciful trademarks. Arbitrary and fanciful trademarks receive the broadest protection, because other companies do not need to use such trademarks. (The categories of trademarks are described in "Choosing A Strong Trademark," earlier in this chapter.)

A trademark may be strong despite its category because of its use in advertising and sales. For example, *McDonald's* is a descriptive trademark, and thus normally would be weaker than other types of marks. However, its extensive use in advertising and high visibility have made it one of the strongest trademarks in the United States.

### *Difference Between the Goods*

Even if two trademarks are identical, there is no confusing similarity (and, thus, no infringement) if the goods are sufficiently different.

- *The use of Pomegranate for earth movers would not prevent the use of Pomegranate for a multimedia product. If Pomegranate was being used for graphic design software, though, its use for a multimedia product would probably infringe the rights of the earlier user.*

The goods on which similar trademarks are used need not be "competitive" for there to be confusing similarity (and, thus, trademark infringement). Confusingly similarity also extends protection against confusion of "association or sponsorship."

- *Although clothing is not competitive with films, the owner of the Star Wars trademark can prevent the use of Star Wars on clothing by Fashion House, Inc. Such use is likely to lead to confusion of "association or sponsorship" because film companies or their licensees frequently sell clothing based on movies titles.*

The scope of protection for trademarks in the computer industry is changing. Originally, courts and the U.S. Patent and Trademark Office ("PTO") took the position that any use of a trademark in the computer industry would prevent its use for another computer product. Recently, the courts and the PTO have recognized that the computer industry is a series of niche markets. They are beginning to permit the use of similar trademarks if the goods or services are sufficiently different. For example, the Trademark Trial and Appeal Board at the PTO found that "Information Finder" and "Knowledge Finder" were not confusingly similar because one mark was used to provide online medical information services to the general public and the other mark was used to provide online medical information services to doctors. This area of law is still evolving. The conservative approach is to avoid adopting a trademark for use on a multimedia product if that trademark is already in use in the computer industry, even if it is used for different goods or services.

### Similarity of the Marks

Similarity can be one of the most important factors in determining the potential for confusion. Whether two trademarks are similar is determined by comparing the sight, sound, and meaning of the two trademarks.

In reviewing two trademarks for similarity, you must carefully analyze the common elements of the two. The use of a common suffix such as "tronics" does not make the two marks similar.

You must also consider the visual appearance of the two trademarks. For example, *Rain Barrel* and *Rain Fresh*, although different in immediate appearance, have a very similar commercial impression.

If two trademarks are "sound alikes," the fact that the products are sold primarily by phone will increase the chance for confusion and the possibility of infringement. In determining whether the trademarks are "sound alikes," you should consider the number of syllables, the stress pattern, the accent, and possible mispronunciations. For example, *Dramamine* and *Bonamine* were found to confusingly similar. The key issue is the commercial impression produced by the mark.

### Evidence of Actual Confusion

If there are examples of actual confusion, such as misdirected phone calls, it will frequently be the critical evidence against the "junior" party. It is very difficult to overcome evidence of actual confusion.

### Marketing Channels

If one product is sold only at wholesale and the other only at retail, the likelihood of confusion may be substantially reduced. Similarly, if one product is sold directly to the consumer while the other one is sold through distributors, the likelihood of confusion may be low.

### Degree of Care Exercised by Purchasers

There is an assumption that a purchaser will exercise greater care in choosing a more expensive product than in choosing an inexpensive product. Consequently, a trademark used on products that are purchased casually, at a low price, is more likely to be found to infringe a similar trademark than the same trademark used on expensive products would be.

> *If Developer adopts the trademark Apiware for his multimedia game that sells for $30, he is likely to be found to infringe Publisher's rights in Apillaware for another computer game that sells for $30. However if Developer uses the same trademark, Apiware, for his multimedia development software that sells for $10,000, he might not infringe Publisher's rights in Apillaware for a multimedia development product which also sells for $10,000.*

### Defendant's Intentions

If the junior party adopted the trademark with the intent of emulating the senior party's trademark, this factor will weigh against the junior party. Although it is permissible to emulate another party's trademark, you take an additional risk in doing so because the courts are more willing to protect the senior party.

### Likelihood of Expansion

The last factor that must be considered in determining whether two trademarks are confusingly similar is whether the senior party is likely to expand its use of the trademark to the products on which the junior party is using the mark. Thus, you must analyze not only the current business of the senior party, but also his or her potential for expansion into different product areas.

> *Developer has adopted the trademark Attiware for its car game software for young children. If Clothing Company adopts Attiware for car toys, it might be an infringement of Developer's rights because many game software companies also sell toys based on their games.*

The analysis of the potential for confusion is one of the most difficult areas in trademark law. Once again, this is one area where it is advisable to obtain the advice of an experienced trademark attorney who is familiar with the court decisions in this area.

## Dilution

Although most trademark rights are based on "likelihood of confusion," certain trademarks may qualify for more extensive protection under a theory called "dilution." Dilution is a separate legal theory that exists under the laws of many states. Dilution laws give owners of very strong trademarks the right to prevent a similar mark from being used on completely different products or services.

> *The Mercedes trademark is one of the best known trademarks in the world. If Developer adopts Mercedes as the title of his game software program, the Mercedes-Benz Company would probably be able to prevent such use under state dilution laws even though Mercedes-Benz does not distribute game software and is unlikely to start distributing such software.*

Dilution laws are meant to address the strong trademark owner's concern that other companies will try to obtain a "free ride" on the trademark's established reputation in fields other than the field in which the owner is using the mark. In the last example, Developer is trying to use the fame of the *Mercedes* trademark to sell his game. Such "free riders" may weaken the distinctiveness of the trademark and damage the reputation of the owner of the original mark.

## International Trademark Protection

Trademark protection outside the United States varies from country to country. Some countries, such as Japan and Germany, provide very few rights for unregistered trademarks. In those countries, only the most famous trademarks, such as *Coca-Cola* and *Mercedes*, will be protected without registration.

Other countries may have a different view of what is confusingly similar. Foreign trademark laws frequently provide broader protection for trademarks in the computer industry than is provided in the United States. You should be aware that registration in the United States will not protect your rights in foreign countries. In fact, in some countries, trademark pirates make a living by registering trademarks of foreign companies and selling them back to the foreign company when its starts to do business in that country.

If you will be selling your product outside the United States, consider registering your trademarks in the countries that are most important to your business. You also should consider registering your trademarks in the countries known for trademark piracy. International trademark registration can be quite expensive. You should analyze the risks and rewards very carefully.

# Using Third-Party Trademarks

You should be careful to avoid using or showing trademarks of other companies in your work without their permission. The trademark owner may object to being associated with your product. For example, Nabisco objected to the use of the *Marlboro* trademark on a billboard in the background of a video game. Similarly, the use of actual car names, such as *Corvette* or *Mustang*, in car-race games has raised objections by the owners of those trademarks.

You should clear the use of third-party trademarks (get permission to use them from their owners) before using them in your multimedia projects. If you cannot clear a trademark, don't use it.

The use of images of actual goods bearing real trademarks in your multimedia product (for example, an airplane with the United Airlines logo) is a gray area. Some trademark owners have taken the position that such use "associates" them with the product in which the images are used and thus gives them the right to grant or deny permission to use the images of trademarked goods. You should be particularly sensitive to such concerns in multimedia products that are viewed as negative or critical about the industry in which the trademark owner is involved (for example, the use of images of airplanes with real logos in a multimedia product that includes plane crashes). The national sports teams have been very aggressive in asserting these rights. If you will be showing a product that includes a national sports team's logo—for example, a "Giants" cap worn by an actor in a video clip—you should contact the team's licensing department about getting a license. Although it is not clear that these organizations have the right, under trademark law, to require a license for merely showing such trademarked products, some of them have taken the position that they do.

# 16

## Protecting Your Intellectual Property Rights

Much of this book has been devoted to how to avoid infringement of others' intellectual property rights. The focus of this chapter is on how you can maximize your own intellectual property protection.

To review the basic principles of copyright law, refer to Chapter 2. The basic principles of patent law, trademark law, and trade secret law are discussed in Chapter 3.

## Copyright Protection

For most multimedia works, copyright law is the primary source of intellectual property protection. As a copyright owner, you have the exclusive right to:

- Reproduce your work.
- Modify your work to create new works (known as derivative works).
- Distribute your work.
- Publicly display your work.
- Publicly perform your work.

(These rights are defined in "The Exclusive Rights," Chapter 2.)

Anyone who wants to exercise any of these exclusive rights in your work needs a license from you. For your own multimedia work, you get to be on the other side—the licensor side—of the rights clearance process described in Chapters 9 and 10.

### Register Early

Copyright protection attaches automatically when an original work of authorship is "fixed." However, the Copyright Act provides an incentive for "timely" registration: To ensure that you can get statutory damages in an infringement suit, you must register your work within three months after first publication of the work.

"Statutory damages" are damages of $500 to $20,000, "as the court considers just."

"Publication" is defined as distribution of copies to the public by sale, rental, lease, or lending. An offer to distribute copies to a group of persons for further distribution or performance is also publication.

Early registration also makes you eligible to receive an award of attorneys' fees (in the court's discretion).

If you don't register your copyright within three months after first publication, your damages in an infringement suit may be limited to the actual damages that you can prove (how much money you lost as a result of the infringement) and any profits of the infringer that are not taken into account in computing your actual damages. It may be difficult to prove your actual damages and the infringer's profits. You will only be able to get statutory damages if the infringement began before publication of the work.

More importantly, if you don't register your copyright within three months of the first publication, you may not be entitled to recover attorney's fees. Even if you can prove your actual damages and the infringer's profits, the total may be too low to cover your legal fees for the lawsuit. You will only be able to get attorney's fees if the infringement began before publication of the work.

*Defendant used 10 seconds of content from Developer's "published" multimedia work in a new multimedia work. Developer sued Defendant for copyright infringement. Developer had registered the copyright on the multimedia work within three months of first publication of her work. Developer opted for statutory damages and asked the court for attorney's fees. The court awarded Developer $10,000 in statutory damages and the entire cost of her legal fees in the case ($15,000). If Developer had not been eligible to opt for statutory damages and receive attorney's fees, it might not have been worth it to file the lawsuit. Developer would have had difficulty proving that she had any damages from Defendant's use of 10 seconds of her work or that Defendant had profited from using 10 seconds of her work. Additionally, she probably would not have received enough in damages to cover her attorney's fees.*

The other reasons to register the copyright in a work are as follows:

- You *will* have to register your work before filing a copyright infringement suit. Citizens of foreign countries whose works are protected in the U.S. by the Berne Convention are exempt from this requirement. Expedited registration costs $220. Regular registration costs $20.

- If you have registered your work, someone who wants permission to use it or buy it will be able to find you by obtaining a Copyright Office registration search. (Copyright Office searches are discussed in "Determining Who Owns the Copyright," Chapter 10.)

- If you intend to assign your copyright, give a lender a security interest in your copyright, or grant exclusive licenses, the other party to the transaction will probably want to record the transaction in the Copyright Office and so will insist that the copyright be registered. The benefits of recording a transaction are discussed in "Assignments" and "Licenses," Chapter 4. Recording the transaction gives constructive notice only if the copyright is registered and the copyright registration number or work's title is included on the recorded document (see "Obtaining a License," Chapter 10.)

- A certificate of registration made within five years of the first publication of the work is legal evidence of the validity of the copyright and of the facts stated in the certificate of registration. If you registered within five years of first publication, the defendant in an infringement suit has the burden of proof in challenging the validity of your copyright (for example, by claiming that your work was not original) or your ownership of the copyright.

## Registration Procedure

To register your work, you have to fill out a two-page application form and send it along with the required deposit of copies of your work (see "Deposit Requirements," later in this chapter). You must enclose a check for the fee ($20) to the Copyright Office.

You can get an application form from the Copyright Office or copy one of the application forms in Appendix G of this book. For most multimedia works, you should use Form PA, which stands for "performing arts." The PA form is also the form for registering motion pictures and audiovisual works in general. If you are registering only the script or software features of your work, you should use Form TX ("literary works"). Don't file both a Form PA and a Form TX for the same multimedia work.

You will find copies of Form PA and Form TX in Appendix G. We have included the Copyright Office's instructions for filling out these forms. We'll give further instructions in the next section. A sample, filled-out Form PA appears in this chapter (pages 169–170).

The Copyright Office will accept an application made on a photocopied blank form so long as it is clear, legible, and on a good grade of 8-1/2 by 11-inch white paper suitable for automatic feeding through a photocopier. The Copyright Office says that "forms should be printed preferably in black ink, head-to-head (so that when you turn the sheet over, the top of page 2 is directly behind the top of page 1)."

You can get up to 10 free copies of the application forms by calling the Copyright Office's Forms Hotline: (202) 707-9100. You may also want to obtain free copies of Copyright Office circulars such as Copyright Basics (Circular 1) and How to Investigate the Copyright Status of a Work (Circular 22). The hotline has an answering machine on which you leave your request, so you should be ready to state what materials you need when you call that number. You should get the material you order within two weeks. If you're not sure what forms and circulars you want, call the Copyright Office's general information number: (202) 707-3000.

## How to Fill Out Form PA

Here's how you fill out Form PA. Use black ink or a typewriter to fill out your application form. (Form TX requires basically the same information.)

### Front Page

*Top right corner*   Don't put anything here. This space is for the Copyright Office staff.

### Space 1   *Title*

If you have already distributed copies under a particular title—for example, *City Tour*—use that title. If you haven't chosen a title, chose one and use it on packaging for copies that you distribute in the future. The Copyright Office will register and index your work under this title.

### Space 2   *Author*

There are separate instructions for works made for hire and for other types of works.

- *Works made for hire.* If the work is a work made for hire (see "The Work Made for Hire Rule," Chapter 4), list the employer or hiring party as the "author." Don't list contributing employees or independent contractors as authors. For Nature of Authorship, just put "author of entire work (employer for whom work for hire was made)."

- *Other types of works.* List the individual author or authors and the nature of each author's contribution. Here are some examples: author of the entire work; co-author of the entire work; author of the software code and user interface; author of the graphics and animation.

If you have licenses to use copyrighted works owned by others, do not put the licensors' names in Space 2. Your licensors are not authors of the work that you are applying to register (and your copyright doesn't cover the work protected by their copyrights). You will mention the types of preexisting works that are included in your work in another section of the application (Space 6).

### Space 3   *Year in which creation was completed*
### *Date and nation of first publication*

Give the date of completion of the version of the work that you are applying to register.

Publication is defined as distribution to the public by sale, rental, lease, or lending. An offer to distribute copies to a group of persons for further distribution is also publication. If the work has not been published, leave this space blank.

# FORM PA
**For a Work of the Performing Arts**
UNITED STATES COPYRIGHT OFFICE

REGISTRATION NUMBER

_____

PA            PAU
_____
EFFECTIVE DATE OF REGISTRATION

_____

Month        Day        Year

**DO NOT WRITE ABOVE THIS LINE. IF YOU NEED MORE SPACE, USE A SEPARATE CONTINUATION SHEET.**

**1**

**TITLE OF THIS WORK ▼**

City Tour

**PREVIOUS OR ALTERNATIVE TITLES ▼**

**NATURE OF THIS WORK ▼** See instructions

Audio Visual Work

**2**

**a**

**NAME OF AUTHOR ▼**

ABC Multimedia, Inc.

**DATES OF BIRTH AND DEATH**
Year Born ▼        Year Died ▼

Was this contribution to the work a "work made for hire"?
☒ Yes
☐ No

**AUTHOR'S NATIONALITY OR DOMICILE**
Name of Country
OR { Citizen of ▶ U.S.
{ Domiciled in ▶

**WAS THIS AUTHOR'S CONTRIBUTION TO THE WORK**
Anonymous?     ☐ Yes ☒ No
Pseudonymous?  ☐ Yes ☒ No
If the answer to either of these questions is "Yes," see detailed instructions.

**NATURE OF AUTHORSHIP** Briefly describe nature of the material created by this author in which copyright is claimed. ▼

Entire work

**NOTE**

Under the law, the "author" of a "work made for hire" is generally the employer, not the employee (see instructions). For any part of this work that was "made for hire" check "Yes" in the space provided, give the employer (or other person for whom the work was prepared) as "Author" of that part, and leave the space for dates of birth and death blank.

**b**

**NAME OF AUTHOR ▼**

**DATES OF BIRTH AND DEATH**
Year Born ▼        Year Died ▼

Was this contribution to the work a "work made for hire"?
☐ Yes
☐ No

**AUTHOR'S NATIONALITY OR DOMICILE**
Name of Country
OR { Citizen of ▶
{ Domiciled in ▶

**WAS THIS AUTHOR'S CONTRIBUTION TO THE WORK**
Anonymous?     ☐ Yes ☐ No
Pseudonymous?  ☐ Yes ☐ No
If the answer to either of these questions is "Yes," see detailed instructions.

**NATURE OF AUTHORSHIP** Briefly describe nature of the material created by this author in which copyright is claimed. ▼

**c**

**NAME OF AUTHOR ▼**

**DATES OF BIRTH AND DEATH**
Year Born ▼        Year Died ▼

Was this contribution to the work a "work made for hire"?
☐ Yes
☐ No

**AUTHOR'S NATIONALITY OR DOMICILE**
Name of Country
OR { Citizen of ▶
{ Domiciled in ▶

**WAS THIS AUTHOR'S CONTRIBUTION TO THE WORK**
Anonymous?     ☐ Yes ☐ No
Pseudonymous?  ☐ Yes ☐ No
If the answer to either of these questions is "Yes," see detailed instructions.

**NATURE OF AUTHORSHIP** Briefly describe nature of the material created by this author in which copyright is claimed. ▼

**3**

**a**
**YEAR IN WHICH CREATION OF THIS WORK WAS COMPLETED** This information must be given in all cases.
1993 ◀ Year

**b**
**DATE AND NATION OF FIRST PUBLICATION OF THIS PARTICULAR WORK** Complete this information ONLY if this work has been published.
Month ▶ Dec.   Day ▶ 15   Year ▶ 1993
U.S.   ◀ Nation

**4**

See instructions before completing this space.

**COPYRIGHT CLAIMANT(S)** Name and address must be given even if the claimant is the same as the author given in space 2.▼

ABC Multimedia, Inc.
100 Lake Boulevard
Any City, CA 90025

**TRANSFER** If the claimant(s) named here in space 4 are different from the author(s) named in space 2, give a brief statement of how the claimant(s) obtained ownership of the copyright.▼

**APPLICATION RECEIVED**

**ONE DEPOSIT RECEIVED**

**TWO DEPOSITS RECEIVED**

**REMITTANCE NUMBER AND DATE**

DO NOT WRITE HERE
OFFICE USE ONLY

**MORE ON BACK ▶**
• Complete all applicable spaces (numbers 5-9) on the reverse side of this page.
• See detailed instructions
• Sign the form at line 8.

**DO NOT WRITE HERE**

Page 1 of _____ pages

| EXAMINED BY | FORM PA |
| --- | --- |
| CHECKED BY | |

☐ CORRESPONDENCE
Yes

FOR COPYRIGHT OFFICE USE ONLY

**DO NOT WRITE ABOVE THIS LINE. IF YOU NEED MORE SPACE, USE A SEPARATE CONTINUATION SHEET.**

**PREVIOUS REGISTRATION** Has registration for this work, or for an earlier version of this work, already been made in the Copyright Office?

☐ Yes ☒ No If your answer is "Yes," why is another registration being sought? (Check appropriate box) ▼

**a.** ☐ This is the first published edition of a work previously registered in unpublished form.

**b.** ☐ This is the first application submitted by this author as copyright claimant.

**c.** ☐ This is a changed version of the work, as shown by space 6 on this application.

If your answer is "Yes," give: **Previous Registration Number** ▼        **Year of Registration** ▼

**5**

**DERIVATIVE WORK OR COMPILATION**   Complete both space 6a & 6b for a derivative work; complete only 6b for a compilation.
**a. Preexisting Material**   Identify any preexisting work or works that this work is based on or incorporates. ▼

_Previously published film footage, graphics, text and music_

**b. Material Added to This Work**   Give a brief, general statement of the material that has been added to this work and in which copyright is claimed. ▼

_Original text, graphics and soundtrack_
_Compilation and editing of preexisting material_

See instructions before completing this space.

**6**

**DEPOSIT ACCOUNT**   If the registration fee is to be charged to a Deposit Account established in the Copyright Office, give name and number of Account.
**Name** ▼        **Account Number** ▼

**7**

**CORRESPONDENCE**   Give name and address to which correspondence about this application should be sent.   Name/Address/Apt/City/State/Zip ▼

_Susan Something_
_ABC Multimedia, Inc._
_100 Lake Boulevard_
_Any City, CA 90025_

Area Code & Telephone Number ▶   _(415) 555-1212_

Be sure to give your daytime phone number ◀

**CERTIFICATION\***   I, the undersigned, hereby certify that I am the
Check only one ▼

☐ author

☐ other copyright claimant

☐ owner of exclusive right(s)

☒ authorized agent of _ABC Multimedia, Inc._
Name of author or other copyright claimant, or owner of exclusive right(s) ▲

**8**

of the work identified in this application and that the statements made
by me in this application are correct to the best of my knowledge.

**Typed or printed name and date** ▼ If this application gives a date of publication in space 3, do not sign and submit it before that date.

_Susan Something_        date ▶ _Dec. 16, 1993_

Handwritten signature (X) ▼   _Susan Something_

**MAIL CERTIFI-CATE TO**

Name ▼   _Susan Something_
_ABC Multimedia, Inc._

Number/Street/Apartment Number ▼
_100 Lake Boulevard_

City/State/ZIP ▼
_Any City, CA 90025_

**Certificate will be mailed in window envelope**

**YOU MUST:**
• Complete all necessary spaces
• Sign your application in space 8
**SEND ALL 3 ELEMENTS IN THE SAME PACKAGE:**
1. Application form
2. Nonrefundable $20 filing fee in check or money order payable to *Register of Copyrights*
3. Deposit material
**MAIL TO:**
Register of Copyrights
Library of Congress
Washington, D.C. 20559

Copyright fees are adjusted at 5-year intervals, based on increases or decreases in the Consumer Price Index. The next adjustment is due in 1995. Contact the Copyright Office in January 1995 for the new fee schedule.

**9**

\* 17 U.S.C. § 506(e): Any person who knowingly makes a false representation of a material fact in the application for copyright registration provided for by section 409, or in any written statement filed in connection with the application, shall be fined not more than $2,500.

▲ June 1992—100,000        ☆U.S. GOVERNMENT PRINTING OFFICE: 1992-312-432/60,003

**Space 4**   *Copyright claimants*

Unless you acquired the copyright in the work by assignment (see "Assignments," Chapter 4), you are both the author and the claimant. Put your name and address here. This information tells potential licensees where to reach you.

If you acquired the copyright by assignment, explain how you acquired the copyright (for example, "by written assignment from the author"). You must indicate that you acquired all of the author's U.S. copyright rights (not just permission to use the work).

## Second Page

**Space 5**   *Previous registration*

Leave this space blank unless an earlier version of the work has been registered, in which case you have to justify filing a new registration application.

**Space 6**   *Derivative work or compilation*

If you used preexisting works in your multimedia works—for example, film clips, music, and photographs—you need to fill out Space 6. If all of the components of your multimedia work were created for your work, you can skip this space.

- *Compilation.* If you created your multimedia work by simply collecting and assembling preexisting materials or data, your work is a compilation and you don't have to fill out "6a." You just have to explain in "6b" what has been compiled—for example, "a compilation of various photographers' photographs of Depression-era poverty scenes with soundtrack consisting of excerpts of musical compositions composed during the Depression." Your goal here is to convince the Copyright Office that there's sufficient originality in your selection, arrangement, and coordination of the material to justify copyright protection. (See "Standards," Chapter 2.)

- *Derivative works.* Most multimedia works are created by editing and combining excerpts of preexisting materials and adding original material (script, soundtrack, and new graphics, for example). Such multimedia works are derivative works (works based on one or more preexisting works). If your multimedia work is a derivative work, you need to fill out "6a" and "6b." In "6a," you need not identify the individual preexisting works that are used in your multimedia work. You can simply state the types of preexisting works that are incorporated in your multimedia work—for example, "previously published film footage, graphics, text, and music." In "6b," state what new material you have added to the preexisting "content" to create your work—for example, "compilation and editing of preexisting material and original text, graphics, and sound track."

**Spaces 7, 8, and 9**   *Deposit account, correspondence, and certification*

Unless you have a deposit account with the Copyright Office, leave Space 7 blank and attach a check for $20 payable to the Register of Copyrights. You can open a deposit account if you have 12 or more transactions each year with the Copyright Office (get Circular R5).

Put your address in Space 8, unless someone else (a copyright attorney, for example) will be handling any questions the Copyright Office staff might have about your application. Read and fill in the certification, print or type your name, and sign below the typed or printed name. If you are signing as agent of a corporation (president, for example), fill in the corporation's name in the space provided, but sign your own name.

Fill out Space 9, the mailing label for your certificate. It will be several weeks before you receive your certificate.

## Deposit Requirements

If your work is in CD-ROM format, the deposit requirement is one complete copy of the CD-ROM package. A complete copy is defined as all of the following items:

- The CD-ROM.

- The operating software.

- Any manuals that go with the material.

- A printed version of the work embodied in the CD-ROM, if the work is fixed in print as well as in a CD-ROM.

For other types of works, the deposit requirement is generally two copies of the work (one copy if the work is unpublished).

## Separate Registrations for Components

You are not required to file separate copyright registrations for the original individual components of your multimedia work (the music, graphics, video footage, software, and so on). The copyright registration on the multimedia work as a whole covers the components. There are two exceptions to this rule: one for stand-alone components and one for exclusively licensed components.

### Stand-Alone Components

Stand-alone components are components that are (or could be) a separate commercial product and that you intend to exploit apart from your multimedia work. An example is a software engine that you use in your multimedia work but also intend to exploit separately by licensing it to other multimedia developers. You should file a separate registration on a stand-alone component to make it easier to identify the component for licensing purposes.

### *Exclusively Licensed Components*

You don't own the copyright in a component for which you have an exclusive license. (This term is defined in "Licenses," Chapter 4.) However, the Copyright Act gives you the right to register a work for which you have an exclusive license. You may wish to do so if you believe that it is likely that the exclusively licensed component will be infringed apart from your work as a whole.

## Copyright Notice and Warnings

Use copyright notice on your packaging and on the title screen. Copyright notice consists of three elements:

- The copyright symbol " ©," the word "Copyright," or the abbreviation "Copr."

- The year of first publication of the work.

- The name of the copyright owner.

The use of copyright notice is optional in the United States. However, there are good reasons for using copyright notice:

- Using notice informs the public—and potential infringers—that the work is copyrighted.

- Notice tells those who might want to get licenses to use your work who owns the copyright (at the time of the publication of the copy with notice).

- In an infringement suit, an infringer who had access to a copy containing notice cannot use an "innocent infringement" defense. This defense, if successful, could result in the court's lowering your statutory damages (discussed in "Register Early," earlier in this chapter) to $200.

- It's difficult to prove "willful" infringement (and get increased statutory damages) if copies of your work don't contain the copyright notice.

- Using notice will get you protection for your work in the approximately 20 countries that still require the use of notice (countries that are not members of the Berne Convention—Russia, for example).

Many people don't understand the rights of copyright owners under the Copyright Act. For example, some people don't know that buying a copy of a copyrighted work doesn't give them permission to copy the work. (This topic is discussed in "Owning a Copy of a Work," Chapter 4.) You should consider adding your own "warning statement" to copies of your work. For example, you could include on your title screen the statement, "No part of this work may be reproduced in whole or in part in any manner without the permission of the copyright owner."

## International Copyright Protection

As was noted in "International Protection," Chapter 2, American authors automatically receive copyright protection in countries that belong to the Berne Convention and the Universal Copyright Convention. Most major countries belong to one of these conventions. You don't need to register your copyrights in Berne or UCC countries to receive copyright protection in those countries. You *do* need to use copyright notice on copies of your work that are distributed in countries belonging to the UCC, but not to Berne.

As of June, 1993, China and Taiwan had not signed either Berne or the UCC. However, the U.S. has bilateral copyright treaties with these countries, and under these treaties, works by U.S. authors are given copyright protection in China and Taiwan. Bolivia and Honduras require a unique form of copyright notice: "All rights reserved." If you plan to distribute your products in these countries, add that phrase at the end of your copyright notice.

## Patent Protection

If your product involves technology that is novel and nonobvious, you may be able to patent it. You should see a patent attorney without delay (and certainly before you publicly distribute or display your product). By delaying, you risk losing your right to get a patent. The basics of patent law are discussed in "Patent Law," Chapter 3.

## Trademark Protection

Trademark law provides protection for words, symbols, slogans, and product configurations that are used in marketing products and services. The basics of trademark law are discussed in "Trademark Law," Chapter 3. Choosing a trademark is discussed in Chapter 15.

Although you can obtain trademark ownership and limited trademark protection in the United States simply by using a trademark in connection with your products, you should obtain federal registrations of your trademarks to receive maximum trademark protection. There are several benefits to federal registration:

- A federal registration gives you rights in your trademark throughout the United States, even in geographical areas in which you are not currently using your trademark (see "Trademark Law," Chapter 3).

- A federal registration is legal evidence of your ownership of the mark and your exclusive right to use it in interstate commerce.

- Federal registrants can file infringement suits in federal court.

- Federal registrants can have U.S. Customs bar the importation of goods bearing infringing trademarks.

- Federal registrants enjoy expanded remedies against counterfeited goods, and they are eligible to receive awards of attorney's fees (in the court's discretion) in infringement actions.

If you plan to spend significant amounts of money advertising your product, you should seriously consider federal registration.

If you are planning on coming out with a line of multimedia products, you should consider registering a "house mark" that you can use on your entire product line. "Adobe" is an example of a house mark used by its owner, Adobe Systems, Inc., on the various items in the owner's product line (for example, Adobe Illustrator and Adobe Photoshop).

Trademark protection can be lost by the action or inaction of the trademark owner, whether or not there is a federal registration. To maintain trademark protection, you as the trademark owner must do the following things:

- *Continuously use the mark.* A trademark must be used continuously to avoid loss of rights. A federally registered trademark is assumed to be "abandoned" if it is not used for a period longer than two years. Once a mark has been abandoned, the trademark owner loses the priority date of the original registration or adoption of the mark.

- *Monitor third-party use.* A trademark owner has a duty to prevent third parties from using the trademark in a way that is confusing to the public. A trademark owner's failure to prevent confusing use of the trademark can result in the mark becoming "generic" and unprotectible. "Aspirin," "escalator," and "thermos" are examples of trademarks that became generic and lost their protection.

- *Exercise quality control over licensees.* Trademarks can be licensed to third parties for their use. However, the trademark owner must exercise quality control over third-party use of the trademark to ensure that the trademark indicates a consistent level of quality of goods or services. The failure to exercise quality control can result in a loss of rights.

- *Avoid improper assignment of the mark.* Trademarks can only be assigned with the associated goodwill of the business in which they are used. An attempt to assign a trademark without the goodwill destroys trademark rights.

## Trade Secret Protection

Trade secret law protects valuable product and business information that is not generally known. The basics of trade secret law are discussed in "Trade Secret Law," Chapter 3.

While developers and publishers don't need to register their trade secrets to establish protection, trade secret protection is lost if reasonable efforts are not made to keep the information from becoming generally known. Measures to maintain secrecy include such steps as marking documents as confidential, restricting employees' and outsiders' access to materials or areas of the company, and requiring employees, independent contractors, and visitors to sign nondisclosure agreements. (Nondisclosure agreements are discussed in "The Contract," Chapter 6, in "Using the Employment Agreement," Chapter 7, and in "Contracts With Independent Contractors," Chapter 8.)

Trade secrets can be licensed to others without losing protection if the licensees are required to maintain the confidentiality of the trade secrets.

# 17

## Sales Law

In every state except Louisiana, a statute known as Article Two of the Uniform Commercial Code applies to all contracts for the sale of goods. This chapter highlights some provisions of Article Two that are important for multimedia developers and publishers.

### The Uniform Commercial Code

After World War II, legal experts proposed that the states adopt a uniform set of legal rules to simplify, clarify, and modernize the laws regarding the sale of goods and other commercial transactions. These rules, known as the Uniform Commercial Code (UCC), are divided into "articles" that cover different types of commercial transactions.

Article Two of the Uniform Commercial Code applies to "transactions in goods." Forty-nine states, the Virgin Islands, and the District of Columbia have adopted it. Louisiana has not adopted it.

In those states that have adopted Article Two, the rules of Article Two displace general contract law (discussed in Chapter 5) for all transactions in goods. Goods are defined as "all things (including specially manufactured goods) which are movable."

Ironically, Article Two of the UCC is not entirely uniform from state to state. California's version, for example, differs slightly from New York's version. For some provisions, the legal experts who drafted the rules gave the states a choice of several options. In addition, many state legislatures added their own variations for particular provisions.

In international transactions, Article Two may be superseded by the United Nations Convention on the International Sale of Goods. This Convention applies to a transaction if both parties are located in countries that have joined the Convention, unless the parties have agreed that the Convention will not apply. The United States joined the Convention on January 1, 1988. Many important commercial states—France and Italy, for example—have joined the Convention.

### Article Two and Multimedia

For Article Two to apply to a transaction, the transaction must involve "goods." If you are selling copies of your multimedia products in CD-ROM form, you are selling goods because the CD-ROMs that embody your product are movable.

If you are creating a custom multimedia work for a client or for a publisher that will be delivered in CD-ROM form, you are probably selling goods because even though creating a custom work involves services rather than goods, the end product will be movable.

If you are creating a product that will only be provided in intangible form—over a network or interactive television, for example—it is unclear whether Article Two applies.

### Merchant

Some of Article Two's provisions apply only to "merchants." A merchant is defined in Article Two as "a person who deals in goods of the kind or otherwise by his occupation holds himself out as having knowledge or skill peculiar to the practices or goods involved in the transaction...." If you are a multimedia developer or publisher, you are probably a merchant for multimedia products.

## Important Provisions of Article Two

Article Two governs the substantive rights of the parties to a transaction. Freedom of contract is the guiding principle of Article Two: The parties to a business transaction may, by agreement, modify most of Article Two's rules.

The balance of this chapter covers four provisions of Article Two that are important for multimedia developers and publishers: the writing requirement for contracts, contract formation, warranties, and remedies.

### The Writing Requirement

According to Article Two, a contract for the sale of goods for $500 or more is not enforceable "unless there is some writing sufficient to indicate that a contract for sale has been made between the parties" and it is signed by the party against whom enforcement is sought. In negotiating contracts for the sale of your multimedia products, remember that if you do not comply with this writing requirement, you may not be able to enforce your contract in court. (Three exceptions to the writing requirement are discussed in "Exceptions to the Writing Requirement," later in this chapter).

To satisfy Article Two's writing requirement, you don't need to get formal written contracts from those who agree to buy your products. (However, we recommend that you use written contracts for all your business relationships. See "Written Contracts," Chapter 5.) All that is required is that the writing be "sufficient to indicate that a contract for sale has been made." The writing need not be signed by both parties, only by the party "against whom enforcement is sought."

⋮ *West Coast Books, Inc., agreed to buy 300 copies of Developer's multimedia encyclopedia for $40 per copy. When Developer attempted to deliver the copies to West Coast Books, he was told that West Coast had changed its mind about buying Developer's product. West Coast Books and Developer did not have a written contract, but Developer has a letter from West Coast Books' purchasing manager that says, "West Coast Books accepts your offer to sell us 300 copies of your multimedia encyclopedia for $40 per copy." If Developer sues West Coast Books to enforce the contract, the letter will satisfy Article Two's writing requirement. The letter is sufficient to indicate that West Coast Books and Developer made a contract, and it is signed by West Coast Books, the party against whom Developer seeks to enforce the contract.*

Something in writing is considered "insufficient" to indicate that a contract was made if it fails to state the quantity term for the sale. If the quantity is stated incorrectly in the writing, the contract can only be enforced for the quantity stated. Make certain that quantity is stated correctly in all written documentation on your sales transactions.

⋮ *Developer and West Coast Books agreed orally that West Coast Books would buy 300 copies of Developer's multimedia encyclopedia at $40 per copy. The signed written agreement states that West Coast Books will buy 200 copies. If West Coast Books denies that it actually agreed to buy 300 copies, Developer can only enforce the contract for 200 copies.*

Something in writing is considered "sufficient" even if it omits terms that were agreed upon orally by the parties (such as price, delivery date, or payment terms).

If the buyer is a "merchant" as defined in Article Two (see "Merchant," earlier in this chapter), you may be able to satisfy Article Two's writing requirement by sending a "confirmation" of an oral agreement to the buyer within a reasonable time. If the buyer receives the confirmation, has reason to know the contents of the confirmation, and does not object within 10 days of receipt of the confirmation, the confirmation will satisfy the writing requirement.

⋮ *Developer and West Coast Books' purchasing manager met and agreed orally that West Coast Books would buy 300 copies of Developer's multimedia encyclopedia at $40 per copy from Developer. The next day, Developer faxed the purchasing manager a letter that said, "I'm writing to confirm our oral agreement, made yesterday, that West Coast will buy 300 copies of my multimedia encyclopedia at $40 per copy." If the purchasing manager does* *not object to the fax within 10 days, Developer's letter satisfies Article Two's writing requirement.*

To avoid disputes about whether or not the buyer is a "merchant," whether the confirmation was sent in a reasonable time, and whether the buyer received the confirmation and had reason to know its contents, you should obtain the buyer's signature on the confirmation. In the example above, Developer could simply add a line to the letter asking that the purchasing manager sign the letter (to indicate that the letter correctly summarized the parties' oral agreement) and send the letter back to the Developer.

### *Exceptions to the Writing Requirement*

There are three exceptions to Article Two's writing requirement that allow an oral agreement to be enforced. They are:

- If the other party admits in court testimony or in a court pleading that the contract was made.

- If payment has been made or accepted or the goods have been received and accepted.

- If the goods are specially manufactured for the buyer and not suitable for sale to others, and the seller has made a substantial beginning on manufacturing the goods before the buyer gives notice that it is repudiating the agreement.

*Big Co. orally agreed to pay Developer $20,000 to create a customized multimedia training work for Big Co. After Developer created the storyboards and script and began production, Big Co. called and cancelled the order. If the training work is not suitable for sale to another client, Developer can enforce the oral contract.*

## Contract Formation ("Battle of the Forms")

According to the traditional common law of contracts, an offer can be accepted only on its exact terms. If the offeree's response to the offer is not a "mirror image" of the offer—for example, if the response includes terms that were not in the offer—the response becomes a counter-offer. A counter-offer terminates the original offer. (The basics of offer and acceptance are discussed in "Offer and Acceptance," Chapter 5.) A contract can then be formed only if the original offeror accepts the counter-offer.

Article Two does not use the common law "mirror image" rule for contract formation. Instead, Article Two states that a "definite and seasonable expression of acceptance...operates as an acceptance even though it states terms additional to or different from those offered or agreed upon, unless acceptance is expressly conditional on assent to the additional or different terms."

*Developer offered to sell West Coast Books 300 copies of Developer's multimedia encyclopedia at $40 per copy. West Coast Books' purchasing manager responded by sending Developer a fax that said, "You've got a deal. Payment due in 120 days." Under the common law of contracts, the parties do not have a contract because the purchasing manager's response contains a new term, "payment due in 120 days," that was not part of the offer. However, because Article Two applies, Article Two's contract formation rule displaces the common law "mirror image" rule. According to Article Two's rule, Developer and West Coast Books formed a contract. The purchasing manager's reply of "you've got a deal" is a "definite and seasonable expression of acceptance."*

According to Article Two, when an acceptance contains terms that were not part of the offer, those additional terms are "proposals for addition to the contract." Between merchants (defined earlier in this chapter in "Merchants"), the additional terms become part of the contract unless one of these situations applies:

- The offer expressly limited acceptance to the terms of the offer.

- The additional terms would materially alter the contract.

- The offeror gives notice of objection to the additional terms.

*In the previous example, the "payment due in120 days" term in the purchasing manager's acceptance is a proposal for addition to the contract. Developer and West Coast Books are both merchants. If Developer does not object to the 120-day payment term, that term is part of the contract unless the term would "materially alter" the contract.*

Whether an additional term "materially alters" a contract is a complex factual determination. That determination must be made after considering Article Two's "default rule" for that type of provision (if any), along with the custom in the industry and prior dealings between the parties (if any). In the last example, Article Two's default rule for when payment is due states that "unless otherwise agreed tender of payment is a condition to the seller's duty to tender and complete any delivery." Developer, using that rule, might argue that giving West Coast Books 120 days to pay would materially alter the contract. West Coast Books, however, might have evidence that the custom in the publishing industry is to permit delayed payment by the buyer, or that in a previous contract, Developer gave West Coast Books 120 days to pay.

Disputes arise frequently over whether additional or different terms contained in an acceptance are part of the contract. This is particularly true when contracts are formed by exchanging forms that contain "fine print" or "boilerplate" terms and conditions. For example, sales contracts are frequently formed based on an exchange of the seller's "quotation" and the buyer's "purchase order." Typically, the "quotation" contains terms designed to protect the seller's interests (for example, "payment due on receipt"). The purchase order contains different and additional terms designed to protect the buyer's interests ("payment due 60 days after buyer has had an opportunity to inspect and test the goods"). Try to avoid "battle of the forms" disputes because they are generally difficult and expensive to resolve. (This problem can come up in development agreements as well as in sales contracts. See "The Contract," Chapter 6.)

If you are the offeror, read the offeree's response to your offer and immediately object to new terms that you do not view as part of your business deal with the offeree. Objections should be made in writing. In the example above, Developer could have avoided a dispute over whether the 120-day payment term proposed by West Coast Books was part of the contract by objecting to that term. If you have sufficient bargaining power, another way to avoid these disputes is to state in your offers that acceptance is limited to the exact terms of your offer.

If you are an offeree and it is important to you that a contract include terms that were not in the offer, make your acceptance conditional on assent to your additional or different terms. By doing that, you are making a counter-offer. You will not have a contract unless the offeror accepts your counter-offer (see "Offer and Acceptance," Chapter 5).

*Developer offered to sell West Coast Books 300 copies of Developer's multimedia encyclopedia for $40 per copy. If West Coast Books' purchasing manager responded by saying, "We've got a deal, but only if you agree to pay shipping," that acceptance would be conditional on Developer's assent to the additional term (it would really be a counter-offer to Developer). If Developer accepts the counter-offer, Developer and West Coast have a contract. If Developer does not accept the offer, the parties do not have an enforceable contract.*

### Warranties

Article Two provides for four types of warranties in connection with the sale of goods:

- Express warranty.
- Implied warranty of merchantability.
- Implied warranty of fitness for particular purpose.
- Implied warranties of title and noninfringement.

You should be familiar with the ways in which express warranties arise. These and other warranties are discussed later in this chapter. For the three types of implied warranties, you should be aware that you are making these warranties every time you sell your product unless you take appropriate steps to exclude the warranties. If your products are being sold through a distributor, make certain that your distributor is aware of these warranties.

Many manufacturers and sellers of consumer products exclude all of Article Two's implied warranties. Instead, they warrant only that the product will, for a limited period of time, be free from defects in materials and craftsmanship under normal use and service. These "standard" warranties are poorly suited for multimedia works and should be avoided. State consumer protection laws and the Magnuson-Moss Warranty Act must be considered in drafting warranty language. The Magnuson-Moss Warranty Act is federal statute that applies to consumer products manufactured after July 4, 1975. Its purpose is to make warranties on consumer products more understandable and enforceable.

### Express Warranties

A seller can create express warranties by making statements of fact or promises to the buyer, by a description of the goods, or by display of a sample or model. An express warranty can be created without using formal words such as "warranty" or "guarantee." All that is necessary is that the statements, description, or sample become part of the "basis of the bargain."

- *Developer told Client, "All of my multimedia products will run on your laptop computer."*
- *Even though Developer did not use the word "warranty," Developer's words created an express warranty. If Client buys one of Developer's products and it will not work on Client's laptop, Developer will be liable to Client for breach of the express warranty.*

To avoid making express warranties that you don't mean to make, you must be careful about what you say—and what your marketing representatives say—in marketing your multimedia works. While many written sales contracts include "merger clauses" (language purporting to exclude from the contract any prior promises made by the seller or seller's representatives that are not in the written contract), some courts have found that such language does not exclude Article Two express warranties. ("Merger clauses" are discussed in "Typical Contract Provisions," Chapter 5.)

An affirmation of the value of the goods or a statement of the seller's opinion or commendation of the goods does not create a warranty.

- *Developer's ads state that Developer's videogame is "the most exciting game currently on the market." That statement does not create an express warranty. It is merely Developer's opinion about the videogame.*

### Implied Warranty of Merchantability

When a merchant (defined in "Merchant," earlier in this chapter) sells goods, a warranty that the goods are "merchantable" is implied in the contract unless that warranty is excluded.

To be merchantable, goods must "pass without objection in the trade" and be "fit for the ordinary purposes for which such goods are used."

> *Big Co. purchased a spreadsheet program that does not add correctly. The program is not "merchantable" because it is not fit for the ordinary purposes for which spreadsheets are used. Unless the seller excluded the implied warranty of merchantability for the sale, the seller gave Big Co. an implied warranty that the program was merchantable. The seller is liable to Big Co. for breaching the implied warranty of merchantability.*

For many types of goods, "merchantability" has been defined through cases decided over a number of years. Grain, for example, is "merchantable" only if it contains less than one-half percent in insect parts. For software and multimedia products, though, the standards of "merchantability" have not yet been defined. While it is well known that software and software-based products generally contain "bugs" when they are sold, it is unclear how many "bugs" a product can contain and still be merchantable.

To avoid disputes over whether goods are merchantable, many manufacturers and sellers of goods exclude the warranty of merchantability. Article Two states that this warranty can be excluded only with language that mentions merchantability. If the exclusion is in writing (and it should be, for evidence purposes), the exclusion must be "conspicuous" (in a different typeface, type size, or color from the rest of the contract). This warranty can also be excluded by making it clear in the contract that the goods are sold "as is."

### *Implied Warranty of Fitness*

The "implied warranty of fitness for particular purpose" is made by a seller when two factors are present:

- The seller has reason to know of a particular purpose for which the buyer requires the goods.

- The buyer relies on the seller's skill or judgment to select suitable goods.

> *Buyer told Software Vendor, "I'm relying on you to make sure that any software you sell me will run on my present computer, a '386." Unless Software Vendor excluded the implied warranty that the software it sold to Buyer would run on Buyer's computer, Vendor made an implied warranty to Buyer that the software would run on Buyer's '386 computer.*

The implied warranty of fitness for particular purpose can be excluded through contract language that explicitly excludes this warranty. It can also be excluded by saying that "there are no warranties which extend beyond the description on the face hereof," or by selling products "as is."

### *Implied Warranties of Title and Noninfringement*

Unless excluded, each contract for the sale of goods includes a warranty by the seller that the seller has the right to transfer title in the goods and that the buyer will get good title. The warranty of title can be excluded only by specific language or by circumstances that give the buyer reason to know that the person selling does not claim full title. This implied warranty is unlikely to be of concern in most multimedia sales transactions (but it could be a problem if you're selling "pirated" copies).

Unless otherwise agreed, a merchant (defined in "Merchant," earlier in this chapter) warrants that the goods sold do not infringe third parties' intellectual property rights. If the buyer furnishes specifications to the seller, the seller is not liable for an infringement claim arising out of the seller's compliance with the specifications.

If you breach the implied warranty of noninfringement, you will have to reimburse the buyer for the damages it pays to the intellectual property owner whose rights are infringed. The damages could far outweigh your profit on the sale.

> *Clothing Manufacturer sold some dresses to a clothing store for $3000. The fabric from which the dresses were made infringed a fabric design copyright owned by a third party. The copyright owner sued the clothing store for infringement, and the clothing store had to pay the copyright owner $30,000 in damages (the store's profits from selling the dresses). Because Clothing Manufacturer had sold the dresses to the clothing store with the implied warranty of noninfringement, Clothing Manufacturer had to reimburse the clothing store for the $30,000 in damages and for the costs of the lawsuit. (This example is based on an actual case.)*

You can exclude this warranty or modify it, but most manufacturers and vendors do not do that (few are even aware of the existence of this warranty). Rather than exposing yourself to the unlimited liability of Article Two's implied warranty of noninfringement, you should exclude this warranty from your sales contracts, offering instead a limited warranty of noninfringement. (See "The Contract," Chapter 6.)

## Remedies

According to Article Two, a buyer can obtain actual damages along with "incidental damages" and "consequential damages" from a seller who breaches a contract. (Breach of contract is discussed in "What is a Contract?," Chapter 5.) Incidental damages are those resulting from the seller's breach of contract, such as expenses incurred in inspecting and transporting rejected goods and obtaining substitute goods. Consequential damages include any loss that could not reasonably be prevented by the buyer that resulted from the buyer's requirements and needs that the seller knew about (or had reason to know about). Consequential damages also include damages for injury to person or property resulting from a breach of warranty.

> *Buyer, a mail-order catalog seller of multimedia products, bought from Seller a telephone system for use in Buyer's mail order business. Seller promised that the system would be installed and operational on January 2. Buyer, relying on that promise, disassembled its old phone system on January 1. The new phone system was not actually operational until February 10. As a result of the delay, Buyer lost $100,000 worth of orders. If Buyer could not reasonably have prevented the loss of the orders (for example, by arranging for an answering service to handle calls), Buyer has consequential damages of $100,000. If Buyer did prevent the loss of orders by having an answering service handle calls between January 2 and February 10, consequential damages are the cost of hiring the answering service.*

Article Two states that a contract may provide for remedies "in addition to or in substitution for those provided in this Article and may limit or alter the measure of damages recoverable under this Article." Unless the contract remedy is the buyer's exclusive remedy, the buyer can choose from the Article Two remedies or the contractual remedy. Many manufacturers and sellers of products limit the buyer's remedy to repair of the defect in the product, replacement of the product, or refund of the purchase price.

Most product manufacturers and sellers try to exclude consequential damages because such liability exposes a seller to a risk of having to pay damages far in excess of the product's price. Consequential damages may be limited or excluded unless the limitation or exclusion is "unconscionable." The term "unconscionable" is not defined in Article Two, but many courts have used the definition created by one of the federal appellate courts: "Unconscionability has generally been recognized to include an absence of meaningful choice on the part of one of the parties together with contract terms which are unreasonably favorable to the other party." In the case of consumer goods, limitation of consequential damages for personal injury is assumed to be unconscionable.

If a seller excludes consequential damages or otherwise contractually limits remedies and then "circumstances cause the...remedy to fail of its essential purpose" (that is, leave the buyer with no real remedy), all of Article Two's normal remedies are available to the buyer, possibly even consequential damages. In one case involving a contractual limitation on damages, the buyer, a hospital, had paid the seller, the software supplier Electronic Data Systems Corporation, over two million dollars for software systems. The software systems were so defective the hospital could not use them. The contract provision limited the hospital's damages to $4000, the amount of the average monthly invoice for the transaction. The court found that because the hospital had paid over two million for unusable software systems, the $4000 limit on damages failed to provide the hospital with an adequate remedy and thus "failed of its essential purpose." To avoid such a determination, many manufacturers and sellers who limit the customer's remedy to repair or replacement also promise that they will refund the purchase price if the product cannot be repaired or replaced. The refund promise is a "backup" remedy.

# 18

## Distribution Agreements

This chapter describes the different forms that multimedia distribution relationships are currently taking. We'll discuss the two choices you have in creating a distribution agreement: assigning the rights or licensing the rights. We'll also cover key issues you'll need to consider in negotiating your agreement, such as what platforms and types of media to include, what the geographic scope of the grant should be, and what ancillary and sequel rights to grant. Other topics include forms of payment, warranties, how to handle credits, and remedies for breach.

### Roles

The term "distribution agreements" has a wide range of meanings in the multimedia industry. At the simplest level, a distribution agreement merely provides for the resale of a multimedia work that has already been copied and packaged. Yet the term "distribution agreements" also includes "publishing agreements" in which the publisher creates the packaging and chooses the product's trademark, then reproduces the multimedia work, packages it, and distributes it.

To better understand the relationship of the parties, it is useful to define the roles of the parties involved in distribution. As used in this chapter, "developer" (or "you") means the party who takes the multimedia product from conception to "gold disk." The "publisher" means the company that makes the product ready for market, packages the product, determines the price, reproduces the product and packaging, and chooses the distribution channels. The "distributor" means the company that warehouses the product, ships it, and takes the financial risk of sales to retailers. The allocation of these functions is not absolute. For example, the "publisher" may take on some of the "distributor's" functions. In addition, some companies may take on multiple roles: A "publisher" may also function as a "distributor," and a "developer" may decide to self-publish, and act as a "publisher."

These distinctions can have an important legal effect. In fact, the distinction between a "publisher" and a "distributor" was critical in a recent case between LucasArts Entertainment Company ("LucasArts") and Humongous Entertainment Company ("HEC"). HEC created a videogame, "Putt Putt Joins the Parade," based on the SCUMM software tool owned by LucasArts (the SCUMM software had been developed by the principals of HEC when they were employed at LucasArts). HEC's license from LucasArts prohibited HEC from selling the game to other publishers for less than a certain price. LucasArts claimed that HEC breached the license agreement's price restriction when it sold the game to Electronic Arts. The court disagreed, holding that Electronic Arts acted as a distributor rather than as a publisher in the transaction.

Most of this chapter deals with the relationship between developers and publishers, because that relationship is the most common one. However, many of the issues raised in "Key Issues in License Agreements," such as geographic scope, media, payment, and warranties, also apply to distribution agreements.

## Scope of the Agreement

The most critical legal issue in the publishing agreement is the scope of the rights being granted. There are two basic choices: assignment and license. (These terms are defined in "Assignments" and "Licenses," Chapter 4.) The choice between these two options will be determined in part by the nature of your multimedia product. For example, if your multimedia product is an interactive training video you specifically designed for a particular company, you may feel comfortable assigning the copyright and other rights in the product to that company. (This topic is discussed in "The Contract," Chapter 6.) For multimedia products that have more general use, the issue becomes more complex because the multimedia industry is young and has not yet established a standard "deal" framework.

## Assigning the Rights

The assignment of all rights in the product by the developer to the "publishing" company is quite common in the film and the book publishing industry. This assignment may have certain exceptions (in the book publishing industry, for example, movie and television rights are often retained by the author), or there may be geographic limitations. Such assignments are also common in the multimedia industry for single or narrow-use applications. You may also find assignment of all rights appropriate for multimedia products with more general applications, depending on the roles of the parties.

*Developer has completed an interactive training program for the sales staff of Big Co. on how to sell their earth moving equipment. Big Co. demands an assignment of all rights in the product. Developer should be willing to assign the rights to Big Co. unless the product includes a software "engine" or other component that Developer wishes to use in a future product.*

For a mass market product in which you assign all rights, a publishing agreement frequently provides that compensation is an initial payment (generally, an advance against royalties) with continuing royalties paid to you. The amount of the royalties will depend on the nature of the product, the market, and your involvement in the product's development. For example, the royalties for the original product on CD-ROM may be quite different than the royalties on clothing or other merchandise articles. This structure can be quite satisfactory for you if you understand its consequences.

In other industries, such as music and book publishing, a limited assignment extending only to certain countries or media is common. However, this approach has not yet been frequently used in the multimedia industry. When an assignment is quite limited, many of the issues discussed in "Licensing the Rights," later in this chapter, become important.

Currently, most assignments in multimedia publishing agreements are for all rights in the work. Once you have assigned all of your rights to the publisher, you will not be able to port the work to a different platform or "reuse" either the multimedia work or its component parts in another multimedia project. Component parts include the underlying software, the storyline, the characters, the user interface, and the photographs. (Reuse of material protected by assigned copyrights is discussed in more detail in "The Contract," Chapter 6.)

If you wish to use those components in other multimedia products, you can obtain a "license back" from the publisher. As a licensee, you will need to address many of the same issues (such as scope of the rights) as a publisher who is a licensee (see "Licensing the Rights," later in this chapter). However, some issues that apply to the publisher, such as performance warranties, would not be relevant to you because you created the multimedia product and are familiar with its performance.

## Licensing the Rights

If you license the rights in your multimedia products instead of assigning them, you must carefully define the scope of the license. The issues can be quite complicated. The multimedia industry is young and there is uncertainty about the ways in which multimedia products will be used and distributed. For example, will the products be distributed on CD-ROMs or supplied over networks? Failure to properly define these rights can lead to problems similar to those in the movie industry: In that industry, disputes continue to the present day about the right to distribute films in videocassette form (in contrast to the "core" right to distribute films for performances in movie theaters). Recently, Time Warner lost a suit about its right to distribute the Beatles' film, *Yellow Submarine*, in videocassette form. The court ordered Time Warner to pay the owner of the copyright $2.3 million dollars as damages for distributing videocassette copies.

Consequently, you should expect that the publisher will wish to obtain the broadest possible grant of rights to avoid uncertainties about product distribution. The most important issues that will arise in the license form of publishing agreements are discussed in "Key Issues in License Agreements," later in this chapter.

### Exclusive and Nonexclusive Licenses

Although license agreements take many forms, the first critical issue is whether the license is exclusive or nonexclusive (these terms are defined in "Licenses," Chapter 4). In most publishing agreements, the publisher will want exclusivity. Unless the publisher is acting only as a simple distributor (such as Merisel, a company that buys and sells finished products), such a request is not unreasonable. Exclusivity ensures the publisher that money spent on promotion will result in revenues to the publisher and not to a second "free riding" publisher. It also prevents confusion regarding pricing and returns (for example, with two publishers of the same product, a distributor might not know to whom to return products). However, you may wish to limit the exclusivity to the markets in which the publisher is best able to exploit the product.

> *Developer developed an interactive history of the Korean War. She granted an exclusive license to distribute the work in CD-ROM and diskette form to Book Publisher Company. However, she granted the exclusive rights to create a television documentary to Film Development Company because Film Development Company had more experience in the television industry.*

In exclusive agreements, make sure that the publisher has a strong incentive to distribute the product. If the publisher changes its corporate strategy or simply fails to market your product, your expected revenues (which are generally based on royalties arising from sales) will be lower than you expected. Such incentives can take a variety of forms: legal obligations, minimum payments, or a combination of both.

The legal obligation to market a product traditionally requires one of four types of effort from the publisher:

- Best efforts.

- Reasonable commercial efforts.

- Efforts in comparison to other types of products.

- More detailed effort requirements (such as advertising budgets and so on).

One problem with this legal obligation to exploit is that most publishers will not agree to employ "best efforts" because the legal standard for "best efforts" is so high that it is very difficult to meet. Unfortunately, the "reasonable commercial efforts" standard is less precise and could be difficult to enforce. The latter two forms of effort may require difficult predictions about what amount of advertising and other promotion efforts are appropriate.

Rather than rely solely on such legal standards, you should ensure that the publisher has a clear economic incentive to market your product and recover its "investment." This can take the form of a large advance to you, minimum royalties, or a combination of the two.

In exclusive agreements, you also should be alert to the remedies for the lack of performance by the publisher. If your only remedy for any failure of performance by the publisher is to terminate the publisher, you may face a difficult choice. Termination will probably be very costly for you because you must find a new publisher and restart an advertising campaign. A new publisher may be reluctant to take on a product that it believes has "failed." Termination could also result in other problems, such as a "flooding" of the market with your product as the original publisher sells off its inventory at discount prices.

## Key Issues in License Agreements

We'll discuss the key issues for license agreements—platforms, types of media, and so on—in this section. These issues may also be important for "license-back" of rights in components (if you have assigned all of your rights in the work to your client), or if you are granting a "limited" assignment of rights to the client or publisher.

### Platforms

The publishing agreement should clearly state the platform or platforms for which you are granting distribution rights. Currently, the Macintosh and IBM platforms are the two most important for most multimedia products. However, some products may be exploited on a variety of other platforms, including Nintendo, Sega, CD-I, Archimedes, and 3DO. You may even divide the platforms among "home" video console systems (such as Super Nintendo Entertainment System), "arcade" systems, and handheld systems (such as GameBoy). You should be confident that the publisher has the ability to exploit your multimedia product on all of the platforms granted in the license.

Another way of splitting fields of use is by operating systems, such as DOS, Windows, Mac, Windows NT, and Solaris. This type of splitting is becoming more difficult due to the number of operating systems that permit "emulation" of other operating systems. For example, Apple Computer has just introduced a computer that also runs Windows programs.

The publisher will want the broadest possible rights to maximize the return on its investment in the product. One common solution is to give the publisher the right to exploit the rights on certain platforms, with a "right of first refusal" to exploit the work on other platforms. A right of first refusal is a right to match a proposed offer or an actual offer from a third party. You can then exploit your product on other platforms if the publisher chooses not to do so. A weaker form of the right of first refusal is a "right of first negotiation." This right requires you to negotiate in good faith with the publisher for a limited time period. You should also recognize that the publisher needs rights on certain minimum platforms to make the distribution of the product economically profitable.

*Developer has developed an interactive "edutainment" product to teach mathematics to first grade students. She granted Publisher an exclusive license to distribute the product on the IBM and Mac platforms. She granted Publisher a right of first refusal to distribute the work on the 3DO, Sega, and Nintendo platforms. She ported the product to the Sega platform and got an offer from Sega to distribute this version. Because Publisher had a right of first refusal for distribution of the Sega version, she offered the same terms to Publisher. When Publisher failed to accept the terms within the 30-day acceptance period in the original agreement, Developer was free to enter into the distribution agreement with Sega for the Sega version of the product. This grant of an exclusive right to Sega will be limited to the Sega platform and will not interfere with the rights granted to Publisher. (Rights of first refusal can be structured in many different ways and this example only describes one of them.)*

### Types of Media

The publishing agreement should define the types of media upon which your product can be exploited by the publisher. Some examples of current media include diskettes, cartridges, and CD-ROMs. Many licenses currently include rights in all media. The clear definition of the scope of these rights is very important because of the uncertainty about the way in which multimedia products will be distributed in the future. As mentioned in "Licensing the Rights," earlier in this chapter, film companies are still involved in disputes about their rights to distribute films in the "new" medium of videocassette. You should try to avoid similar problems.

You and the publisher should carefully determine what restrictions are appropriate and define them carefully. You also need to consider other forms of media such as distribution via cable or telephone companies and use on interactive television and computer networks.

### Geographic Scope

Most multimedia publishing agreements currently give worldwide rights to the publisher. However, it may be appropriate to grant more limited rights if you believe that the publisher does not have the capability to distribute your product worldwide. If you decide to include such limits, it is very important to describe the exact nature of the geographic rights. The "leakage" of products outside of distribution territories is not uncommon. For example, many software vendors were surprised to discover their products were being sold in South American countries even though they had not established any publishers or distributors in those countries. They discovered that it was common for computer software dealers in Florida to purchase products for further distribution in South America. To avoid such problems, the publishing agreement should carefully limit distribution of the product to distribution for use in a particular country or area.

- *Developer granted Publisher an exclusive United States right to distribute his game software. Developer may find that his game software is being sold in the United States by Publisher for use in arcades in South America with the Publisher's knowledge. It is not clear that Developer can stop such resales without a more limited distribution right in the original agreement with the Publisher. To avoid this problem, Developer should have granted Publisher an exclusive right to distribute his game software for use in arcades located in the United States (instead of the exclusive right to distribute the game software in the United States). Then, Developer would have the legal right to prevent such distribution outside of the United States.*

If the multimedia product can be broadcast by television (or satellite) or used on a network, you should impose appropriate geographic restrictions on this type of distribution. You should also be aware of any geographic limitations imposed by content licenses authorizing your use of third-party works. (License terms are discussed in "Obtaining a License," Chapter 10.)

- *Developer created an education game to teach French to high school students. He licensed French songs for use in his game to help the students learn the language. His song license is limited to reproduction and distribution in Canada and the United States (the music publisher that granted the license only has the right to license the songs in the United States and Canada). If Developer distributes the product in the United Kingdom and Ireland, he will be violating his license with the music publisher. The music publisher may terminate the license agreement for breach. The Developer also may be sued by the owner of the copyrights in the songs in the United Kingdom and Ireland.*

## Ancillary Rights

Your multimedia product may have the potential for significant revenue from "ancillary" rights. Ancillary rights are rights to exploit the storyline, characters, or settings in other media, such as books, television, merchandising, and films. For example, sale of "hint books" for videogames can be very lucrative. Many Hollywood films now make more from merchandising the characters in their films than they make from the actual box office receipts. For example, the original *Batman* movie grossed approximately $400 million worldwide from performance in movie theaters, but earned over $500 million through merchandising sales of clothing, toys, games, and videocassettes.

## Sequel Rights

If the multimedia work is one that lends itself to sequels, sequel rights are very important to you and the publisher. Many game programs, because of the characters in their games, present rich opportunities for sequels. Frequently, each sequel will out-sell the previous product. For example, Broderbund has been very successful in exploiting sequels of *Carmen Sandiego*. In fact, Broderbund has expressly stated that its corporate strategy is to "develop products that may be expanded into families of related sequel or complementary products that achieve sustained consumer appeal and brand name recognition." In the film industry, the *Star Wars* trilogy has been very successful.

You must decide if you wish to grant sequel rights to the publisher and what the terms will be. You may decide to use the terms of the original license agreement for the sequel, or you can provide for a separate negotiation at the time the sequels are ready for development. A common solution is to give the publisher a "right of first refusal" to distribute sequels (see the explanation of this term in "Platforms," earlier in this chapter). This compromise is advantageous for both parties because the publisher is already familiar with the original work and its marketing, and you avoid the expense of working with a new publisher. At the same time, you can feel comfortable that the right of first refusal ensures that you will receive market value for your sequel.

If you grant sequel rights, pay careful attention to the definition of the scope of sequel rights. Is a sequel a product that includes the use of a single character, theme, or setting, or must it include the entire ensemble of characters as well as identical themes and settings in the original product? The contract provision on sequel rights should also deal with the publisher's rights to propose sequels, and the terms for the creation and distribution of such sequels by the publisher.

This issue takes a different form when you have assigned all of your rights to the publisher. In that structure, the publisher has the right to create sequels because one of the rights that you assigned is the "modification" right (see "The Exclusive Rights," Chapter 2). You then need to include contract provisions to give you the right to participate in creating and distributing sequels.

### Foreign Language and Other Platforms

The distribution agreement should address the "porting" of the original multimedia product to other platforms and "localizing" to foreign languages. You should consider how much control you wish to retain over such new versions. For example, you may want the right to create such new versions both for economic and quality control reasons. However, you should recognize that the publisher also needs the ability to create such new versions to maximize the return on its investment. If you cannot or do not wish to create such new versions, the publisher should have the right to do so.

A common solution gives you, the developer, a right of first refusal to create such versions upon the request of the publisher. If you fail to exercise your right of first refusal, the publisher can create such works directly or through third parties. However, if the publisher creates such a work, it will own the copyright in the translation, and you should obtain an assignment of such rights to you. If your trademark or tradename is used on publisher-created versions, it is important that you ensure that these products meet your quality standards. (See "Trademark Protection," Chapter 16.)

### Unrelated Works

You may want to enter into a broader relationship with a publisher. In such a relationship, the publisher has an option to develop and distribute a limited number of your future projects (or any projects that you create during a certain period), whether or not they are related to one another. (This type of agreement is common in the film industry.) The distribution agreement should state clearly what information you must provide to the publisher about a future project and what procedure the publisher must follow to exercise its option on a project. You should clearly define the term of the "acceptance period" during which the publisher must make the decision—frequently it is a period after receipt of the project's description. The agreement also should describe the scope of the publisher's obligations once it has exercised the option for a proposal.

### Trademarks

You should remember that the use of your trademarks or tradenames on a product requires you to exercise quality control over the product. If the relationship permits the publisher to develop new versions of the products (whether they are multimedia works or merchandising articles, such as clothes), you must ensure that such products meet the quality control standards that you have established for your trademarks. Failure to exercise quality control could result in the trademarks becoming "generic." In other words, you could lose your right to enforce your trademarks. (See "Trademark Protection," Chapter 16.)

## Payment

You should ensure that the calculation and timing of payments are very clearly described in the distribution agreement. Generally, payment is divided into two categories: advances and royalties. You may also receive separate payment of "expenses" to license content.

### Advances

Advances are the initial payment that you receive from the publisher before distribution of the product. Advances can be paid in a lump-sum payment or a series of payments tied to milestones in the development of a product.

Advances are determined in a variety of ways: They can be arbitrary amounts set to encourage the publisher to exploit the product, or they can be tied to the expense of developing a particular product. These expenses can include traditional costs, such as employee and independent contractor salaries, and third-party license fees. They can also include less traditional expenses, such as the premiums for "errors and omission" insurance or purchase of needed equipment.

*Developer is a small company that is negotiating its first transaction with Publisher. Publisher is willing to pay Developer an advance to cover the expenses of developing the product. However, Developer needs a Silicon Graphics computer and a scanner to create the new product. Publisher may be willing to increase the size of the advance to permit Developer to purchase or lease the necessary equipment.*

One of the most important issues for you is whether the advances are refundable or nonrefundable. Refundable means you may have to repay the advances to the publisher for certain defined reasons. It may be appropriate to repay the advances if you are unsuccessful in creating the multimedia product for certain reasons under your control, such as loss of employees or accepting additional work. However, a requirement to refund the advances if your multimedia product is not successful in the marketplace is unreasonable. Such a requirement would mean that you would lose both the money and the time that you spent in developing the product.

Frequently, advances are nonrefundable, but recoupable from the royalties due to you. Recoupment can take many forms. The most common form requires withholding of all your royalties until all of the advances from the publisher have been repaid. The potential problem with this approach is that you will not have any cash flow from royalties after the delivery of the multimedia product until all of the advances are repaid. Depending on the amount of the advances, this repayment could take months or even years. One compromise is to permit recoupment of a designated percentage of your royalties so that the publisher receives repayment of advances (although more slowly than under the prior structure) and you receive revenue immediately from the distribution of the multimedia product.

*Publisher paid Developer a $200,000 advance which is recoupable from a 10 percent royalty on net revenues from the sale of the product. The royalties due to Developer were $50,000 in the first quarter, $70,000 in the second quarter, $100,000 in the third quarter, $120,000 in the fourth quarter, and $170,000 in the fifth quarter. If all advances are recouped from royalties before any payment of royalties to Developer, Publisher will be repaid its advances by the third quarter. Developer will not be paid royalties until the third quarter. The first payment will be $20,000. If the Publisher agrees that recoupment will be limited to 50 percent of the royalties due to Developer, Developer will receive payments immediately: $25,000 in the first quarter, $35,000 in the second quarter, $50,000 in the third quarter, $60,000 in the fourth quarter, and $140,000 in the fifth quarter. Publisher will not be repaid until the fifth quarter (instead of in the third quarter).*

When you are contemplating a publishing agreement for a series of products, the issue of cross-recoupment (sometimes referred to as "cross-collateralization") frequently arises. Cross-recoupment is the right of the publisher to obtain repayment of advances on one product from royalties for another product. Cross-recoupment permits the publisher to spread its risk among several products, some of which may be less successful than others. This request is generally reasonable because it permits the parties to share the risks and rewards more equally.

## Royalties

Royalties can take many forms. In fact, they represent one of the most flexible means of allocating a financial return between the parties. The balance of this section will discuss the most common issues that arise in determining royalties.

### Royalty Base

Although many developers focus on what "percentage" they will get of the royalty base, the definition of the royalty base is the more important issue. The initial question in this definition is whether royalties will be paid on gross or net revenues. Gross revenues are all revenues received from the distribution of the product, without any deductions. The problem with the use of gross revenues is that they don't reflect the profits of the publisher. The multimedia industry is young, and many of the distribution expenses are not yet well defined. The publisher is likely to be very conservative in setting royalties based on gross revenues because of uncertainties about what the actual profit will be. This problem can be particularly acute for the publisher if the multimedia product includes significant amounts of "third party" content for which the publisher is responsible for paying license fees. (See "Obtaining a License," Chapter 10.) In this situation, the publisher may have great difficulty in estimating its profits on the product in advance.

The advantage to you of royalties paid on gross revenues is that gross revenues are relatively easy to calculate. Unlike "net profits," gross revenues are not really subject to manipulation. The recent dispute between Art Buchwald and a major movie studio regarding a "net profits" agreement illustrates the manipulation problem. Art Buchwald contributed a brief story idea to the studio for an initial $10,000 payment. He was to get a fixed fee and a share in the "net profits" if the idea was used in a film. Eventually, the idea was used for the Eddie Murphy movie, *Coming to America*. The studio denied that the idea was the basis for the movie, but a judge disagreed. The studio then stated that though the movie grossed over $350 million worldwide, the movie had a deficit of $18 million under the net profits definition. Art Buchwald challenged the studio over their calculation of net profits. The trial revealed many examples of the studio marking up the costs of services it provided to cover its overhead and make further profits. For example, the deductions included a 10 percent advertising overhead that was not related to actual costs, and a 15 percent overhead charge that was found not even "remotely" to correspond to actual costs. The judge described a 15 percent overhead charge on an operational allowance for Eddie Murphy Productions as "charging overhead on overhead."

Nonetheless, net revenue is the most frequent royalty base in multimedia publishing agreements. If properly defined, this royalty base poses little risk to you. The use of net revenues may actually mean a greater return to you: The publisher may be willing to pay a higher percentage of the net revenue. The critical issue is the list of what items are deducted from gross revenues to calculate net revenue. The most common deductions are:

- Sales and use taxes.
- Shipping charges.
- Shipping insurance.
- Returns and stock balancing.
- Discounts (including cooperative advertising, credits, and rebates).
- Costs of manufacturing.

For multimedia products that will have significant international sales, net revenues may also include a deduction for royalty payments that cannot be brought back into the United States because of currency control or similar laws of foreign countries. (Some countries do not permit revenues earned in that country to be converted into dollars and transferred out of the country.) If the publisher creates a "ported" or "localized" version of the product, the royalty rate on such a version may be reduced to reflect the publisher's greater investment.

You should review the components of net revenue very carefully for deductions that are controlled by affiliates or subsidiaries of the publisher. These types of deductions may not reflect the market costs of the goods or services being provided.

To reflect the true price of your product, the price used to calculate gross revenues or net revenues should be fixed in a market transaction. Avoid having this price based on sales by the publisher to its related companies, such as sales subsidiaries, because that price may be quite different from market price due to taxes and other concerns.

### *Payment Mechanics*

The royalty provision also should state when the royalties become due. The two most common choices are the date products are shipped and the date the payment is received. These choices involve different risks for you and for the publisher.

The date of shipment is an easy date to determine. However, the publisher's distributors will not pay the publisher immediately for the product—they may take an additional 30 to 90 days (or even 120 days for some foreign sales) after receipt of the product to pay. Consequently, the publisher may be reluctant to adopt the date of shipment as the date royalties are due. This is because it requires that the publisher finance your royalty payments on products for which it has not yet received payment (and will not receive payment for several months).

On the other hand, if the payment becomes due on the date of receipt of payment by the publisher, you share the collection risk with the publisher. Publishers prefer this payment method because it reduces their risk. Moreover, if multimedia products are treated like books, retail distributors will have the right to return all of the copies they have "bought." Such a return policy could make the payment of royalties that are based on "sales" very erratic when the royalty payments are reduced to reflect returns. You should ensure that if returns exceed shipments, you do not have an obligation to repay any of your prior royalty payments. Under this method, you risk not receiving a royalty payment for copies sent by the publisher to a distributor who sells the product but doesn't pay the publisher, or who enters bankruptcy before payment. Nonetheless, this arrangement is the most common one because the publisher is clearly motivated to obtain payment.

The publishing agreement should also state how frequently payments are to be made, and the nature of reports that will accompany the payment. At a minimum, the report should indicate the period of the report, the amount of sales, and the calculation of royalties. If the publishing agreement covers more than one product, the report should provide this information for each product by stock balancing unit (SKU) (*e.g.*, 5.25" and 3.5" versions). The most common time periods for payment for many game products is monthly (quarterly or semi-annually for many CD-ROM products). For more complex agreements, you also may wish to have the report include geographic information on sales, if it is available. You should recognize that such information may not be available, particularly due to the relative newness of the distribution channels.

### Bundled Products

"Bundled" products are those that are distributed with the hardware or software of the publisher or a third party. They need to be handled differently in the royalty provision than "retail" products. The compensation the publisher receives from bundled products may be difficult to calculate. For example, a publisher could provide a "free" product for bundling with another product for premiums or a preloaded game on a computer. The amount of payment, if any, received per bundled copy is generally much less than the amount received for a retail sale. One common solution is to provide for payment of a fixed dollar amount per bundled copy rather than a percentage of royalties or a different percentage.

### Minimum Unit Royalties

You may wish to consider a per-unit minimum royalty on retail copies. If the royalty is set as a percentage of the publisher's net revenues, your royalty payments may be much lower than you expect if the publisher sells the product for less than you expect. On the other hand, this reduced price may reflect the true market price of your product.

Both you and the publisher share a desire to maximize the revenue from the distribution of the product. In many cases, such per-unit minimums will not be necessary. If you decide to request such minimums, set them carefully to take into account the publisher's potential return and the realities of the marketplace. For example, multimedia products are rarely sold at the "suggested retail price." Minimum royalties based on the assumption that the publisher is receiving the suggested retail price are likely to be unrealistic because the publisher typically receives between 50–60 percent of the "suggested retail price" from the distributors. You can use the suggested retail price as the basis for this calculation, but you should recognize that the publisher will not be receiving the full amount. You may also wish to provide for a reduction in the per-unit royalty if the distribution price is reduced over time. Finally, you should recognize that the publisher may need to sell off older versions at less than normal retail prices.

Developers occasionally have tried to get the same per-copy royalty for both bundled and retail copies. This either sets the royalty rate too low for retail sales or too high for bundled sales. Generally, the result is a high per-copy royalty that deters the publisher from distributing bundled copies of the product.

### *Annual Minimums*

The requirement of minimum royalty payments is one of the most effective devices to ensure that the publisher remains committed to exploiting the product. Such minimums may be less necessary if you have received a sufficiently large advance. Minimum royalty payments set clear expectations between you and the publisher. Generally, such minimums are set on a calendar-year basis. The amount varies depending on the price of the product and the sales expectations. On the other hand, you and the publisher may have very different expectations for the product, and it may be very difficult to agree on an amount acceptable to both parties. Annual minimums are rarely used in nonexclusive licenses.

## Warranties

A "warranty" is simply a legal promise that certain facts are true. Most distribution agreements include a warranty section in which the publisher asks you to warrant certain facts. You can provide a warranty even for facts that are not within your control.

As discussed in "The Contract," Chapter 6, warranties come in different levels of certainty. The most common types of warranties are:

- Absolute.

- Know or should know.

- Actual knowledge.

"Absolute" warranties have the highest degree of certainty. These warranties have no exceptions and do not depend on your actual knowledge. Publishers prefer this type of warranty because proving that you had knowledge of a certain matter may be difficult.

Other warranties are qualified by statements such as "know or should have known" or "actual knowledge." Such qualifiers try to limit your duty to investigate the facts. The "know or should have known" warranty imposes on the warrantor a greater duty to investigate and "know" the status of the facts warranted than the "actual knowledge" warranty.

Whether to provide an absolute or a qualified warranty will depend on the subject of the warranty. For example, an absolute warranty that there are no pending lawsuits about the multimedia product is quite reasonable because you should know such information. However, a qualified warranty may be more appropriate for a warranty of noninfringement of third-party patents because you can infringe a patent innocently without any knowledge of the patent or the infringement.

The term "warranty" has a different meaning under the Uniform Commercial Code. (See "Important Provisions of Article Two," Chapter 17.)

The warranties most commonly requested by a publisher are discussed in the balance of this section.

### Ownership or Right to Grant the License

Depending on the nature of the multimedia product, the publisher may demand a warranty that you are the sole and exclusive owner of all intellectual property rights in the product, or simply that you have the right to grant the licenses in the distribution agreement. For example, for a work that has significant third-party content, you would not be able to warrant that you are the owner of the copyright of the entire work because it includes copyrightable material owned by third parties. However, a publisher will want to ensure that you have obtained the right to distribute third party materials contained in your work (see "Obtaining a License," Chapter 10). If you haven't gotten appropriate licenses from third parties, the publisher will infringe third-party copyrights by distributing your work. In fact, the publisher is likely to request copies of licenses and other contracts with third parties to ensure that you have the rights you need. This process is called "due diligence." (For more information, see "Due Diligence," Chapter 19.)

If you are granting an assignment or an exclusive license, the publisher wants to be certain that you can actually grant exclusive rights in the product. The publisher does not want " "free riders" who also have the right to distribute the product and take advantage of the publisher's advertising. If you have failed to obtain appropriate assignments from the individuals who helped to create the product (see "Using the Employment Agreement," Chapter 7, and "Copyright Ownership," Chapter 8), those individuals may have "joint" ownership of the copyright in the product. This joint ownership will permit them to grant other publishers the right to distribute the product (see "Joint Authorship and Ownership," Chapter 4). Such "parallel" rights would undermine the exclusivity of the original publisher.

### Noninfringement of Third-Party Rights

A warranty of noninfringement of third-party rights is one of the most important ones for a publisher because of the complex nature of multimedia products and the frequent use of third-party content. The publisher wants to ensure that you have obtained all of the rights necessary to distribute the product and that the product, as created, does not infringe third-party rights. Even though the publisher receives these warranties from you, it is still liable to third parties for infringement of their rights if you are wrong.

Different types of intellectual property call for different levels of certainty in the warranty. You should be willing to provide strong warranties regarding noninfringement of trade secrets and copyrights because these types of infringements are within your control.

The most difficult issue for you is the warranty about the noninfringement of patents. Unlike the infringement of copyrights or misappropriation of trade secrets, you can infringe patents without your knowledge. The problem is complicated by the youth of the multimedia industry and the lack of information about potentially applicable patents. In addition, patent applications in the United States are maintained in confidence until they are actually issued, a period of secrecy that may last several years. On the other hand, you are clearly more knowledgeable about how the product was developed than the publisher. The appropriate allocation of this risk requires careful negotiation between the parties.

### Performance

Warranties about the performance of the product arise under Article Two of the Uniform Commercial Code. Most multimedia products would be considered "goods" under the Uniform Commercial Code and, therefore, would be subject to the rules imposed by that statute. (See "Important Provisions of Article Two," Chapter 17.) You should be familiar with Article Two's "express" and "implied" warranties to determine the scope of your obligations.

Although you should be prepared to provide limited performance warranties, you should describe carefully the scope of your responsibilities for correcting errors in your product. You will also want to disclaim the "implied" performance warranties of "fitness for a particular purpose" and "merchantability" (see "Important Provisions of Article Two," Chapter 17) because of their ambiguity for software products. Virtually all software products have bugs, and the question of how many bugs are permitted in "merchantable" software is still open. Finally, you will probably be providing an express indemnity for infringement of third-party intellectual property rights, so you should disclaim the statutory warranty of noninfringement. Otherwise you would be providing two separate indemnities (see "Important Provisions of Article Two," Chapter 17).

## Credits

If the publisher has the right to reproduce your product or is providing packaging, you should ensure that you receive appropriate credit. Credits are very important. The Writers Guild of America has established elaborate rules in the movie and television industries regarding appropriate credits for writers and others involved in the creation of films and television programs, but no such rules currently exist in the multimedia industry. The most frequent form of credits are "written by" and "developed by" on the title screen and the packaging. You should also recognize that the publisher will be very interested in maintaining control of the packaging of its products. Consequently, you should not make unrealistic demands about size and placement of credits. If you are providing only one part of a larger work, you should ensure that you review the final placement of credits prior to duplication to avoid having your credits buried in optional screens.

## Remedies

Remedies are the relief for the failure ("breach") of a party's obligations under the distribution agreement. (Breach of contract is discussed in "What is a Contract?," Chapter 5.) Pay careful attention to the remedies in the distribution agreement. Termination of the agreement is a "blunt" remedy. It may not be an effective remedy for many lesser breaches of obligations under the distribution agreement. If you terminate the distribution agreement, you must then find a new publisher and start the advertising and distribution process once again.

You should consider what type of "intermediate" remedies should be available to you for a less than complete failure on the part of the publisher. For example, if the publisher is successfully distributing your multimedia product in the United States but not in Europe, you will have a difficult decision if your choices are limited to taking no action or terminating the entire agreement. Instead, you should consider an "intermediate" remedy that permits termination in the countries in which the publisher is not performing successfully. Intermediate remedies should be put in place at the time the agreement is drafted.

You also should be aware of remedies that may be imposed on you for the breach of your obligations. One of the most common and most important remedies is an indemnity of the publisher for infringements of third-party intellectual property rights. The costs of defending and paying damages in an infringement case could far exceed the revenues you receive under the distribution agreement. The most efficient way of avoiding this liability is to properly clear any third-party content before using it (see Chapters 9, 10, 11, and 12).

One basis for allocating risks under a contract is to allocate them to the party best able to reduce them. As the developer, you are best able to assess the risk of infringement of third-party intellectual property rights and to reduce the risk. If you have a dispute with third parties, you can reduce your liability by including a requirement in the distribution agreement that permits you to demand that the publisher suspend distribution of the product in countries where challenges by third parties have been brought. For example, if a foreign corporation has brought a trademark infringement claim against the publisher in France based on your trademark, you should be able to demand that the publisher cease distributing the product in France (or remove the trademark for copies distributed in France) to avoid increasing your liability for damages.

In addition, you may wish to try to limit your liability for damages under this obligation. For example, you could ask to limit your liability under the agreement to the amount of your royalties. However, the publisher may be very reluctant to permit such a limit. This is because the publisher's liability is likely to be significantly greater than the sum of all of the royalties paid to you. (The publisher's liability will be based on its profits, not royalty payments to you.) Two potential compromises are to set a limit of a large amount based on the predicted sales or obtain insurance against this risk. Unfortunately, at the current time, it is difficult to obtain insurance for this type of risk. The issue of limiting your liability for infringement of third-party intellectual property rights may be one of the most contentious ones in your negotiations with the publisher.

# 19

## Publishers' Concerns

The structure of transactions between multimedia developers and publishers is still in flux. The still-young multimedia industry draws on conflicting traditions from the book publishing, television, film, and software industries. There is currently no industry framework to use as a guide.

The multimedia publisher must deal with the same issues as the developer, but will have a different perspective. This chapter will describe key issues from the publisher's point of view.

Other chapters also discuss a number of issues that are relevant to the publisher.

### Scope of Rights

The question of whether the distribution agreement should be structured as an assignment or a license (see "Scope of the Agreement," Chapter 18) is probably the most difficult and important issue between publishers and developers.

The advantage of an assignment is that it provides the publisher with all rights in the product, and it does not require the publisher to predict which rights will be most valuable in the future (see "Assigning the Rights," Chapter 18). Even a general assignment should state clearly whether it includes an assignment of rights in the characters and settings in the product. Characters and settings could have significant value in sequels and other media.

If the publisher does not have the negotiating leverage to obtain an assignment, it will have to be satisfied with a license (see "Licensing the Rights," Chapter 18). In that case, the publisher should ensure that it gets a right of first refusal to exploit the multimedia product in media other than the "core" product form which it has licensed. The most common core product forms are CD-ROM and diskette. The most common noncore product rights, discussed in the balance of this section, are:

- Right to port to other platforms.

- Right to localize for other languages.

- Right to develop publisher-originated sequels.

- Right to distribute developer-originated sequels.

- Right to complete an unfinished work.

- Merchandising and ancillary rights.

### Rights to Porting and Localization

In many cases, the publisher may only receive the right to reproduce and distribute the product. However, the publisher should be very careful to obtain the right to modify the multimedia product for other platforms and other languages, even if the developer is not currently interested in such modifications. The current uncertainty about which platform will be the most important reinforces the importance of the porting and localization right. The publisher should also try to ensure that localization is made easier by having easy access to text files and text fields large enough for translations which are longer than English text.

As discussed in "Assignments," Chapter 4, copyright rights are divisible. If the publisher does not obtain the right to modify the product to create ported versions or foreign language versions of the product, the publisher will not have porting or localization rights. (The modification right and other exclusive rights are discussed in "The Exclusive Rights," Chapter 2.) In that case, the publisher may miss significant opportunities for increased revenue.

On the other hand, the developer may wish to control the creation of such ports and localized products. A frequent compromise is to provide the developer with a "right of first refusal" to create such works (see "Key Issues in License Agreements," Chapter 18). However, to avoid a separate negotiation for each new version, the publisher should try to establish the terms upon which it will be able to distribute such new versions (generally, the publisher will prefer the same terms as those for the original version).

The publisher should also consider whether the developer should be permitted to make these modifications for platforms with which the developer is not familiar. In other words, does the publisher wish to subsidize the developer's learning to create a product for a new platform? The publisher also should establish what materials—such as source code, graphics files, and camera-ready art—the developer will provide if the publisher (or the publisher's contractor) creates the modifications. Access to the developer's materials could substantially reduce the cost of creating these new versions.

### Rights to Sequels

Many multimedia products offer significant opportunities to create a series of products based on the same theme, characters, or settings. The ability to market a series instead of a single product can substantially increase the return for the publisher. Consequently, the right to distribute sequels is critical for the publisher.

The publisher should establish the terms on which such sequel rights will be made available in as much detail as possible. If the publisher cannot obtain an absolute right to distribute sequels, a "right of first refusal" is the next best alternative, preferably based upon the same terms as those for distribution of the initial product. The disadvantage to the publisher of simply getting a right of first refusal is that it creates an "auction" with third parties, a situation that may not recognize the publisher's contribution to the value of the original product.

The publisher should try to get the following minimum information from the developer to decide whether to exercise its right of first refusal to distribute sequels:

- A written proposal (including a budget) from the developer to create the sequel.

- The royalty percentage for the sequel (if not already established).

- The advances for the sequel (if not already established).

- Other appropriate distribution terms.

If the publisher decides not to exercise the right of first refusal on a proposal, the developer should be allowed to offer rights in the sequel on the same terms to a third party for a limited period of time—typically from 30 to 120 days. If this time period is not limited, the publisher takes the risk that over time the initial product will become more successful and the original terms for the sequel will become more attractive. To ensure that the publisher and third parties compete on an equal basis for the sequel rights, the term during which the developer can offer such terms should be limited.

As an alternative, the publisher should try to include a "right of last look." This right gives the publisher a final opportunity to obtain rights in the sequel if the developer is about to enter into an agreement with a third party. A "right of last look" generally offers the publisher the opportunity to obtain the rights on the same terms as the third party. It is usually of very short duration (frequently five or fewer business days).

The publisher should also try to ensure that it has the right to develop sequels based on its own ideas. For example, the developer may decide not to create any further sequels, for reasons not based on the economic success of the original product. The publisher may believe that a sequel would be successful, and the publisher should have the right to invest in such a sequel. To avoid conflict with the developer, the publisher should consider offering the developer the right of first refusal to create that sequel based on the publisher's ideas. However, if the developer does not exercise that right, the publisher should be able to make the sequel. Naturally, the royalties paid to the developer for a sequel based on the publisher's ideas should be less than those for the original product.

### Rights to Complete

Many developers are thinly capitalized organizations that may not be able to complete a project if a key developer leaves. Consequently, the publisher should ensure that it has the right to complete a multimedia product if the developer is unsuccessful. Completion rights should also apply to ported versions, foreign language versions (localizations), and sequels whose development was begun by the developer. Once again, if the publisher does not have an assignment of rights in the product or the explicit right to modify the product, the publisher will not have the right to complete a product. At the same time, the developer may not have the resources to repay any advances. Thus, the publisher will be left with an unfinished product and an unrecoverable advance. This potential problem emphasizes the importance of having an escrow with source code and other components.

### Rights to Merchandising and Ancillary Products

Depending on the type of multimedia product, the rights to ancillary products—books, clothing, television, and film—may be more valuable than the rights to the original multimedia product on CD-ROM or diskette. If the multimedia product creates popular characters, the potential returns in this market may be enormous. The publisher should obtain the exclusive rights to license these characters, or at least a right of first refusal to exploit them.

## Due Diligence

"Due diligence" is the shorthand term for the investigation of facts and legal issues undertaken by lawyers (or others) as part of a business transaction. In publishing agreements, the most important part of the publisher's due diligence is ensuring that the developer has properly done two things:

- Cleared any rights to third-party content used in the product. (See Chapters 9, 10, and 12.)
- Obtained the necessary assignments from the individuals who helped to create the product. (See Chapters 7 and 8.)

The publisher will be liable for infringement if it distributes a product that includes third-party material without appropriate permission. Ignorance or warranties from the developer are not a defense to copyright infringement by the publisher. The publisher will have a substantially greater liability for mistakes on these issues than the developer. Damages awards to third parties will be calculated on the publisher's profits, not on those of the developer (or the royalties paid by publisher to developer). Damages are discussed in "Copyright Protection," Chapter 16.

*Developer used a videoclip from the film Terminator in a multimedia product on sales training without clearing the rights to use the clip. Publisher got a warranty from Developer of ownership of all rights in the product and a warranty of noninfringement of third-party rights in the publishing agreement. The Publisher distributed the product to retail stores. The studio will probably sue both Developer and Publisher. Even though Publisher got a warranty that the product did not infringe third-party rights, both parties will be liable for copyright infringement because Developer failed to get a license to use the clip. Publisher may also have a claim against Developer for its damages.*

In addition, the third party whose intellectual property rights are infringed may obtain a court order to prevent distribution of the product and destroy existing copies of the product. In October, 1993, Berkeley Systems obtained an injunction against Delrina for the use of Berkeley Systems' famous "Flying Toasters" in a "spoof" screen saver in which Delrina's Opus character shot down "Flying Toasters." One Delrina officer stated that the order to cease distribution and destroy existing copies of the Delrina product had cost the company hundreds of thousands of dollars.

Although the publisher can obtain warranties from the developer that no intellectual property infringement problems exist, warranties will not protect the publisher against embarrassment and business problems arising from the unauthorized use of third-party materials. (Warranties are discussed in "Warranties," Chapter 18.) The publisher may also find that the developer does not have the resources to defend or reimburse the publisher for damages paid to such a third party, despite having a legal obligation to do so.

To avoid "buying" a lawsuit, the publisher or its attorney should understand how the multimedia product was developed, review third-party content licenses, and review the developer's agreements with its employees and independent contractors. (License terms are discussed in "Obtaining a License," Chapter 10.) It is much cheaper to discover and resolve problems before beginning distribution of the product.

*Publisher performed "due diligence" on a golf game it wanted to distribute. Publisher reviewed the assignment agreements with the individuals who created the game and the golf celebrity who licensed his name to be used on it. Publisher discovered that several of the individuals involved in the development of the game were not full-time employees of Developer at the time they worked on the game and they had not executed assignment agreements. The golf celebrity has licensed his name only for a year and the license is limited to IBM computers. Before licensing the product, the Publisher should ensure that the individuals have executed appropriate assignment agreements. Publisher may also wish to extend the term of the celebrity license and broaden its scope.*

Once again, because the legal issues are complicated and the industry is new, there are no industry standards about what rights are needed. The burden is on the publisher to ensure that the developer has taken appropriate steps to obtain the rights necessary to develop and distribute the work. (This topic is discussed in "Determining What Rights You Need," Chapter 10.)

## Payment

Most multimedia distribution agreements provide for the payment of an advance against royalties, and for royalties on per-copy sales. (See "Payment," Chapter 18.)

### Royalties

The publisher should ensure that the method of calculating royalties is clearly defined. As discussed in "Payment," Chapter 18, the publisher will generally prefer royalties based on net revenues rather than on gross revenues because it is less risky for the publisher.

In most cases, advances will be recouped against royalties. The procedure for recoupment of advances requires a careful balance of developer and publisher concerns. The publisher will want its advance repaid as rapidly as possible, a goal best achieved by withholding all of the royalty payments due to the developer until the advance is repaid. However, the publisher should recognize the potential problem this may create for the developer. Many developers are thinly capitalized and may depend on the revenue from the product being distributed while they work on other projects. By simply decreasing the percentage of the royalty payments used to recoup the advance from 100 percent to a lower percentage, the publisher can ensure that the developer continues to have a revenue stream. If the publishing agreement includes the right to distribute multiple products from the same developer, the publisher should ensure that it can "cross-recoup" (sometimes referred to as "cross-collateralize") its advances—recoup advances for one product against another product.

### Bundling

Bundling may be a very important distribution channel for the publisher. There are a wide variety of financial arrangements in bundling—ranging from small payments to non-monetary accommodations, such as cross licenses of other products. The publisher should ensure that royalties for bundling are calculated in a way that does not prevent bundling by requiring too high a payout. Minimum royalties per copy can be very dangerous in bundling if not set realistically. Some publishers use a fixed-dollar-per-copy royalty. A fixed-dollar royalty is attractive for its simplicity when compared with the difficulty of attempting to calculate the value of "non-monetary" compensation to determine the amount of a "percentage" of revenue royalty.

### Completed Versions and New Versions

The publisher should try to establish in advance the reduction in royalties for derivative products that it develops on its own or on products that it must complete. Obviously, the royalty for such products should be less than the royalties for those products that the developer has successfully completed. These concerns extend to ported and foreign language versions created by the publisher, as well as to new "sequels" developed by the publisher.

## Bankruptcy

If the publisher has received an assignment of all rights in the intellectual property of a product, then it is relatively well protected against the consequences of the developer's bankruptcy. However, a problem could arise in identifying the materials (source code, graphics files, and so forth) to which the publisher has rights if the developer is also simultaneously creating other products when bankruptcy occurs. To avoid this problem, the publisher should consider an escrow arrangement in which all materials are deposited on a regular basis with a third-party escrow agent.

Bankruptcy of a developer poses potentially serious problems for the publisher if the publisher has a license rather than an assignment. Many developers are thinly capitalized and, thus, the chances of bankruptcy are real.

Generally, a United States bankruptcy court can terminate a license agreement if it is considered to be "executory"—one in which both parties have continuing obligations. Virtually every multimedia license agreement would be considered executory. For example, the publisher's obligation to pay royalties and the developer's indemnity of the publisher for intellectual property infringement is sufficient to make the license agreement executory. If the trustee in bankruptcy determines that the license is "burdensome" on the bankrupt company, the trustee can terminate the license and make the licensee (in this case, the publisher) an unsecured creditor with no further rights under the agreement and only a claim for damages. An unsecured creditor generally is paid only a small percentage of the amount of its claim.

In addition, the trustee can then relicense the product to a third party. In the United States, this problem was partially solved by amendment to the Bankruptcy Code in 1988. This amendment (found in 11 U.S.C. § 365[n] in the United States Code) provides that a licensee can retain its right under a license agreement so long as it continues to pay royalties and waives the right to future performance from the bankrupt party (for example, correction of errors) and certain other rights.

Unfortunately, this amendment solves only part of the problems for a publisher. Three other problems exist:

- First, this amendment applies only to intellectual property rights arising under United States law. Thus, if the publishing agreement includes the right to distribute the product outside of the United States, such rights would be subject to bankruptcy laws of each foreign country.

- Second, this amendment does not apply to trademark licenses. At the request of the United States Trademark Association (now the International Trademark Association), trademarks were excluded from this provision. Thus, the trustee in bankruptcy is still able to terminate the trademark license if the trustee can convince the bankruptcy court that the license is burdensome.

- Third, the amendment may not apply to exclusive copyright licenses in the United States. Such licenses are a "transfer of interest in copyright" and not a mere license. (See "Licenses," Chapter 4.) The most effective way of protecting an exclusive copyright license is to register the copyright and record the existence of the exclusive license against the registration. (See "Assignments," Chapter 4.) Once such a transfer is recorded, it will give "constructive notice" of the transfer and prevent future assignees or licensees from obtaining superior rights. (See "Assignments," Chapter 4.) Although the effect of a bankruptcy on an exclusive copyright license is not clear at the present time, an exclusive copyright license that is properly recorded should survive bankruptcy.

The solution to the problem of possible developer bankruptcy is difficult and will vary depending on the nature of the rights granted and your negotiating leverage. You should contact your legal counsel on how to deal with this problem.

## Right to Sue Third-Party Infringers

Once the publisher has paid for the right to distribute the product, it should be able to stop third-party infringers or require the developer to do so by requiring that the developer sue third parties to stop the sale of infringing products. The right to sue "offensively" generally belongs to the owner of the copyright (or trademark). Thus, unless the publisher has received an assignment of all rights in the product, this right to sue will reside with the developer. An important exception to this rule in the United States permits an exclusive *copyright* licensee to sue third parties for infringement. However, the right of an exclusive licensee to sue varies depending on the country and the type of intellectual property (patent, trade secret, copyright, or trademark). Consequently, the publisher should deal with this issue expressly in the publishing agreement.

Another problem in the right to sue third parties for infringement arises for components of the product that the developer does not own, such as photographs or characters. If the developer has only licensed such rights and those licenses are nonexclusive, then the developer (and, consequently, the publisher) will not have the right to sue for infringement of rights in those components. Unless the developer obtained the right to sue for infringement of components in its license agreements, the developer will only have the right to sue third parties for copying of the "whole work," not for copying of components. (These rights under trademark law are a little different because they are based on "confusing similarity," discussed in "Scope of Trademark Rights," Chapter 15.)

- *Developer has nonexclusively licensed a photograph of Marilyn Monroe for her celebrity trivia game. She used the photograph prominently on the front package of her game. A competitor with a similar game used the same photograph on the front of the package of his game, but without a license. Developer will not be able to sue her competitor for copyright infringement without the permission of the copyright owner of the photograph because she only has a nonexclusive license.*

Generally, the publishing agreement should state whether the publisher or the developer has the first right to sue a third party for infringement. If that party decides not to bring suit within a limited time period, the other party should have the right to bring the suit. The agreement should also provide that the party not bringing the suit will assist the other party. Finally, the publishing agreement should allocate the division of any damages received from such a lawsuit. The failure to do so can lead to litigation between the developer and the publisher. One common solution provides that the damages, after deductions for the expense of the lawsuit (including attorneys' fees), should be split in some fixed percentage between the parties.

If the developer retains ownership of the intellectual property in the multimedia product, the developer may wish to have authority to approve any lawsuit settlements to avoid settlements that would adversely affect its rights. If the developer refuses to approve the settlement, the developer should have the obligation to take over the litigation and pay the publisher for the amounts spent in the litigation. Otherwise, the developer could block settlement of the lawsuit and force the publisher to continue the lawsuit without bearing any expense itself.

# Appendices

# The Copyright Act of 1976, Selected Provisions

## §101. Definitions

"Audiovisual works" are works that consist of a series of related images which are intrinsically intended to be shown by the use of machines or devices such as projectors, viewers, or electronic equipment, together with accompanying sounds, if any, regardless of the nature of the material objects, such as films or tapes, in which the works are embodied.

A "collective work" is a work, such as a periodical issue, anthology, or encyclopedia, in which a number of contributions, constituting separate and independent works in themselves, are assembled into a collective whole.

A "compilation" is a work formed by the collection and assembling of preexisting materials or of data that are selected, coordinated, or arranged in such a way that the resulting work as a whole constitutes an original work of authorship. The term "compilation" includes collective works.

A "computer program" is a set of statements or instructions to be used directly or indirectly in a computer in order to bring about a certain result.

"Copies" are material objects, other than phonorecords, in which a work is fixed by any method now known or later developed, and from which the work can be perceived, reproduced, or otherwise communicated, either directly or with the aid of a machine or device. The term "copies" includes the material object, other than a phonorecord, in which the work is first fixed.

A "derivative work" is a work based upon one or more preexisting works, such as a translation, musical arrangement, dramatization, fictionalization, motion picture version, sound recording, art reproduction, abridgment, condensation, or any other form in which a work may be recast, transformed, or adapted. A work consisting of editorial revisions, annotations, elaborations, or other modifications which, as a whole, represent an original work of authorship, is a "derivative work."

To "display" a work means to show a copy of it, either directly or by means of a film, slide, television image, or any other device or process or, in the case of a motion picture or other audiovisual work, to show individual images nonsequentially.

A work is "fixed" in a tangible medium of expression when its embodiment in a copy or phonorecord, by or under the authority of the author, is sufficiently permanent or stable to permit it to be perceived, reproduced, or otherwise communicated for a period of more than transitory duration. A work consisting of sounds, images, or both, that are being transmitted, is "fixed" for purposes of this title if a fixation of the work is being made simultaneously with its transmission.

A "joint work" is a work prepared by two or more authors with the intention that their contributions be merged into inseparable or interdependent parts of a unitary whole.

"Literary works" are works, other than audiovisual works, expressed in words, numbers, or other verbal or numerical symbols or indicia, regardless of the nature of the material objects, such as books, periodicals, manuscripts, phonorecords, film, tapes, disks, or cards, in which they are embodied.

"Motion pictures" are audiovisual works consisting of a series of related images which, when shown in succession, impart an impression of motion, together with accompanying sounds, if any.

To "perform" a works means to recite, render, play, dance or act it, either directly or by means of any device or process or, in the case of a motion picture or other audiovisual work, to show its images in any sequence or to make the sounds accompanying it audible.

"Phonorecords" are material objects in which sounds, other than those accompanying a motion picture or other audiovisual work, are fixed by any method now known or later developed, and from which the sounds can be perceived, reproduced, or otherwise communicated, either directly or with the aid of a machine or device. The term "phonorecords" includes the material object in which the sounds are first fixed.

"Pictorial, graphic, and sculptural works" include two-dimensional and three-dimensional works of fine, graphic, and applied art, photographs, prints and art reproductions, maps, globes, charts, diagrams, models, and technical drawings, including architectural plans. Such works shall include works of artistic craftsmanship insofar as their form but not their mechanical or utilitarian aspects are concerned; the design of a useful article, as defined in this section, shall be considered a pictorial, graphic, or sculptural work only if, and only to the extent that, such design incorporates pictorial, graphic, or sculptural features that can be identified separately from, and are capable of existing independently of, the utilitarian aspects of the article.

"Publication" is the distribution of copies or phonorecords of a work to the public by sale or other transfer of ownership, or by rental, lease, or lending. The offering to distribute copies or phonorecords to a group of persons for purposes of further distribution, public performance, or public display, constitutes publication. A public performance or display of a work does not of itself constitute publication.

To perform or display a work "publicly" means—
(1) to perform or display it at a place open to the public or at any place where a substantial number of persons outside of a normal circle of a family and its social acquaintances is gathered; or
(2) to transmit or otherwise communicate a performance or display of the work to a place specified by clause (1) or to the public, by means of any device or process, whether the members of the public capable of receiving the performance or display receive it in the same place or in separate places and at the same time or at different times.

"Sound recordings" are works that result from the fixation of a series of musical, spoken, or other sounds, but not including the sounds accompanying a motion picture or other audiovisual work, regardless of the nature of the material objects, such as disks, tapes, or other phonorecords, in which they are embodied.

A "transfer of copyright ownership" is an assignment, mortgage, exclusive license, or any other conveyance, alienation, or hypothecation of a copyright or of any of the exclusive rights comprised in a copyright whether or not it is limited in time or place of effect, but not including a nonexclusive license.

A "useful article" is an article having an intrinsic utilitarian function that is not merely to portray the appearance of the article or to convey information. An article that is normally a part of a useful article is considered a "useful article."

A "work of visual art" is

(1) a painting, drawing, print, or sculpture, existing in a single copy, in a limited edition of 200 copies or fewer that are signed and consecutively numbered by the author, or, in the case of a sculpture, in multiple cast, carved, or fabricated sculptures of 200 or fewer that are consecutively numbered by the author and bear the signature or other identifying mark of the author; or

(2) a still photographic image produced for exhibition purposes only, existing in a single copy that is signed by the author, or in a limited edition of 200 copies or fewer that are signed and consecutively numbered by the author.

A work of visual art does not include—

(A)  (i) any poster, map, globe, chart, technical drawing, diagram, model, applied art, motion picture or other audiovisual work, book, magazine, newspaper, periodical, data base, electronic information service, electronic publication, or similar publication;

(ii) any merchandising item or advertising, promotional, descriptive, covering, or packaging material or container;

(iii) any portion or part of any item described in clause (i) or (ii);

(B) any work made for hire; or

(C) any work not subject to copyright protection under this title.

A "work made for hire" is—

(1) a work prepared by an employee within the scope of his or her employment; or

(2) a work specially ordered or commissioned for use as a contribution to a collective work, as a part of a motion picture or other audiovisual work, as a translation, as a supplementary work, as a compilation, as an instructional text, as a test, as answer material for a test, or as an atlas, if the parties expressly agree in a written instrument signed by them that the work shall be considered a work made for hire. For the purpose of the foregoing sentence, a "supplementary work" is a work prepared for publication as a secondary adjunct to a work by another author for the purpose of introducing, concluding, illustrating, explaining, revising, commenting upon, or assisting in the use of the other work, such as forewords, afterwords, pictorial illustrations, maps, charts, tables, editorial notes, musical arrangements, answer material for tests, bibliographies, appendixes, and indexes, and an "instructional text" is a literary, pictorial, or graphic work prepared for publication and with the purpose of use in systematic instructional activities.

## §102. Subject matter of copyright: In general

(a) Copyright protection subsists, in accordance with this title, in original works of authorship fixed in any tangible medium of expression, now known or later developed, from which they can be perceived, reproduced, or otherwise communicated, either directly or with the aid of a machine or device. Works of authorship include the following categories:

(1) literary works;

(2) musical works, including any accompanying words;

(3) dramatic works, including any accompanying music;

(4) pantomimes and choreographic works;

(5) pictorial, graphic, and sculptural works;

(6) motion pictures and other audiovisual works;

(7) sound recordings; and

(8) architectural works.

(b) In no case does copyright protection for an original work of authorship extend to any idea, procedure, process, system, method of operation, concept, principle, or discovery, regardless of the form in which it is described, explained, illustrated, or embodied in such work.

## §103.  Subject matter of copyright: Compilations and derivative works.

(a) The subject matter of copyright as specified by section 102 includes compilations and derivative works, but protection for a work employing preexisting material in which copyright subsists does not extend to any part of the work in which such material has been used unlawfully.

(b) The copyright in a compilation or derivative work extends only to the material contributed by the author of such work, as distinguished from the preexisting material employed in the work, and does not imply any exclusive right in the preexisting material. The copyright in such work is independent of, and does not affect or enlarge the scope, duration, ownership, or subsistence of any copyright protection in the preexisting material.

## §106.  Exclusive rights in copyrighted works

Subject to sections 107 through 120, the owner of copyright under this title has the exclusive rights to do and to authorize any of the following:

(1) to reproduce the copyrighted work in copies or phonorecords;

(2) to prepare derivative works based upon the copyrighted work;

(3) to distribute copies or phonorecords of the copyrighted work to the public by sale or other transfer of ownership, or by rental, lease, or lending;

(4) in the case of literary, musical, dramatic, and choreographic works, pantomimes, and motion pictures and other audiovisual works, to perform the copyrighted work publicly; and

(5) in the case of literary, musical, dramatic, and choreographic works, pantomimes, and pictorial, graphic, or sculptural works, including the individual images of a motion picture or other audiovisual work, to display the copyrighted work publicly.

## §106A.  Rights of certain authors to attribution and integrity

(a) RIGHTS OF ATTRIBUTION AND INTEGRITY.   Subject to section 107 and independent of the exclusive rights provided in section 106, the author of a work of visual art—

(1) shall have the right—

(A) to claim authorship of that work, and

(B) to prevent the use of his or her name as the author of any work of visual art which he or she did not create;

(2) shall have the right to prevent the use of his or her name as the author of the work of visual art in the event of a distortion, mutilation, or other modification of the work which would be prejudicial to his or her honor or reputation; and

(3) subject to the limitations set forth in section 113(d), shall have the right—

(A) to prevent any intentional distortion, mutilation, or other modification of that work which would be prejudicial to his or her honor or reputation, and any intentional distortion, mutilation, or modification of that work is a violation of that right, and

(B) to prevent any destruction of a work of recognized stature, and any intentional or grossly negligent destruction of that work is a violation of that right.

(b) SCOPE AND EXERCISE OF RIGHTS.   Only the author of a work of visual art has the rights conferred by subsection (a) in that work, whether or not the author is the copyright owner. The authors of a joint work of visual [art] are coowners of the rights conferred by subsection (a) in that work.

(d) DURATION OF RIGHTS   (1) With respect to works of visual art created on or after the effective date set forth in section 9(a) of the Visual Artists Rights Act of 1990, the rights conferred by subsection (a) shall endure for a term consisting of the life of the author.

(2) With respect to works of visual art created before the effective date set forth in section 9(a) of the Visual Artists Rights Act of 1990, but title to which has not, as of such effective date, been transferred from the author, the rights conferred by subsection (a) shall be coextensive with, and shall expire at the same time as, the rights conferred by section 106.

(3) In the case of a joint work prepared by two or more authors, the rights conferred by subsection (a) shall endure for a term consisting of the life of the last surviving author.

(4) All terms of the right conferred by subsection (a) run to the end of the calendar year in which they would otherwise expire.

(e) TRANSFER AND WAIVER.   (1) The rights conferred by subsection (a) may not be transferred, but those rights may be waived if the author expressly agrees to such waiver in a written instrument signed by the author. Such instrument shall specifically identify the work, and uses of that work, to which the waiver applies, and the waiver shall apply only to the work and uses so identified. In the case of a joint work prepared by two or more authors, a waiver of rights under this paragraph made by one such author waives such rights for all such authors.

(2) Ownership of the rights conferred by subsection (a) with respect to a work of visual art is distinctive from ownership of any copy of that work, or of a copyright or any exclusive right under a copyright in that work. Transfer of ownership of any copy of a work of visual art, or of a copyright or any exclusive right under a copyright, shall not constitute a waiver of the rights conferred by subsection (a). Except as may otherwise be agreed by the author in a written instrument signed by the author, a waiver of the rights conferred by subsection (a) with respect to a work of visual art shall not constitute a transfer of ownership of any copy of that work, or of ownership of a copyright or of any exclusive rights under a copyright in that work.

## §107.  Limitations on exclusive rights: Fair use

Notwithstanding the provisions of sections 106 and 106A, the fair use of a copyrighted work, including such use by reproduction in copies or phonorecords or by any other means specified by that section, for purposes such as criticism, comment, news reporting, teaching (including multiple copies for classroom use), scholarship, or research, is not an infringement of copyright. In determining whether the use made of a work in any particular case is a fair use the factors to be considered shall include—

(1) the purpose and character of the use, including whether such use is of a commercial nature or is for nonprofit educational purposes;

(2) the nature of the copyrighted work;

(3) the amount and substantiality of the portion used in relation to the copyrighted work as a whole; and

(4) the effect of the use upon the potential market for or value of the copyrighted work.

## §109.  Limitations on exclusive rights: Effect of transfer of particular copy or phonorecord

(a) Notwithstanding the provisions of section 106(3), the owner of a particular copy or phonorecord lawfully made under this title, or any person authorized by such owner, is entitled, without the authority of the copyright owner, to sell or otherwise dispose of the possession of that copy or phonorecord.

## §201.  Ownership of copyright

(a) INITIAL OWNERSHIP.   Copyright in a work protected under this title vests initially in the author or authors of the work. The authors of a joint work are coowners of copyright in the work.

(b) WORKS MADE FOR HIRE. In the case of a work made for hire, the employer or other person for whom the work was prepared is considered the author for purposes of this title, and, unless the parties have expressly agreed otherwise in a written instrument signed by them, owns all of the rights comprised in the copyright.

(c) CONTRIBUTIONS TO COLLECTIVE WORKS.   Copyright in each separate contribution to a collective work is distinct from copyright in the collective work as a whole, and vests initially in the author of the contribution. In the absence of an express transfer of the copyright or of any rights under it, the owner of copyright in the collective work is presumed to have acquired only the privilege of reproducing and distributing the contribution as part of that particular collective work, any revision of that collective work, and any later collective work in the same series.

(d) TRANSFER OF OWNERSHIP.
   (1) The ownership of a copyright may be transferred in whole or in part by any means of conveyance or by operation of law, and may be bequeathed by will or pass as personal property by the applicable laws of intestate succession.
   (2) Any of the exclusive rights comprised in a copyright, including any subdivision of any of the rights specified by section 106, may be transferred as provided by clause (1) and owned separately. The owner of any particular exclusive right is entitled, to the extent of that right, to all of the protection and remedies accorded to the copyright owner by this title.

## §202.  Ownership of copyright as distinct from ownership of material object

Ownership of a copyright, or of any of the exclusive rights under a copyright, is distinct from ownership of any material object in which the work is embodied. Transfer of ownership of any material object, including the copy or phonorecord in which the work is first fixed, does not of itself convey any rights in the copyrighted work embodied in the object; nor, in the absence of an agreement, does transfer of ownership of a copyright or of any exclusive rights under a copyright convey property rights in any material object.

## §204. Execution of transfers of copyright ownership

(a) A transfer of copyright ownership, other than by operation of law, is not valid unless an instrument of conveyance, or a note or memorandum of the transfer, is in writing and signed by the owner of the rights conveyed or such owner's duly authorized agent.

(b) A certificate of acknowledgement is not required for the validity of a transfer, but is prima facie evidence of the execution of the transfer if—

(1) in the case of a transfer executed in the United States, the certificate is issued by a person authorized to administer oaths within the United States; or

(2) in the case of a transfer executed in a foreign country, the certificate is issued by a diplomatic or consular officer of the United States, or by a person authorized to administer oaths whose authority is proved by a certificate of such an officer.

## §205. Recordation of transfers and other documents

(a) CONDITIONS FOR RECORDATION.   Any transfer of copyright ownership or other document pertaining to a copyright may be recorded in the Copyright Office if the document filed for recordation bears the actual signature of the person who executed it, or if it is accompanied by a sworn or official certification that it is a true copy of the original, signed document.

(b) CERTIFICATE OF RECORDATION.   The Register of Copyrights shall, upon receipt of a document as provided by subsection (a) and of the fee provided by section 708, record the document and return it with a certificate of recordation.

(c) RECORDATION AS CONSTRUCTIVE NOTICE.   Recordation of a document in the Copyright Office gives all persons constructive notice of the facts stated in the recorded document, but only if

(1) the document, or material attached to it, specifically identifies the work to which it pertains so that, after the document is indexed by the Register of Copyrights, it would be revealed by a reasonable search under the title or registration number of the work; and

(2) registration has been made for the work.

(d) PRIORITY BETWEEN CONFLICTING TRANSFERS.   As between two conflicting transfers, the one executed first prevails if it is recorded, in the manner required to give constructive notice under subsection (c), within one month after its execution in the United States or within two months after its execution outside the United States, or at any time before recordation in such manner of the later transfer. Otherwise the later transfer prevails if recorded first in such manner, and if taken in good faith, for valuable consideration or on the basis of a binding promise to pay royalties, and without notice of the earlier transfer.

(e) PRIORITY BETWEEN CONFLICTING TRANSFER OF OWNERSHIP AND NONEXCLUSIVE LICENSE.   A nonexclusive license, whether recorded or not, prevails over a conflicting transfer of copyright ownership if the license is evidenced by a written instrument signed by the owner of the rights licensed or such owner's duly authorized agent; and if

(1) the license was taken before execution of the transfer; or

(2) the license was taken in good faith before recordation of the transfer and without notice of it.

## §302. Duration of copyright: Works created on or after January 1, 1978

(a) IN GENERAL.   Copyright in a work created on or after January 1, 1978, subsists from its creation and, except as provided by the following subsections, endures for a term consisting of the life of the author and fifty years after the author's death.

(b) JOINT WORKS.   In the case of a joint work prepared by two or more authors who did not work for hire, the copyright endures for a term consisting of the life of the last surviving author and fifty years after such last surviving author's death.

(c) ANONYMOUS WORKS, PSEUDONYMOUS WORKS, AND WORKS MADE FOR HIRE.   In the case of an anonymous work, a pseudonymous work, or a work made for hire, the copyright endures for a term of seventy-five years from the year of its first publication, or a term of one hundred years from the year of its creation, whichever expires first.

## §401. Notice of copyright: Visually perceptible copies

(a) GENERAL PROVISIONS.   Whenever a work protected under this title is published in the United States or elsewhere by authority of the copyright owner, a notice of copyright as provided by this section may be placed on publicly distributed copies from which the work can be visually perceived, either directly or with the aid of a machine or device.

(b) FORM OF NOTICE.   If a notice appears on the copies, it shall consist of the following three elements:

(1) the symbol © (the letter C in a circle), or the word "Copyright," or the abbreviation "Copr."; and

(2) the year of first publication of the work; in the case of compilations or derivative works incorporating previously published material, the year date of first publication of the compilation or derivative work is sufficient. The year date may be omitted where a pictorial, graphic, or sculptural work, with accompanying text matter, if any, is reproduced in or on greeting cards, postcards, stationery, jewelry, dolls, toys, or any useful articles; and

(3) the name of the owner of copyright in the work, or an abbreviation by which the name can be recognized, or a generally known alternative designation of the owner.

(c) POSITION OF NOTICE.   The notice shall be affixed to the copies in such manner and location as to give reasonable notice of the claim of copyright. The Register of Copyrights shall prescribe by regulation, as examples, specific methods of affixation and positions of the notice on various types of works that will satisfy this requirement, but these specifications shall not be considered exhaustive.

(d) EVIDENTIARY WEIGHT OF NOTICE.   If a notice of copyright in the form and position specified by this section appears on the published copy or copies to which a defendant in a copyright infringement suit had access, then no weight shall be given to such a defendant's interposition of a defense based on innocent infringement in mitigation of actual or statutory damages, except as provided in the last sentence of section 504(c)(2).

## §408. Copyright registration in general

(a) REGISTRATION PERMISSIVE.   At any time during the subsistence of the first term of copyright in any published or unpublished work in which the copyright was secured before January 1, 1978, and during the subsistence of any copyright secured on or after that date, the owner of copyright or of any exclusive right in the work may obtain registration of the copyright claim by delivering to the Copyright Office the deposit specified by this section, together with the application and fee specified by sections 409 and 708. Such registration is not a condition of copyright protection.

## §411. Registration and infringement actions

(a) Except for actions for infringement of copyright in Berne Convention works whose country of origin is not the United States and an action brought for violation of the rights of the author under section 160A(a), and subject to the provisions of subsection (b), no action for infringement of the copyright in any work shall be instituted until registration of the copyright claim has been made in accordance with this title. In any case, however, where the deposit, application, and fee required for registration have been delivered to the Copyright Office in proper form and registration has been refused, the applicant is entitled to institute an action for infringement if notice thereof, with a copy of the complaint, is served on the Register of Copyrights. The Register may, at his or her option, become a party to the action with respect to the issue of registrability of the copyright claim by entering an appearance within sixty days after such service, but the Register's failure to become a party shall not deprive the court of jurisdiction to determine that issue.

## §412. Registration as prerequisite to certain remedies for infringement

In any action under this title, other than an action brought for a violation of the rights of the author under section 106a(a) or an action instituted under section 411(b), no award of statutory damages or of attorney's fees, as provided by sections 504 and 505, shall be made for

> (1) any infringement of copyright in an unpublished work commenced before the effective date of its registration; or
>
> (2) any infringement of copyright commenced after first publication of the work and before the effective date of its registration, unless such registration is made within three months after the first publication of the work.

## §501. Infringement of copyright

(a) Anyone who violates any of the exclusive rights of the copyright owner as provided by sections 106 through 118 or of the author as provided in section 106A, or who imports copies or phonorecords into the United States in violation of section 602, is an infringer of the copyright or right of the author, as the case may be. For purposes of this chapter (other than section 506), any reference to copyright shall be deemed to include the rights conferred by section 106A(a).

## §504. Remedies for infringement: Damages and profits

(a) IN GENERAL.   Except as otherwise provided by this title, an infringer of copyright is liable for either

> (1) the copyright owner's actual damages and any additional profits of the infringer, as provided by subsection (b); or
>
> (2) statutory damages, as provided by subsection (c).

(b) ACTUAL DAMAGES AND PROFITS.   The copyright owner is entitled to recover the actual damages suffered by him or her as a result of the infringement, and any profits of the infringer that are attributable to the infringement and are not taken into account in computing the actual damages. In establishing the infringer's profits, the copyright owner is required to present proof only of the infringer's gross revenue, and the infringer is required to prove his or her deductible expenses and the elements of profit attributable to factors other than the copyrighted work.

(c) STATUTORY DAMAGES.

(1) Except as provided by clause (2) of this subsection, the copyright owner may elect, at any time before final judgment is rendered, to recover, instead of actual damages and profits, an award of statutory damages for all infringements involved in the action, with respect to any one work, for which any one infringer is liable individually, or for which any two or more infringers are liable jointly and severally, in a sum of not less than $500 or more than $20,000 as the court considers just. For the purposes of this subsection, all the parts of a compilation or derivative work constitute one work.

(2) In a case where the copyright owner sustains the burden of proving, and the court finds, that infringement was committed willfully, the court in its discretion may increase the award of statutory damages to a sum of not more than $100,000. In a case where the infringer sustains the burden of proving, and the court finds, that such infringer was not aware and had no reason to believe that his or her acts constituted an infringement of copyright, the court in its discretion may reduce the award of statutory damages to a sum of not less than $200.

## §505. Remedies for infringement: Costs and attorney's fees

In any civil action under this title, the court in its discretion may allow the recovery of full costs by or against any party other than the United States or an officer thereof. Except as otherwise provided by this title, the court may also award a reasonable attorney's fee to the prevailing party as part of the costs.

# Appendix B

# Form Contracts

These contracts have been used for actual transactions. However, they should be considered samples rather than "model" agreements that will fit all of your needs. You should review them (and the chapters to which they relate) to understand the issues that you need to address.

The contracts included here may not fit your needs in a particular transaction. Consult with an experienced attorney prior to using any of these contracts.

These contracts are provided for your personal use or use by your company. They cannot be reproduced or modified for use by third parties.

## *1*  Nondisclosure Agreement (Protecting Developer's Confidential Information)

This agreement is used when the developer is disclosing confidential information during discussions of a potential business project. When both parties are disclosing confidential information, use the Mutual Nondisclosure Agreement (see Form 5). The agreement permits the information to be used only for evaluation.

## NONDISCLOSURE AGREEMENT
(Protecting Developer's Confidential Information)

This nondisclosure agreement ("Agreement") is entered into as of _____ ("Effective Date") by and between Development Company ("Devco") and _____ ("Recipient"). Devco and Recipient are engaged in discussions in contemplation of or in furtherance of a business relationship. In order to induce Devco to disclose its confidential information during such discussions, Recipient agrees to accept such information under the restrictions set forth in this Agreement.

1. **Disclosure of Confidential Information.**   Devco may disclose, either orally or in writing, certain information which Recipient knows or has reason to know is considered confidential by Devco relating to _____ _____ ("Devco Confidential Information"). Devco Confidential Information shall include, but not be limited to, trade secrets, know-how, inventions, techniques, processes, algorithms, software programs, schematics, software source documents, contracts, customer lists, financial information, sales and marketing plans and business plans.

2. **Confidentiality.**   Recipient agrees to maintain in confidence Devco Confidential Information. Recipient will use Devco Confidential Information solely to evaluate the commercial potential of a business relationship with Devco. Recipient will not disclose the Devco Confidential Information to any person except its employees or consultants to whom it is necessary to disclose the Devco Confidential Information for such purposes. Recipient agrees that Devco Confidential Information will be disclosed or made available only to those of its employees or consultants who have agreed in writing to receive it under terms at least as restrictive as those specified in this Agreement. Recipient will take reasonable measures to maintain the confidentiality of Devco Confidential Information, but not less than the measures it uses for its confidential information of similar type. Recipient will immediately give notice to Devco of any unauthorized use or disclosure of the Devco Confidential Information. Recipient agrees to assist Devco in remedying such unauthorized use or disclosure of the Devco Confidential Information. This obligation will not apply to the extent that Recipient can demonstrate that:
   (a) the Devco Confidential Information at the time of disclosure is part of the public domain;
   (b) the Devco Confidential Information became part of the public domain, by publication or otherwise, except by breach of the provisions of this Agreement;
   (c) the Devco Confidential Information can be established by written evidence to have been in the possession of Recipient at the time of disclosure;
   (d) the Devco Confidential Information is received from a third party without similar restrictions and without breach of this Agreement; or

(e) the Devco Confidential Information is required to be disclosed by a government agency to further the objectives of this Agreement, or by a proper court of competent jurisdiction; provided, however, that Recipient will use its best efforts to minimize the disclosure of such information and will consult with and assist Devco in obtaining a protective order prior to such disclosure.

3. **Materials.**   All materials including, without limitation, documents, drawings, models, apparatus, sketches, designs and lists furnished to Recipient by Devco and any tangible materials embodying Devco Confidential Information created by Recipient shall remain the property of Devco. Recipient shall return to Devco or destroy such materials and all copies thereof upon the termination of this Agreement or upon the written request of Devco.

4. **No License.**   This Agreement does not grant Recipient any license to use Devco Confidential Information except as provided in Article 2.

5. **Term.**

    (a) This Agreement shall terminate ninety (90) days after the Effective Date unless terminated earlier by either party. Devco may extend the term of the Agreement by written notice to Recipient. Either party may terminate this Agreement, with or without cause, by giving notice of termination to the other party. The Agreement shall terminate immediately upon receipt of such notice.

    (b) Upon termination of this Agreement, Recipient shall cease to use Devco Confidential Information and shall comply with Article 3 within twenty (20) days of the date of termination. Upon the request of Devco, an officer of Recipient shall certify that Recipient has complied with its obligations in this Section.

    (c) Notwithstanding the termination of this Agreement, Recipient's obligations in Article 2 shall survive such termination.

6. **General Provisions.**

    (a) This Agreement shall be governed by and construed in accordance with the laws of the United States and of the State of California as applied to transactions entered into and to be performed wholly within California between California residents. Except as provided in Section 6(b), any dispute arising out of or relating to this Agreement, or the breach, termination or validity thereof, will be submitted by the parties to arbitration, to take place in _____, by the American Arbitration Association under the commercial rules then in effect for that Association except as provided in this Section. All proceedings will be held in English and a transcribed record prepared in English. Depositions may be taken and discovery obtained in any such arbitration proceedings in accordance with California Code of Civil Procedure Sections 1283.05 and 1283.1, which is incorporated herein by this reference. Judgment upon the award rendered by the arbitrator(s) may be entered in any court having jurisdiction thereof.

(b) Notwithstanding Section 6(a), Devco shall have the right to obtain a preliminary relief on any equitable claim in any court of competent jurisdiction, where such judgment is necessary to preserve its property and/or proprietary rights under this Agreement.

(c) Any notice provided for or permitted under this Agreement will be treated as having been given when (a)delivered personally, (b)sent by confirmed telex or telecopy, (c)sent by commercial overnight courier with written verification of receipt, or (d)mailed postage prepaid by certified or registered mail, return receipt requested, to the party to be notified, at the address set forth below, or at such other place of which the other party has been notified in accordance with the provisions of this Section. Such notice will be treated as having been received upon the earlier of actual receipt or five (5) days after posting.

(d) Recipient agrees that the breach of the provisions of this Agreement by Recipient will cause Devco irreparable damage for which recovery of money damages would be inadequate. Devco will, therefore, be entitled to obtain timely injunctive relief to protect Devco's rights under this Agreement in addition to any and all remedies available at law.

(e) Neither party may assign its rights under this Agreement.

(f) This Agreement may be amended or supplemented only by a writing that is signed by duly authorized representatives of both parties.

(g) No term or provision hereof will be considered waived by either party, and no breach excused by either party, unless such waiver or consent is in writing signed on behalf of the party against whom the waiver is asserted. No consent by either party to, or waiver of, a breach by either party, whether express or implied, will constitute a consent to, waiver of, or excuse of any other, different, or subsequent breach by either party.

(h) If any part of this Agreement is found invalid or unenforceable, that part will be amended to achieve as nearly as possible the same economic effect as the original provision and the remainder of this Agreement will remain in full force.

(i) This Agreement constitutes the entire agreement between the parties relating to this subject matter and supersedes all prior or simultaneous representations, discussions, negotiations, and agreements, whether written or oral.

IN WITNESS WHEREOF, the parties have executed this Agreement as of the Effective Date.

"RECIPIENT":                                    "DEVCO":

_____            DEVELOPMENT COMPANY


By: _____            By: _____

_____            _____
Typed name                                      Typed name

_____            _____
Title                                           Title

Address:                                        Address:

_____            _____

_____            _____

_____            _____

_____            _____

## *2* **Short Form Assignment by Developer**

This agreement is used to record the transfer of a copyright by the developer in the Copyright Office. The assignee, generally the client, must include either the registration number or title of the copyrightable work to have "constructive notice" of the transfer (see "Obtaining a License" Chapter 10). This short form assignment can also be used to record an assignment of less than all rights in the work (for example, an assignment of audio visual rights or motion picture rights).

# SHORT FORM ASSIGNMENT BY DEVELOPER

The developer, _____, ("Developer") for good and valuable consideration, the receipt of which is acknowledged, grants to Client Company ("Client"), its successors and assigns all right, title and interest in the copyrightable work named _____ ("Work") owned by Developer. Developer authorizes the recordation of this notice with the Copyright Office. The [registration number/name] of the Work is _____.

CLIENT:                                              DEVELOPER:

CLIENT COMPANY                                       _____


By: _____             By: _____

_____             _____
Typed name                                          Typed name

_____             _____
Title                                               Title

Address:                                             Address:

_____             _____

_____             _____

_____             _____

_____             _____

# 3 Quitclaim

This letter is used in community property states to "quitclaim" any rights which a spouse may have in a copyright. It should be used when obtaining a copyright assignment from a married individual in a community property state. (see "Community Property," Chapter 4.)

# QUITCLAIM

_____

_____

_____

Dear [Husband/Wife]:

Your [Husband/Wife] is assigning all rights (including the copyright) in _____ ("Work") to Developer Company ("Devco"). Under certain interpretations of the law, you may have partial ownership rights in the Work. In order to avoid any doubt and in consideration for our payment to [Husband/Wife], you agree to assign all of such rights, if any, in the Work to Devco and to quitclaim all rights in the Work. Please indicate your agreement by signing below. Thank you for your assistance.

Sincerely yours,

Developer Company

_Read and Agreed:_

_____

# *4* Nondisclosure Agreement (Protecting Third-Party Confidential Information)

This agreement is used when the developer is receiving confidential information during discussions of a potential business project. When both parties are disclosing confidential information use the Mutual Nondisclosure Agreement (see Form 5). The agreement permits the information to be used only for evaluation.

## NONDISCLOSURE AGREEMENT
### (Protecting Third-Party Confidential Information)

This nondisclosure agreement ("Agreement") is entered into as of _____ ("Effective Date") by and between _____ ("Disclosing Company") and Development Company ("Devco"). Disclosing Company and Devco are engaged in discussions in contemplation of or in furtherance of a business relationship. In order to induce Disclosing Company to disclose its confidential information during such discussions, Recipient agrees to accept such information under the restrictions set forth in this Agreement.

1. **Disclosure of Confidential Information.** Disclosing Company may disclose, either orally or in writing, certain information relating to _____ ("Disclosing Company Confidential Information") which is disclosed to Devco in written form and marked "Confidential" or, if disclosed orally, summarized in writing where such summary is marked "Confidential" and sent to Devco within thirty (30) days of the oral disclosure. Disclosing Company Confidential Information shall include, but not be limited to, trade secrets, know-how, inventions, techniques, processes, algorithms, software programs, schematics, software source documents, contracts, customer lists, financial information, sales and marketing plans and business plans.

2. **Confidentiality.** Devco agrees to maintain in confidence Disclosing Company Confidential Information. Devco will use Disclosing Company Confidential Information solely to evaluate the commercial potential of a business relationship with Disclosing Company. Devco will not disclose the Disclosing Company Confidential Information to any person except its employees or consultants to whom it is necessary to disclose the Disclosing Company Confidential Information for such purposes. Devco agrees that Disclosing Company Confidential Information will be disclosed or made available only to those of its employees or consultants who have agreed in writing to receive it under terms at least as restrictive as those specified in this Agreement. Devco will take reasonable measures to maintain the confidentiality of Disclosing Company Confidential Information, but not less than the measures it uses for its confidential information of similar type. This obligation will not apply to the extent that Devco can demonstrate that:
   (a) the Disclosing Company Confidential Information at the time of disclosure is part of the public domain;
   (b) the Disclosing Company Confidential Information became part of the public domain, by publication or otherwise, except by breach of the provisions of this Agreement;
   (c) the Disclosing Company Confidential Information can be established by written evidence to have been in the possession of Devco at the time of disclosure;
   (d) the Disclosing Company Confidential Information is received from a third party without similar restrictions and without breach of this Agreement; or

(e) the Disclosing Company Confidential Information is required to be disclosed by a government agency to further the objectives of this Agreement, or by a proper court of competent jurisdiction; provided, however, that Devco will use its best efforts to minimize the disclosure of such information and will consult with and assist Disclosing Company in obtaining a protective order prior to such disclosure.

3. **Materials**.   All materials including, without limitation, documents, drawings, models, apparatus, sketches, designs and lists furnished to Devco by Disclosing Company and any tangible materials embodying Disclosing Company Confidential Information created by Devco shall remain the property of Disclosing Company. Devco shall return to Disclosing Company or destroy such materials and all copies thereof upon the termination of this Agreement or upon the written request of Disclosing Company.

4. **No License**   This Agreement does not grant Devco any license to use Disclosing Company Confidential Information except as provided in Article 2.

5. **Term.**

    a) This Agreement shall terminate ninety (90) days after the Effective Date unless terminated earlier by either party. Disclosing Company may extend the term of the Agreement by written notice to Devco. Either party may terminate this Agreement, with or without cause, by giving notice of termination to the other party. The Agreement shall terminate immediately upon receipt of such notice.

    (b) Upon termination of this Agreement, Devco shall cease to use Disclosing Company Confidential Information and shall comply with Article 3 within twenty (20) days of the date of termination. Upon the request of Disclosing Company, an officer of Devco shall certify that Devco has complied with its obligations in this Section.

    (c) Notwithstanding the termination of this Agreement, Devco's obligations in Article 2 shall survive for _____ years after such termination.

6.    **General Provisions.**

    (a) This Agreement shall be governed by and construed in accordance with the laws of the United States and of the State of California as applied to transactions entered into and to be performed wholly within California between California residents. Except as provided in Section 6(b), any dispute arising out of or relating to this Agreement, or the breach, termination or validity thereof, will be submitted by the parties to arbitration, to take place in _____, by the American Arbitration Association under the commercial rules then in effect for that Association except as provided in this Section. All proceedings will be held in English and a transcribed record prepared in English. Depositions may be taken and discovery obtained in any such arbitration proceedings in accordance with California Code of Civil Procedure Sections 1283.05 and 1283.1, which is incorporated herein by this reference.

Judgment upon the award rendered by the arbitrator(s) may be entered in any court having jurisdiction thereof.

(b) Notwithstanding Section 6(a), Disclosing Company shall have the right to obtain a preliminary relief on any equitable claim in any court of competent jurisdiction, where such judgment is necessary to preserve its property and/or proprietary rights under this Agreement.

(c) Any notice provided for or permitted under this Agreement will be treated as having been given when (a) delivered personally, (b) sent by confirmed telex or telecopy, (c) sent by commercial overnight courier with written verification of receipt, or (d) mailed postage prepaid by certified or registered mail, return receipt requested, to the party to be notified, at the address set forth below, or at such other place of which the other party has been notified in accordance with the provisions of this Section. Such notice will be treated as having been received upon the earlier of actual receipt or five (5) days after posting.

(d) Devco agrees that the breach of the provisions of this Agreement by Devco will cause Disclosing Company irreparable damage for which recovery of money damages would be inadequate. Disclosing Company will, therefore, be entitled to obtain timely injunctive relief to protect Disclosing Company' rights under this Agreement in addition to any and all remedies available at law.

(e) Neither party may assign its rights under this Agreement.

(f) This Agreement may be amended or supplemented only by a writing that is signed by duly authorized representatives of both parties.

(g) No term or provision hereof will be considered waived by either party, and no breach excused by either party, unless such waiver or consent is in writing signed on behalf of the party against whom the waiver is asserted. No consent by either party to, or waiver of, a breach by either party, whether express or implied, will constitute a consent to, waiver of, or excuse of any other, different, or subsequent breach by either party.

(h) If any part of this Agreement is found invalid or unenforceable, that part will be amended to achieve as nearly as possible the same economic effect as the original provision and the remainder of this Agreement will remain in full force.

(i) This Agreement constitutes the entire agreement between the parties relating to this subject matter and supersedes all prior or simultaneous representations, discussions, negotiations, and agreements, whether written or oral.

IN WITNESS WHEREOF, the parties have executed this Agreement as of the Effective Date.

"DISCLOSING COMPANY":          "DEVCO":

_____     DEVELOPMENT COMPANY

By: _____     By: _____

_____     _____

Typed name                         Typed name

_____     _____

Title                                Title

Address:                       Address:

_____     _____

_____     _____

_____     _____

## 5   Mutual Nondisclosure Agreement

This agreement is used when both your company and the other company are disclosing confidential information to one another. The agreement permits the information to be used only for evaluation.

# MUTUAL NONDISCLOSURE AGREEMENT

This mutual non-disclosure agreement (the "Agreement") is made as of the _____ day of _____, 19____, between [ _____ ] ("Other Company"), a _____ corporation, having a principal place of business at _____, and Development Company ("Devco"), a _____ corporation, having a principal place of business at <u>c</u>.

## RECITALS

WHEREAS, Other Company and Devco are engaged in discussions in contemplation of a business relationship or in furtherance of a business relationship;

WHEREAS, in the course of dealings between Other Company and Devco, each party may have access to or have disclosed to it information which is of a confidential nature as that term is later defined in this Agreement; and

WHEREAS, Other Company and Devco each desire to establish and set forth their individual obligations with respect to the other's Confidential Information.

## AGREEMENT

In consideration of the foregoing, [ _____ ] and Devco mutually agree as follows:

1. **Disclosure of Confidential Information.** Either party ("Disclosing Party") may disclose to the other party ("Receiving Party"), either orally or in writing, certain information relating to the following subject(s): _____ which it believes is confidential ("Confidential Information"). Confidential Information as used in this Agreement shall mean the information of either Disclosing Party which is disclosed to the Receiving Party pursuant to this Agreement in written form and marked "Confidential" or, if disclosed orally, the Disclosing Party shall send a written summary of such information to the Receiving Party within forty (40) days of disclosure and mark such summary "Confidential." Confidential Information shall include, but not be limited to, trade secrets, know-how, inventions, techniques, processes, algorithms, software programs, schematics, designs, contracts, customer lists, financial information, sales and marketing plans and business information.

2. **Confidentiality.** The Receiving Party will use the Disclosing Party's Confidential Information solely to evaluate the commercial potential of a business relationship with the Disclosing Party. The Receiving Party will not disclose the Confidential Information of the Disclosing Party to any

person except to its employees or consultants to whom it is necessary to disclose the Disclosing Party's Confidential Information for such purposes. The Receiving Party agrees that the Disclosing Party's Confidential Information will be disclosed or made available only to those of its employees or consultants who have agreed in writing to receive it under terms at least as restrictive as those specified in this Agreement. The Receiving Party will take reasonable measures to maintain the confidentiality of the Disclosing Party's Confidential Information, but not less than the measures it uses for its confidential information of similar type. The Receiving Party will immediately give notice to the Disclosing Party of any unauthorized use or disclosure of the Disclosing Party's Confidential Information. The Receiving Party agrees to assist the Disclosing Party in remedying such unauthorized use or disclosure of the Disclosing Party's Confidential Information. This confidentiality obligation will not apply to the extent that the Receiving Party can demonstrate that:

(a) the Confidential Information of the Disclosing Party is, at the time of disclosure, part of the public domain;

(b) the Confidential Information of the Disclosing Party became part of the public domain, by publication or otherwise, except by breach of the provisions of this Agreement;

(c) the Confidential Information of the Disclosing Party can be established by written evidence to have been in the possession of the Receiving Party at the time of disclosure;

(d) the Confidential Information of the Disclosing Party is received by the Receiving Party from a third party without similar restrictions and without breach of this Agreement;

(e) the Confidential Information of the Disclosing Party was developed by employees or agents of the Receiving Party independently of and without reference to any Confidential Information of the Disclosing Party (the Receiving Party shall bear the burden of proving such independent development); or

(f) the Confidential Information of the Disclosing Party is required to be disclosed by a government agency to further the objectives of this Agreement, or by a proper court of competent jurisdiction; provided, however, that the Receiving Party will use its best efforts to minimize the disclosure of such information and will consult with and assist the Disclosing Party in obtaining a protective order prior to such disclosure.

3. **Materials**.   All materials including, without limitation, documents, drawings, models, apparatus, sketches, designs and lists furnished to the Receiving Party by the Disclosing Party and any tangible embodiments of the Disclosing Party's Confidential Information created by the Receiving Party shall remain the property of the Disclosing Party. The Receiving Party shall return to the Disclosing Party or destroy such materials and all copies thereof upon the termination of this Agreement or upon the written request of the Disclosing Party.

4. **No License**.   This Agreement does not grant the Receiving Party any license to use the Disclosing Party's Confidential Information except as provided in Article 2.

5. **Term.**

   (a) This Agreement shall terminate _____(____) days after the Effective Date unless terminated earlier by either party. Either party may terminate this Agreement, with or without cause, by giving notice of termination to the other party. The Agreement shall terminate immediately upon receipt of such notice.

   (b) Upon termination of this Agreement, the Receiving Party shall cease to use the Disclosing Party's Confidential Information and shall comply with Article 3 within twenty (20) days of the date of termination. Upon the request of the Disclosing Party, an officer of the Receiving Party shall certify that the Receiving Party has complied with its obligations in this Section.

   (c) Notwithstanding the termination of this Agreement, the Receiving Party's obligations in Article 2 shall survive such termination.

6. **General Provisions.**

   (a) This Agreement shall be governed by and construed in accordance with the laws of the United States and of the State of California as applied to transactions entered into and to be performed wholly within California between California residents. Except as provided in Section 6(b), any dispute arising out of or relating to this Agreement, or the breach, termination or validity thereof, will be submitted by the parties to arbitration, to take place in the city of _____, by the American Arbitration Association under the commercial rules then in effect for that Association except as provided in this Section. All proceedings will be held in English and a transcribed record prepared in English. Depositions may be taken and discovery obtained in any such arbitration proceedings in accordance with California Code of Civil Procedure Sections 1283.05 and 1283.1, which is incorporated herein by this reference. Judgment upon the award rendered by the arbitrator(s) may be entered in any court having jurisdiction thereof.

   (b) Notwithstanding Section 6(a), the Disclosing Party shall have the right to obtain preliminary relief on any equitable claim in any court of competent jurisdiction, where such judgment is necessary to preserve its property and/or proprietary rights under this Agreement.

   (c) Any notice provided for or permitted under this Agreement will be treated as having been given when (a) delivered personally, (b) sent by confirmed telex or telecopy, (c) sent by commercial overnight courier with written verification of receipt, or (d) mailed postage prepaid by certified or registered mail, return receipt requested, to the party to be notified, at the address set forth below, or at such other place of which the other party has been notified in accordance with the provisions of this Section. Such notice will be treated as having been received upon the earlier of actual receipt or five (5) days after posting.

   (d) The Receiving Party agrees that the breach of the provisions of this Agreement by the Receiving Party will cause the Disclosing Party irreparable damage for which recovery of money damages would be inadequate. The Disclosing Party will, therefore, be entitled to obtain timely injunctive relief to protect the Disclosing Party's rights under this Agreement in addition to any and all remedies available at law.

   (e) Neither party may assign its rights under this Agreement.

(f)  This Agreement may be amended or supplemented only by a writing that is signed by duly authorized representatives of both parties.

(g)  No term or provision hereof will be considered waived by either party, and no breach excused by either party, unless such waiver or consent is in writing signed on behalf of the party against whom the waiver is asserted. No consent by either party to, or waiver of, a breach by either party, whether express or implied, will constitute a consent to, waiver of, or excuse of any other, different, or subsequent breach by either party.

(h)  If any part of this Agreement is found invalid or unenforceable, that part will be amended to achieve as nearly as possible the same economic effect as the original provision and the remainder of this Agreement will remain in full force.

(i)  This Agreement constitutes the entire agreement between the parties relating to this subject matter and supersedes all prior or simultaneous representations, discussions, negotiations, and agreements, whether written or oral.

IN WITNESS WHEREOF, the parties have executed this Agreement as of the Effective Date.

"OTHER COMPANY":                           "DEVCO":

[(FULL CORPORATE NAME)]                     DEVELOPMENT COMPANY


By: _____        By: _____

_____            _____
Typed name                                   Typed name

_____            _____
Title                                        Title

Address:                                     Address:

_____            _____

_____            _____

_____            _____

_____            _____

# *6* **Employee Nondisclosure and Assignment Agreement**

This agreement is used to ensure that the developer's employee maintains the developer's information in confidence and assigns to developer all proprietary rights developed during the term of his or her employment. This agreement prohibits the employee from engaging in employment, consulting or other activity in a business competitive with the developer. It should be signed on an employee's first day of work for the developer. The "employee" is referred to in the first person (as "I"). The developer is referred to as Development Company ("Devco").

# EMPLOYEE NONDISCLOSURE AND ASSIGNMENT AGREEMENT

This Agreement is intended to set forth in writing my responsibility to Development Company ("Devco"). I recognize that Devco is engaged in a continuous program of research, development, and production respecting its business, present and future. As part of my employment with Devco, I have certain obligations relating to inventions that I develop during my employment.

In return for my employment by Devco, I acknowledge and agree that:

1. **Effective Date**. This agreement ("Agreement") shall be effective on _____, 19____, the first day of my employment with Devco.

2. **Confidentiality**. I will maintain in confidence and will not disclose or use, either during or after the term of my employment, any proprietary or confidential information or know-how belonging to Devco ("Confidential Information"), whether or not in written form, except to the extent required to perform duties on behalf of Devco. Confidential Information refers to any information, not generally known in the relevant trade or industry, which was obtained from Devco, or which was learned, discovered, developed, conceived, originated or prepared by me in the scope of my employment. Such Confidential Information includes, but is not limited to, software, technical and business information relating to Devco's inventions or products, research and development, production processes, manufacturing and engineering processes, machines and equipment, finances, customers, marketing, and production and future business plans and any other information which is identified as confidential by Devco. Upon termination of my employment or at the request of my supervisor before termination, I will deliver to Devco all written and tangible material in my possession incorporating the Confidential Information or otherwise relating to Devco's business. These obligations with respect to Confidential Information extend to information belonging to customers and suppliers of Devco who may have disclosed such information to me as the result of my status as an employee of Devco.

3. **Work Products.**

   *3.1 Definition of Work Products.* As used in this Agreement, the term "Work Product" means any new work of authorship, new or useful art, discovery, contribution, finding or improvement, whether or not patentable, and all related know-how. Work Product includes, but is not limited to, all storylines, characters, computer software, designs, discoveries, formulae, processes, manufacturing techniques, inventions, improvements, and ideas.

   *3.2 Disclosure of Work Products and Assignment of Proprietary Rights.*

       (a) The "Devco Work Product" is defined as any Work Product that I may solely or jointly conceive, develop or reduce to practice during the period of my employment, (i) that relates, at the time of conception, development, or reduction to practice of the Work

Product, to Devco's business or actual or demonstrably anticipated research or development; (ii) that was developed, in whole or in part, on Devco's time or with the use of any of Devco's equipment, supplies, facilities, or trade secret information; or (iii) that resulted from any work I performed for Devco. I will promptly disclose and describe to Devco all Devco Work Product.

(b)  (i)    I hereby irrevocably assign, convey and otherwise transfer to Devco, and its respective successors and assigns, all rights, title, and interests worldwide in and to the Devco Work Product and all proprietary rights therein, including, without limitation, all copyrights, trademarks, design patents, trade secret rights, moral rights, and all contract and licensing rights, and all claims and causes of action of any kind with respect to any of the foregoing, whether now known or hereafter to become known.

(ii)   In the event I have any right in and to the Devco Work Product that cannot be assigned to Devco, I hereby unconditionally and irrevocably waive the enforcement of all such rights, and all claims and causes of action of any kind with respect to any of the foregoing against Devco, its distributors and customers, whether now known or hereafter to become known and agree, at the request and expense of Devco and its respective successors and assigns, to consent to and join in any action to enforce such rights and to procure a waiver of such rights from the holders of such rights.

(iii)  In the event I have any rights in and to the Devco Work Product that cannot be assigned to Devco and cannot be waived, I hereby grant to Devco, and its respective successors and assigns, an exclusive, worldwide, royalty-free license during the term of the rights to reproduce, distribute, modify, publicly perform and publicly display, with the right to sublicense and assign such rights in and to the Devco Work Product including, without limitation, the right to use in any way whatsoever the Devco Work Product.

(iv)  I retain no rights to use the Devco Work Product and agree not to challenge the validity of the ownership by Devco of the Devco Work Product.

(v)   I do not assign or agree to assign any Work Product created by me prior to my employment by Devco.

(c)  Unless I specifically state such an exception in *Exhibit A*, if I use Work Product that I created prior to my employment with Devco during my employment with Devco, I grant an irrevocable, nonexclusive, royalty-free, worldwide license to Devco, with the right to sublicense, to reproduce, modify, distribute, publicly perform and publicly display such works as part of Devco's products.

(d)  I recognize that Work Product relating to my activities while working for Devco and conceived or made by me, alone or with others, within one year after termination of my employment may have been conceived in significant part while employed by Devco. Accordingly, I agree that such Work Products shall be presumed to have been conceived during my employment with Devco and are to be assigned to Devco as a Devco

Work Product unless and until I have established the contrary. I agree to disclose promptly in writing to Devco all Work Product made or conceived by me for one (1) year after my term of employment, whether or not I believe such Work Product is subject to this Agreement, to permit a determination by Devco as to whether or not the Work Product should be the property of Devco. Any such information will be received in confidence by Devco.

*3.3 **Nonassignable Work Products**.*    This Agreement does not apply to any Work Product which qualifies fully as a nonassignable invention under the provisions of Section 2870 of the California Labor Code.

4. **Devco's Materials.**    Upon termination of my employment with Devco or at any other time upon Devco's request, I will promptly deliver to Devco, without retaining any copies, all documents and other materials furnished to me by Devco or prepared by me for Devco.

5. **Competitive Employment.**    During the term of my employment with Devco, I will not engage in any employment, consulting, or other activity in any business competitive with Devco without Devco's written consent.

6. **Non-solicitation.**    During the term of my employment with Devco and for a period of two (2) years thereafter, I will not solicit or encourage, or cause others to solicit or encourage, any employees of Devco to terminate their employment with Devco.

7. **Acts to Secure Proprietary Rights.**
    *7.1 **Further Acts**.*    I agree to perform, during and after my employment, all acts deemed necessary or desirable by Devco to permit and assist it, at its expense, in perfecting and enforcing the full benefits, enjoyment, rights and title throughout the world in the Devco Work Product. Such acts may include, but are not limited to, execution of documents and assistance or cooperation in the registration and enforcement of applicable patents and copyrights or other legal proceedings.

    *7.2 **Appointment of Attorney-In-Fact**.*    In the event that Devco is unable for any reason whatsoever to secure my signature to any lawful and necessary document required to apply for or execute any patent, copyright or other applications with respect to any Work Product (including improvements, renewals, extensions, continuations, divisions or continuations in part thereof), I hereby irrevocably appoint Devco and its duly authorized officers and agents as my agents and attorneys-in-fact to execute and file any such application and to do all other lawfully permitted acts to further the prosecution and issuance of patents, copyrights or other rights thereon with the same legal force and effect as if executed by me.

8. **No Conflicting Obligations.**    My performance of this Agreement and as an employee of Devco does not and will not breach any agreement to keep in confidence proprietary information, knowledge or data acquired by me prior to my employment with Devco. I will not disclose to

Devco, or induce Devco to use, any confidential or proprietary information or material belonging to any previous employer or other person or entity. I am not a party to any other agreement which will interfere with my full compliance with this Agreement. I will not enter into any agreement, whether written or oral, in conflict with the provisions of this Agreement.

9. **Survival.** Notwithstanding the termination of my employment, Section 3.2 and Articles 2, 6, and 7 shall survive such termination. This Agreement does not in any way restrict my right or the right of Devco to terminate my employment at any time, for any reason or for no reason.

10. **Specific Performance.** A breach of any of the promises or agreements contained herein will result in irreparable and continuing damage to Devco for which there will be no adequate remedy at law, and Devco shall be entitled to injunctive relief and/or a decree for specific performance, and such other relief as may be proper (including monetary damages if appropriate).

11. **Waiver.** The waiver by Devco of a breach of any provision of this Agreement by me will not operate or be construed as a waiver of any other or subsequent breach by me.

12. **Severability.** If any part of this Agreement is found invalid or unenforceable, that part will be amended to achieve as nearly as possible the same economic effect as the original provision and the remainder of this Agreement will remain in full force.

13. **Governing Law.** This Agreement will be governed by and construed in accordance with the laws of the United States and the State of California as applied to agreements entered into and to be performed entirely within California between California residents.

14. **Choice of Forum.** The parties hereby submit to the jurisdiction of, and waive any venue objections against, the United States District Court for the Northern District of California, San Jose Branch and the Superior and Municipal Courts of the State of California, Santa Clara County, in any litigation arising out of the Agreement.

15. **Entire Agreement.** This Agreement, including all Exhibits to this Agreement, constitutes the entire agreement between the parties relating to this subject matter and supersedes all prior or simultaneous representations, discussions, negotiations, and agreements, whether written or oral. This Agreement may be amended or modified only with the written consent of both me and Devco. No oral waiver, amendment or modification will be effective under any circumstances whatsoever.

16. **Assignment.** This Agreement may be assigned by Devco. I may not assign or delegate my duties under this Agreement without Devco's prior written approval. This Agreement shall be binding upon my heirs, successors, and permitted assignees.

EMPLOYEE:

_____
Date

Signature

_____
Printed Name


DEVCO:

DEVELOPMENT COMPANY

_____
Date:

By: _____

Title: _____

Address:

_____

_____

_____

## LIMITED EXCLUSION NOTIFICATION

THIS IS TO NOTIFY you in accordance with Section 2872 of the California Labor Code that the above Agreement between you and Devco does not require you to assign to Devco, any invention for which no equipment, supplies, facility or trade secret information of Devco was used and which was developed entirely on your own time, and (a) which does not relate (1) to the business of Devco or (2) to Devco's actual or demonstrably anticipated research or development, or (b) which does not result from any work performed by you for Devco. This limited exclusion does not apply to any patent or invention covered by a contract between Devco and the United States or any of its agencies requiring full title to such patent or invention to be in the United States.

I ACKNOWLEDGE RECEIPT of a copy of this notification.

_____

Signature

_____

Printed Name of Employee

_____

Date

WITNESSED BY:

DEVELOPMENT COMPANY

_____

Representative

_____

Date

# EXHIBIT A

## Prior Work Products

# 7 Independent Contractor Agreement

This agreement is used when the independent contractor will perform a project for a multimedia company. The agreement assumes that the project is a simple one that does not include detailed milestones and acceptance provisions.

## INDEPENDENT CONTRACTOR AGREEMENT

THIS AGREEMENT ("Agreement") is entered into by and between Development Company ("Devco"), a _____ corporation, and the undersigned (the "Contractor").

1. **Engagement of Services.**   Contractor agrees to perform services for Devco as follows:

_____

_____

_____

_____

("Project"). Devco selected Contractor to perform these services based upon Devco receiving Contractor's personal service and therefore Contractor may not subcontract or otherwise delegate its obligations under this Agreement without Devco's prior written consent. Contractor agrees to perform the services in a professional manner.

2. **Compensation.**

   *2.1 Fees and Approved Expenses.*   Devco will pay Contractor the fee set forth in *Exhibit A* for services rendered by Contractor pursuant to this Agreement. Contractor will not be reimbursed for any expenses incurred in connection with the performance of services under this Agreement, unless those expenses are approved in advance and in writing by Devco.

   *2.2 Timing.*   Devco will pay Contractor for services and will reimburse Contractor for previously approved expenses within thirty (30) days of the date of Contractor's invoice.

3. **Independent Contractor Relationship.**   Contractor and Devco understand, acknowledge, and agree that Contractor's relationship with Devco will be that of an independent contractor and nothing in this Agreement is intended to or should be construed to create a partnership, joint venture, or employment relationship.

4. **Trade Secrets—Intellectual Property Rights.**

   *4.1 Disclosure.*

   (a)   Contractor agrees to disclose promptly in writing to Devco, or any person designated by Devco, all work product, including but not limited to computer programs, processes, know-how and other copyrightable material, that is conceived, developed, made or reduced to practice by Contractor within the scope of the Project.

   (b)   Contractor represents that his performance of all of the terms of this Agreement does not and will not breach any agreement to keep in confidence proprietary information, knowledge or data of a third party and Contractor will not disclose to Devco, or induce

Devco to use, any confidential or proprietary information belonging to third parties unless such use or disclosure is authorized in writing by such owners.

(c) Contractor represents that any inventions or copyrighted works relating to Devco's actual or anticipated business or research and development which Contractor has conceived, developed, made, or reduced to practice at the time of signing this Agreement, have been disclosed in writing to Devco and attached to this Agreement as *Exhibit B*. These inventions and copyrighted works are not assigned to Devco. However, if Contractor uses such inventions or copyrighted works in the Project, Contractor grants to Devco a royalty-free, worldwide, perpetual, irrevocable, non-exclusive license, with the right to sublicense, to reproduce, distribute, modify, publicly perform and publicly display such inventions and copyrighted works in Devco's products based on the Project.

**4.2 *Confidential Information.*** Contractor agrees during the term of this Agreement and thereafter to take all steps reasonably necessary to hold in trust and confidence information which he knows or has reason to know is considered confidential by Devco ("Confidential Information"). Contractor agrees to use the Confidential Information solely to perform the project hereunder. Confidential Information includes, but is not limited to, technical and business information relating to Devco's inventions or products, research and development, manufacturing and engineering processes, and future business plans. Contractor's obligations with respect to the Confidential Information also extend to any third party's proprietary or confidential information disclosed to Contractor in the course of providing services to Devco. This obligation shall not extend to any information which becomes generally known to the public without breach of this Agreement. This obligation shall survive the termination of this Agreement.

**4.3 *No Conflict of Interest.*** Contractor agrees during the term of this Agreement not to accept work or enter into a contract or accept an obligation, inconsistent or incompatible with Contractor's obligations or the scope of services rendered for Devco under this Agreement.

**4.4 *Assignment of Work Product.***

(a) "Work Product" means the storyline, characters, computer software, designs, discoveries, works of authorship, formulae, processes, manufacturing techniques, inventions, improvements and ideas solely or jointly conceived, developed or reduced to practice during the Project. Contractor hereby irrevocably assigns, conveys and otherwise transfers to Devco, and its respective successors and assigns, all rights, title and interests worldwide in and to the Work Product and all proprietary rights therein, including, without limitation, all copyrights, trademarks, design patents, trade secret rights, moral rights, and all contract and licensing rights, and all claims and causes of action of any kind with respect to any of the foregoing, whether now known or hereafter to become known. In the event Contractor has any rights in and to the Work Product that cannot be assigned to Devco, Contractor hereby unconditionally and irrevocably waives the enforcement of all such rights, and all claims and causes of action of any kind with respect to any of the foregoing against Devco, its distributors and customers, whether now known or hereafter to become known and agrees, at the request and expense of Devco and its respective successors and assigns, to consent to and join in any action to enforce such rights and to procure a waiver of such rights from the holders of such rights. In the event Contractor has any rights in and to the Work Product that cannot be assigned to Devco and cannot be waived, Contractor hereby grants to Devco, and its respective successors and assigns, an exclusive, worldwide, royalty-free license during the term of the rights to reproduce, distribute, modify, publicly perform and publicly display, with the right to sublicense and assign such rights in and to the Work Product including, without limitation, the right to use in any way whatsoever the Work Product. Contractor retains no rights to use the Work Product and agrees not to challenge the validity of the ownership by Devco in the Work Product.

(b)   Contractor agrees to assist Devco in any reasonable manner to obtain and enforce for Devco's benefit patents, copyrights, and other property rights covering the Work Product in any and all countries. Contractor agrees to execute, when requested, patent, copyright, or similar applications and assignments to Devco, and any other lawful documents deemed necessary by Devco to carry out the purpose of this Agreement. Contractor further agrees that the obligations and undertaking stated in this Section 4.4(b) will continue beyond the termination of Contractor's service to Devco. If called upon to render assistance under this Section 4.4(b), Contractor will be entitled to a fair and reasonable fee in addition to reimbursement of authorized expenses incurred at the prior written request of Devco.

(c)   In the event that Devco is unable for any reason whatsoever to secure Contractor's signature to any lawful and necessary document required to apply for or execute any patent, copyright or other applications with respect to any Work Product (including improvements, renewals, extensions, continuations, divisions or continuations in part thereof), Contractor hereby irrevocably designates and appoints Devco and its duly authorized officers and agents as his agents and attorneys-in-fact to act for and in his behalf and instead of Contractor, to execute and file any such application and to do all other lawfully permitted acts to further the prosecution and issuance of patents, copyrights or other rights thereon with the same legal force and effect as if executed by Contractor.

**4.5 *Return of Devco's Property.***   Contractor acknowledges that Devco's sole and exclusive property includes all documents, such as drawings, manuals, notebooks, reports, sketches, records, computer programs, employee lists, customer lists and the like in his custody or possession, whether delivered to Contractor by Devco or made by Contractor in the performance of services under this Agreement, relating to the business activities of Devco or its customers or suppliers and containing any information or data whatsoever, whether or not Confidential Information. Contractor agrees to deliver promptly all of Devco's property and all copies of Devco's property in Contractor's possession to Devco at any time upon Devco's request.

*4.6 **Warranties***.   Contractor represents and warrants that:

(a)   the Work Product was created solely by him, his full-time employees during the course of their employment, or independent contractors who assigned all right, title and interest in their work to Contractor;

(b)   Contractor is the owner of all right, title and interest in the tangible forms of the Work Product and all intellectual property rights protecting them  The Work Product and the intellectual property rights protecting them are free and clear of all encumbrances, including, without limitation, security interests, licenses, liens, charges or other restrictions except as set forth in *Exhibit C*;

(c)   Contractor has maintained the Work Product in confidence;

(d)   the use, reproduction, distribution, or modification of the Work Product does not and will not violate the rights of any third parties in the Work Product including, but not limited to, trade secrets, trademarks, publicity, privacy, copyrights, and patents;

(e)   the Work Product is not in the public domain;

(f)   Contractor has full power and authority to make and enter into this Agreement.

*4.7 **Performance***.   Contractor represents and warrants that for a period of _____ following acceptance of the Work Product (i) the _____ will be free from defects in workmanship and materials under normal use, and (ii) that the _____ will perform in accordance with the specifications in *Exhibit A*.

*4.8 **Indemnification***.   Contractor agrees to defend, indemnify, and hold harmless Devco, their officers, directors, sublicensees, employees and agents, from and against any claims, actions or demands, including without limitation reasonable legal and accounting fees, alleging or resulting from the breach of the warranties in Section 4.6. Devco shall provide notice to Contractor promptly of any such claim, suit, or proceeding and shall assist Contractor, at Contractor's expense, in defending any such claim, suit or proceeding.

5.   **Termination—Noninterference with Business.**

*5.1 **Termination by Devco***.   Devco may terminate this Agreement for material breach at any time upon fifteen (15) days prior written notice to Contractor. Devco also may terminate this Agreement immediately in its sole discretion upon Contractor's material breach of Article 4 and/or Section 5.3 of this Agreement and/or upon any acts of gross misconduct by Contractor directly affecting this Agreement or the independent contractor relationship.

*5.2 **Termination by Contractor***.   Contractor may terminate this Agreement for material breach at any time upon fifteen (15) days prior written notice to Devco.

*5.3 **Noninterference with Business***.   During and for a period of two (2) years immediately following termination of this Agreement by either party, Contractor agrees not to solicit or induce any employee or independent contractor to terminate or breach an employment, contractual or other relationship with Devco.

6. **General Provisions.**    This Agreement will be governed by and construed in accordance with the laws of the United States and the State of California as applied to agreements entered into and to be performed entirely within California between California residents. This Agreement, including all Exhibits to this Agreement, constitutes the entire agreement between the parties relating to this subject matter and supersedes all prior or simultaneous representations, discussions, negotiations, and agreements, whether written or oral. No term or provision hereof will be considered waived by either party, and no breach excused by either party, unless such waiver or consent is in writing signed on behalf of the party against whom the waiver is asserted. No consent by either party to, or waiver of, a breach by either party, whether express or implied, will constitute a consent to, waiver of, or excuse of any other, different, or subsequent breach by either party. Contractor may not assign its rights or obligations arising under this Agreement without Devco's prior written consent. Devco may assign its rights and obligations under this Agreement. This Agreement will be for the benefit of Devco's successors and assigns, and will be binding on Contractor's heirs, legal representatives and permitted assignees. If any dispute arises between the parties with respect to the matters covered by this Agreement which leads to a proceeding to resolve such dispute, the prevailing party in such proceeding shall be entitled to receive its reasonable attorneys' fees, expert witness fees and out-of-pocket costs incurred in connection with such proceeding, in addition to any other relief to which it may be entitled. All notices, requests and other communications required to be given under this Agreement must be in writing, and must be mailed by registered or certified mail, postage prepaid and return receipt requested, or delivered by hand to the party to whom such notice is required or permitted to be given. Any such notice will be considered to have been given when received, or if mailed, five (5) business days after it was mailed, as evidenced by the postmark. The mailing address for notice to either party will be the address shown on the signature page of this Agreement. Either party may change its mailing address by notice as provided by this Section. The following provisions shall survive termination of this Agreement: Article 4 and Section 5.3. This Agreement is effective as of _____, 19____, and will terminate on _____, 19____, unless terminated earlier in accordance with Section 5 above.


"DEVCO":                                          "CONTRACTOR":

DEVELOPMENT COMPANY                               _____


By: _____            By: _____

_____         _____
Typed name                                        Typed name

_____         _____
Title                                             Title

Address:                                    Address:

_____          _____

_____          _____

_____          _____

EXHIBIT A
Project and Specifications

EXHIBIT B
Prior Work Product Disclosure

EXHIBIT C
Exceptions

# *8* **Work Made For Hire Agreement (To Developer—Includes Representations)**

This agreement is used a short form transfer of copyright in contributions to products which are eligible for treatment as "commissioned works made for hire." To be effective, the agreement must be signed before the commencement of work on the product. It includes a "back-up" assignment to ensure transfer of rights in copyright if the product does not fall within the limited categories of "commissioned works for hire" and in foreign countries which do not have "commissioned works for hire." It also includes representations about ownership and other important issues.

## WORK FOR HIRE AGREEMENT
### (To Developer-Includes Representations)

THIS AGREEMENT ("Agreement") is dated as of _____ by and between

_____ ("Author") and Development

Company, _____ with its principal

place of business at _____ ("Devco").

WHEREAS, Devco is a developer of interactive art, literature, and entertainment products; and

WHEREAS, Author will contribute certain material to Devco for the multimedia product

_____ ("Work") and the parties intend that

Devco be the owner of all rights in Work. The agreement will confirm such understanding.

NOW THEREFORE, the parties agree as follows:

1.  The Work is a commissioned "work for hire" which will be owned by Devco. If the Work is deter-
    mined not to be a "work for hire" or such doctrine is not effective, the Author hereby irrevocably
    assigns, conveys and otherwise transfers to Devco, and its respective successors, licensees, and
    assigns, all right, title and interest worldwide in and to the Work and all proprietary rights there-
    in, including, without limitation, all copyrights, trademarks, design patents, trade secret rights,
    moral rights, and all contract and licensing rights, and all claims and causes of action of respect
    to any of the foregoing, whether now known or hereafter to become known. In the event, I have
    any right in the Work which cannot be assigned, I agree to waive enforcement worldwide of such
    right against Devco, its distributors, and customers or, if necessary, exclusively because such
    right, worldwide to Devco with the right to sublicense. These rights are assignable by Devco.

2.  Author represents and warrants that: (a)the Work will be created solely by him, his full-time
    employees during the course of their employment, independent contractors who will assign
    all right, title and interest in their work to Author;(b) Author will be the owner of all right, title
    and interest in the tangible forms of the Work and all intellectual property rights protecting
    them. (c) the Work and the intellectual property rights protecting them will be free and clear
    of all encumbrances, including, without limitation, security interests, licenses, liens, charges or
    other restrictions; (d) the use, reproduction, distribution, or modification of the Work will not
    violate the rights of any third parties in the Work including, but not limited to, trade secrets,
    publicity, privacy, copyrights and patents; (e) the Work will not be in the public domain; and
    (f) Author has full power and authority to make and enter into this Agreement. Author agrees to
    defend, indemnify and hold harmless Devco, its officers, directors and employees for any claims,
    suits or proceedings alleging a breach of these warranties.

2.  Author agrees that he or she will take all actions and execute any and all documents as may be
    requested by Devco, at Devco's expense, from time to time to fully vest in Devco all rights, title
    and interests worldwide in and to the Work.

3. In consideration of the foregoing, Devco agrees to pay to Author the sum of _____ Dollars ($_____).

DEVCO:                                          AUTHOR:

DEVELOPMENT COMPANY

_____
Printed name

By: _____     By: _____

_____
Printed name

_____
Title

Address:                                        Address:

_____     _____

_____     _____

_____     _____

# *9* Assignment Agreement (To Developer—Includes Representations)

This agreement is used an assignment of copyright. It includes standard representations about ownership and other important issues.

ASSIGNMENT AGREEMENT
(Includes Representations)

THIS AGREEMENT ("Agreement") is dated as of _____ by and between _____ ("Assignor") and Development Company, _____ with its principal place of business at _____ ("Devco").

WHEREAS, Devco is a developer of interactive art, literature, and entertainment products; and

WHEREAS, Assignor has contributed certain material to Devco for the multimedia product _____ ("Work"), and the parties intended that Devco be the owner of all rights in Work. The agreement will confirm such understanding.

NOW THEREFORE, the parties agree as follows:

1. Assignor hereby irrevocably assigns, conveys and otherwise transfers to Devco, and its respective successors, licensees, and assigns, all right, title and interest worldwide in and to the Work and all proprietary rights therein, including, without limitation, all copyrights, trademarks, design patents, trade secret rights, moral rights, and all contract and licensing rights, and all claims and causes of action of respect to any of the foregoing, whether now known or hereafter to become known. In the event, Assignor has any right in the Work which cannot be assigned, Assignor agrees to waive enforcement worldwide of such right against Devco, its distributors, and customers or, if necessary, exclusively license such right worldwide to Devco, with the right to sublicense. These rights are assignable by Devco.

2. Assignor represents and warrants that: (a) the Work was created solely by Assignor, Assignor's full-time employees during the course of their employment, or independent contractors who assigned all right, title and interest in their work to Assignor; (b) Assignor is the owner of all right, title and interest in the tangible forms of the Work and all intellectual property rights protecting them; (c) the Work and the intellectual property rights protecting them are free and clear of all encumbrances, including, without limitation, security interests, licenses, liens, charges or other restrictions; (d) the use, reproduction, distribution, or modification of the Work does not and will not violate the rights of any third parties in the Work including, but not limited to, trade secrets, publicity, privacy, copyrights, and patents; (e) the Work is not in the public domain; and (f) Assignor has full power and authority to make and enter into this Agreement. Assignor agrees to defend, indemnify, and hold harmless Devco, its officers, directors and employees for any claims, suits or proceedings alleging a breach of these warranties.

3. Assignor agrees that he or she will take all actions and execute any and all documents as may be requested by Devco, at Devco's expense, from time to time, to fully vest in Devco all rights, title and interests worldwide in and to the Work.

4.   In consideration of the foregoing, Devco agrees to pay to Assignor the sum of _____
     Dollars ($_____).

DEVCO:                                          ASSIGNOR:

DEVELOPMENT COMPANY
                                                _____
                                                Printed name

By: _____           By: _____

_____
Printed name

_____
Title

Address:                                        Address:

_____       _____

_____       _____

_____       _____

# *10* Assignment Agreement
# (To Developer—No Representations)

This agreement is used as an assignment of copyright. It does not include any representations about ownership and other important issues. It is the minimum assignment which a developer should use for multimedia works.

## ASSIGNMENT AGREEMENT
### (To Developer—No Representations)

THIS AGREEMENT ("Agreement") is dated as of _____ by and between
_____ ("Assignor") and Development
Company, _____ with its principal
place of business at _____ ("Devco").

WHEREAS, Devco is a developer of interactive art, literature, and entertainment products; and

WHEREAS, Assignor has contributed certain material to Devco for the multimedia product
_____ ("Work"), and the parties intended
that Devco be the owner of all rights in Work. The agreement will confirm such understanding.

NOW THEREFORE, the parties agree as follows:

1. Assignor hereby irrevocably assigns, conveys, and otherwise transfers to Devco, and its respective successors, licensees, and assigns, all right, title and interest worldwide in and to the Work and all proprietary rights therein, including, without limitation, all copyrights, trademarks, design patents, trade secret rights, moral rights, and all contract and licensing rights, and all claims and causes of action of respect to any of the foregoing, whether now known or hereafter to become known. In the event, Assignor has any right in the Work which cannot be assigned, Assignor agrees to waive enforcement worldwide of such right against Devco, its distributors, and customers or, if necessary, exclusively license such right worldwide to Devco, with the right to sublicense. These rights are assignable by Devco.

2. Assignor agrees that he or she will take all actions and execute any and all documents as may be requested by Devco, at Devco's expense, from time to time, to fully vest in Devco all rights, title and interests worldwide in and to the Work.

3. In consideration of the foregoing, Devco agrees to pay to Assignor the sum of _____ Dollars ($_____).

DEVCO:                                          ASSIGNOR:

DEVELOPMENT COMPANY                              _____
                                                Printed name

By: _____             By: _____

_____
Printed name

_____
Title

Address:                                        Address:

_____               _____

_____               _____

_____               _____

## *11*  Still Photograph and Trademark License Agreement

This agreement is used to select photographs from a larger collection and use them in a multimedia work. It also includes a trademark license because many photographers have a reputation which can be valuable in selling the developer's product. The license is exclusive for the use of the photographs in a particular type of product.

## STILL PHOTOGRAPH AND TRADEMARK LICENSE AGREEMENT

THIS LICENSE AGREEMENT ("Agreement"), dated as of this _____ day of _____, 19____, between _____ ("Licensor"), a _____ corporation with its principal place of business located at _____ and Development Company ("Devco"), a _____ corporation with its principal place of business at _____.

### Recitals

WHEREAS, Licensor has certain copyrights and other proprietary rights in still photographs described in *Exhibit A* (the "Photographs"), and Devco desires to use the Photographs as part of certain products;

WHEREAS, Licensor has and will have certain copyrights and other proprietary rights in still photographs, both in existence on the Effective Date and to be created in the future (including the right to license or sublicense said photographs) (the "Collection"), and Licensee desire to use certain still photographs from the Collection as part of certain products.

WHEREAS, Licensor has rights in the trademarks _____ ("Trademark") for _____ and Devco desires to use the Trademark in connection with such products.

WHEREAS, Licensee wishes to use, and Licensor wishes to allow the use of, certain photographs from the Collection, to be chosen as set forth below (the "Photographs"), as well as the Trademark (either alone or as an element of Licensee's trademarks) in and on Licensee's Product as defined below, including the initial version and on subsequent versions, ports to different platforms, and translations to foreign languages of said products (collectively, the "Licensed Products"), as well as in and on any accompanying manuals, packaging, promotional and advertising materials for said software products (collectively, the "Products Materials"), all in connection with and only in connection with the manufacture, sale, offering for sale, advertising, promotion and distribution of the Licensed Products.

### Agreement

NOW, THEREFORE, in consideration of the foregoing and of the mutual promises contained herein, the parties hereby agree as follows:

1. **Rights Granted.**

   (a) Licensor hereby grants to Devco an exclusive, worldwide license to use the Trademark on packages for software which _____ ("Field of Use") ("Product") and the Product Materials.

(b) Licensor hereby grants to Devco an exclusive, worldwide license in the Field of Use, with the right to sublicense through multiple chains of distribution, to reproduce, have reproduced, distribute, modify, publicly display, and publicly perform each of the Photographs as part of and in connection with the Licensed Products.

2. **License Fee**.

   (a) During the term of this Agreement, Devco shall pay to Licensor a royalty payment of _____ percent (____%) Devco's Net Revenues from the Licensed Product sold as Retail Copies. Retail Copies are copies of the Licensed Products sold alone, either directly or indirectly, to end users.

   (b) "Net Revenues" means the sums received or due to Devco with respect to the Licensed Products distributed as Retail Copies less: (1) Cost of Goods, as defined below; (2) shipping; (3) insurance; (4) credit for discounts; (5) invoiced amounts for copies of the Licensed Products provided as replacements or revisions (but not as back-ups), whether provided under a warranty or maintenance policy or otherwise; (6) taxes; and (7) price reduction related to co-op advertising.

   (c) "Cost of Goods" means the cost of optical or magnetic media upon which the program is recorded, packaging materials, manuals and other collateral materials and program components, CD-ROM or magnetic disk duplication services, printing and binding of manuals and other materials included in or with the finished Licensed Product and pre-distribution shipping costs, plus standard labor costs for Licensed Product manufacture.

   (d) The royalty for Bundled Copies of the Licensed Product shall be $_____ per Bundled Copy. Bundled Copies means the copies of the Licensed Product distributed together with hardware or software of Devco or a third party. Bundled Copies shall not include Retail Copies.

   (e) Royalties shall be due forty-five (45) days after the end of the calendar quarter in which Devco receives its Net Revenues or distributes the Bundled Copy.

3. **Ownership of the Trademark and Rights in the Photographs.**   Licensor shall retain all rights in the Trademark and Photographs, other than those licensed in this Agreement. Devco's use of the Trademark shall inure to the benefit of and be on behalf of Licensor.

4. **Further Assurances.**   Licensor shall take reasonable measures to protect the Trademark for Licensed Products in the following countries _____.

5. **Quality Control**.   The nature and quality of the Licensed Products and Product Materials sold by Devco using the Trademark shall conform to standards set by Licensor. Devco shall supply Licensor with samples of each Licensed Product and Product Materials prior to distribution. Unless Licensor objects to such samples in writing within ten (10) days, the samples shall be deemed approved. Licensor's approval shall not be unreasonably withheld. In the event that the quality standards referred to above are not met, then Licensor may serve notice on Devco that

Devco has sixty (60) days after receipt of notice to meet such standards. In the event that Devco fails to meet such quality standards within the sixty (60) day period, then upon written notice from Licensor, Devco shall immediately discontinue the use of the Trademark on all future copies of that particular Licensed Product or Product Materials. This termination shall be on a Licensed Product by Licensed Product basis.

6. **Infringement by Third Parties of the Photographs or Trademarks.**

   (a) Licensor shall have the sole right to file any action alleging that a third party has infringed the rights granted to Licensee in any of the Photographs and Trademarks within the first sixty (60) days after Licensor receives notice of such infringement. If Licensor elects to file such an action, it shall pay the entire cost of such action and shall be entitled to all of any monetary recovery related thereto. Licensor shall defend, indemnify, and hold harmless Licensee from any claim, suit or proceeding (including, but not limited to, counterclaims) against Licensee arising from any action brought by Licensor against a third party, but only to the extent that said counterclaim relates to an actual or alleged breach of any of Licensor's warranties herein except for claims based on Licensor's warranties.

   (b) If Licensor advises Licensee in writing within thirty (30) days after Licensor receives notice of such infringement that it intends to take no action with regard thereto, then Licensee shall have the right to file any action alleging that a third party has infringed the rights of Licensee in any of the Photographs and Trademarks. If Licensor does not so advise Licensee within thirty (30) days, and if Licensor does not in fact elect to file such an action with sixty (60) days after receiving notice of such infringement, then Licensee shall have the right to file an action alleging that a third party has infringed the rights of Licensee in any of the Photographs and Trademarks. If Licensee elects to file such an action, it shall pay the entire cost of such action and shall be entitled to recover the entire costs of the such action, including attorney's fees, from such recovery, and shall pay to Licensor _____ percent (____%) of the remaining balance of the recovery and shall be entitled to keep _____ percent (____%) of the remaining balance of the recovery. Licensor shall provide Licensee with reasonable assistance, at Licensee's expense, in bringing such action, including making its personnel available to testify. Licensee shall defend, indemnify and hold harmless Licensor from any claim, suit or proceeding (including, but not limited to, counterclaims) against Licensor arising from any action brought by Licensee against a third party.

   (c) If Licensee elects to file an action, it will provide Licensor with notice of such proceedings. If Licensor subsequently wishes to assume control of the action, then Licensor may do so upon reasonable notice to Licensee and on the condition that prior to asserting such control Licensor reimburses Licensee for the full amount of attorneys' fees and costs incurred by Licensee in pursuing the action.

7. **Warranties.** Licensor warrants that it is the sole owner of the Trademark and the sole owner of all rights in the Photographs. None of the Trademark or the Photographs: (i) are subject to any restrictions or to any mortgages, liens, pledges, charges, security interests, encumbrances or encroachments, or to any rights of others of any kind or nature whatsoever which would prevent the grant of this license; (ii) infringe any copyrights, trademarks, trade secrets or other proprietary rights of third parties, (iii) are the subject of any notice of such infringement received by Licensor; and (iv) are the subject of agreements or arrangements between Licensor and any third party that have any effect upon Licensor's rights to license the Trademark and/or the Photographs as set forth in this Agreement. Licensor has obtained clearances that will permit the use of the Photographs in the Licensed Products from all individuals who are recognizable in the Photographs.

8. **Indemnification.** Licensor agrees to defend, indemnify and hold harmless Devco, its officers, directors, sublicensees, employees and agents, from and against any claims, actions or demands alleging, including without limitation reasonable legal and accounting fees, resulting from the breach of the warranties in Section 7. Devco shall provide notice to Licensor promptly of any such claim, suit or proceeding and shall assist Licensor, at Licensor's expense, in defending any such claim, suit or proceeding.

9. **Assignability and Transferability.** This Agreement shall be binding on, and shall inure to the benefit of, the parties hereto and their respective heirs, legal representatives, successors and assigns. Any party may assign this Agreement without the prior written consent of the other party as part of a sale of all or substantially all of its assets, corporate reorganization, consolidation or merger. Otherwise, neither party may assign, voluntarily, by operation of law, or otherwise, any rights or delegate any duties under this Agreement (other than the right to receive payments) without the other party's prior written consent (which will not be unreasonably withheld), and any attempt to do so without that consent will be void.

10. **Term.** Unless terminated earlier pursuant to Paragraph 11, this Agreement shall commence on the Effective Date and shall _____ in effect for a period of _____ calendar years after the date that Devco begins commercial distribution of a Licensed Product (the "Initial Term"). Thereafter, this Agreement shall be automatically renewed for one two-year period ("Renewal Term"), unless terminated by Devco upon written notice ninety (90) days prior to the end of the Initial Term.

11. **Termination.**
    (a) Each party shall have the right to terminate this Agreement upon thirty (30) days written notice, if the other are in material breach of any provision of this Agreement and if such breach is not cured within such thirty (30) day period.

(b) Upon termination of this Agreement, all rights to use the Trademark and the Photographs in the manner provided for in this Agreement shall revert automatically to Licensor, and Devco shall promptly discontinue all uses of the Trademark and of the Photographs. Licensee shall have the right to sell any Licensed Products manufactured prior to the effective date of termination for six months after the date of such termination.

12. **Notice**.   All notices or other communications pursuant to this Agreement shall be in writing and shall be deemed to have been given when (a) delivered personally; (b) sent by confirmed telex or telecopy; (c) sent by commercial overnight courier with written verification of receipt; or (d) mailed postage prepaid by certified or registered mail, return receipt requested, to the party to be notified at the address set forth above, or at such other place at which the other party has been notified in accordance with the provisions of this paragraph. Such notice shall be treated as having been received upon the earlier of actual receipt or five (5) days after posting.

13. **Choice of Law**.   This Agreement shall be governed by and construed in accordance with the laws of the United States and the State of California as applied to agreements entered into and to be performed entirely within California by California residents.

14. **Amendment.**   This Agreement may be amended or supplemented only by a writing signed by duly authorized representatives of both parties on behalf of both parties.

15. **Severability.**   In the event that any provision of this Agreement shall be unenforceable or invalid under any applicable law or be so held by applicable court decision, such unenforceability or invalidity shall not render this Agreement unenforceable or invalid as a whole, and, in such event, such provision shall be changed and interpreted so as to best accomplish the objectives of such unenforceable or invalid provision without the limits of applicable law or applicable court decisions.

16. **Entire Agreement**.   This Agreement constitutes the entire agreement between the parties relating to the subject matter and supersedes all prior or simultaneous representations, discussions, negotiations and agreements, whether written or oral.

17. **Waiver.**   No term or provision hereof will be considered waived by either party, unless such waiver or consent is in writing signed on behalf of the party against whom the waiver is asserted. No consent by either party to, or waiver of, a breach by either party, whether express or implied, will constitute a consent to, waiver of, or excuse of any other, different, or subsequent breach by either party.

IN WITNESS WHEREOF, the parties hereto have caused this Agreement to be executed on the date first written above.

LICENSOR:

LICENSING COMPANY

By: _____

Title: _____

Date: _____


LICENSEE:

DEVELOPMENT COMPANY

By: _____

Title: _____

Date: _____

EXHIBIT A
Photographs

## *12*  **Short Form Exclusive License to Developer**

This agreement is used to record an exclusive license of a copyright in the Copyright Office. The developer must include either the registration number or title of the copyrightable work to have "constructive notice" of the exclusive license (see "Obtaining a License," Chapter 10).

## SHORT FORM EXCLUSIVE LICENSE TO DEVELOPER

The author, _____, ("Author") for good and valuable consideration, the receipt of which is acknowledged, grants to Development Company ("Devco"), its successors and assigns an exclusive license [to distribute/create derivative works/reproduce/publicly perform/ publicly display] the [audio-visual rights, motion picture rights, music composition rights] in the copyrightable work named _____ ("Work") owned by Author. Author authorizes the recordation of this notice with the Copyright Office. The [registration number/name] of the Work is _____.

DEVCO:

DEVELOPMENT COMPANY

By: _____


_____
Printed name


_____
Title


Address:

_____

_____

_____

AUTHOR:

_____
Printed name


By: _____


Address:

_____

_____

_____

## *13*  **Short Form Assignment to Developer**

This agreement is used to record the transfer of a copyright to the developer in the Copyright Office. The developer must include either the registration number or title of the copyrightable work to have "constructive notice" of the transfer (see "Obtaining a License" Chapter 10). This short form assignment can also be used to record an assignment of less than all rights in the work (for example, an assignment of audio visual rights or motion picture rights). (See Form 12.)

## SHORT FORM ASSIGNMENT TO DEVELOPER

The author, _____, ("Author") for good and valuable consideration, the receipt of which is acknowledged, grants to Developer Company ("Devco"), its successors and assigns all right, title and interest in the copyrightable work named _____ ("Work") owned by Auhor. Author authorizes the recordation of this notice with the Copyright Office. The [registration number/name] of the Work is _____.

DEVCO:                                          AUTHOR:

DEVELOPMENT COMPANY                 _____
                                                Printed name

By: _____   By: _____

_____
Printed name

_____
Title

Address:                                        Address:

_____   _____

_____   _____

_____   _____

# *14* **Software Component License**

This agreement is used when the developer is licensing software for use in its product. The agreement limits the use of the software to the developer's product or other products distributed by developer.

It includes the right to receive enhancements during the term of the agreement and a "most favored nation" clause (provision that gives the developer the right to receive the enhancements on the best terms offered by the licensor).

## SOFTWARE COMPONENT LICENSE

THIS AGREEMENT ("Agreement") entered into as of _____, 19____, by and between Software Supplier Company ("SSC"), having its principal place of business at _____ and Development Company, a _____ corporation, having a place of business at _____ ("Devco").

NOW, THEREFORE, the parties agree as follows:

1.  **Definitions.**   The terms used in this Agreement shall have the following definitions:

    *1.1 End User Documentation*   means the manuals and other documentation relating to the Program for the end user.

    *1.2 Future Version*   means any modifications and updates, except Error Corrections, if any, to the Initial Release in object code form distributed by SSC.

    *1.3 Error Corrections*   means bug fixes to the Initial Release and in the Enhancements.

    *1.4 Devco's Products*   mean finished computer software or other products distributed by Devco. A Devco Product will consist of the original product and any new versions of such original product.

    *1.5 Product Specifications*   mean (a), for the Initial Release, SSC's product specification sheet set forth on *Exhibit A* for the Program on the Effective Date; and (b), for Enhancements, SSC's product specification sheet, if any, for the Enhancements or if SSC has not published a product specification sheet for the Enhancements, the most recent version of SSC's product specification sheet for the Program.

    *1.6 Program*   means the Initial Release, Error Corrections, and Enhancements.

    *1.7 Source Code*   means the source code form of the Program.

2.  **Term of Agreement.**   The term of this Agreement will commence on the Effective Date and, unless earlier terminated as provided below, will continue for the term of the copyrights in the Program.

3.  **Scope of Rights.**

    *3.1 Software License.*

    (a)   SSC grants to Devco a perpetual, irrevocable, worldwide, nonexclusive, license, with right to sublicense, during the term of this Agreement, to do the following:

       (1)   Reproduce, modify, and distribute the Program for use as part of Devco's Products;

       (2)   Reproduce and use the Program for Devco's internal purposes.

    (b)   Devco shall be the sole and exclusive owner of all rights in the modifications of the Program and Source Code developed by Devco.

*3.2 Error Correction*.   During the term of the Agreement, SSC will provide all of the Error Corrections and reasonable technical assistance to Devco without cost.

*3.3 Enhancements.*   During the term of the Agreement, SSC shall give Devco the Enhancements as soon as they are distributed to other parties. SSC shall make Enhancements available to Devco on the most favorable terms which it offers to third parties. If SSC subsequently offers more favorable terms for an Enhancement to a third party, such terms shall retroactively apply to Devco.

*3.4 Documentation*.   SSC grants to Devco a non-exclusive, worldwide, royalty-free license to use the End User Documentation for its own internal purposes and to reproduce, modify and distribute the End User Documentation to customers for the Devco's Products.

4.  **Delivery and Acceptance.**   SSC shall deliver to Devco one copy of the Initial Release (and Source Code) on magnetic media and one copy of the End User Documentation for the Program within ten days of the Effective Date. If Devco has the right to receive Enhancements, SSC shall deliver to Devco one copy of the Enhancement (and Source Code) on magnetic media and one copy of the End User Documentation for the Enhancement. Devco shall have thirty (30) days to review the Initial Release or Enhancement to ensure that it meets the Product Specifications. If the Initial Release or Enhancement fails to meet the Product Specifications, Devco may return such Initial Release or Enhancement and receive a refund of the royalty paid for it.

5.  **Order and Payment.**   Devco shall pay SSC the sum of _____ for the first Devco Product which includes the Program ten days after the distribution of the Devco Product incorporating the Program. Devco shall pay SSC $_____ for each additional Devco Product that incorporates the Program ten days after the first distribution of such additional Devco Product. An additional Devco Product is a program that includes significantly different functions, not new versions of the original Devco Product.

6.  **Warranty**.   SSC warrants to Devco that the Initial Release and Enhancements (and the Source Code versions thereof) received during the Agreement will perform in accordance with the Program Specifications during the Agreement. SSC warrants that the End User Documentation shall be free of material errors during the warranty period of the Initial Release or Enhancement with which it is associated. Devco agrees to report in writing any failure to meet the warranties ("Error") to SSC. In the event Devco discovers and gives written notice of an Error within the relevant warranty period, SSC will, at its own expense, correct the Error within five (5) days of notice of the Error. If the Error cannot be corrected within such period, SSC will provide a workaround. Errors will be reported to SSC in a form and with supporting information reasonably requested by SSC to enable it to verify, diagnose and correct the Error. SSC DISCLAIMS ALL OTHER REPRESENTATIONS AND WARRANTIES, INCLUDING THE WARRANTIES OF MERCHANTABILITY AND FITNESS FOR A PARTICULAR PURPOSE.

7. **SSC's Warranty and Indemnification for Infringement of Proprietary Rights.**   SSC represents and warrants that it is the sole and exclusive owner of all rights in the Program. Further, SSC represents and warrants that: (i) the Program is not subject to any restrictions or to any mortgages, liens, pledges, charges, security interests, encumbrances or encroachments, or to any rights of others of any kind or nature whatsoever which would prevent the grant of this license; (ii) the Program does not encroach or infringe any copyrights, trademarks, trade secrets or other proprietary rights of third parties; (iii) SSC has not received any notice of such encroachment or infringement; and (iv) SSC has not entered into any agreements or arrangements between SSC and any third party that have any effect upon SSC's rights to license the Program, as set forth in this Agreement. SSC agrees to indemnify and hold harmless Devco, its officers, directors, employees and agents against any claims, actions, or demands alleging that the modification, reproduction, or distribution of the Program (or Source Code) infringes any patents, copyrights, or trade secrets of any third parties.

8. **Termination.**   This Agreement shall terminate upon the ninetieth (90th) day after either party gives the other notice of a material breach by the other of any term or condition of this Agreement, unless the breach is cured before that day.

9. **General Provisions.**

   *9.1 Assignment.*   Devco may assign its rights under this Agreement to any person to whom it transfers all or substantially all of its proprietary rights in any of the Devco Product (it may assign its rights to different parties if it assigns rights in Devco Products to different parties). This Agreement will bind and inure to the benefit of the parties and their respective successors and permitted assigns. This Agreement will be governed by and construed in accordance with the laws of the United States and the State of California as applied to agreements entered into and to be performed entirely within California between California residents.

   *9.2 Notice.*   Any notice provided for or permitted under this Agreement will be treated as having been given when (a) delivered personally, (b) sent by confirmed telex or telecopy, (c) sent by commercial overnight courier with written verification of receipt, or (d) mailed postage prepaid by certified or registered mail, return receipt requested, to the party to be notified, at the address set forth above, or at such other place of which the other party has been notified in accordance with the provisions of this Section.

   *9.3 Entire Agreement.*   This Agreement, including all Exhibits to this Agreement, constitutes the entire agreement between the parties relating to this subject matter and supersedes all prior or simultaneous representations, discussions, negotiations and agreements, whether written or oral.

IN WITNESS WHEREOF, the parties have executed this Agreement as of the Effective Date.

"SSC":                                      "DEVCO":

SOFTWARE SUPPLIER COMPANY                   DEVELOPMENT COMPANY

By: _____        By: _____

_____        _____
Printed name:                               Printed name:

_____        _____
Title:                                      Title:

EXHIBIT A

Initial Release Description

Product Specifications for the Initial Release

## *15*  **Music License for CD-ROMs by Harry Fox**

This agreement is the license used by the Harry Fox Agency to license synchronization rights in music for multimedia rights. (see "Methods of Obtaining Rights," Chapter 12). If the developer needs public performance rights, he or she will need a separate license.

The Harry Fox Agency, Inc.
205 East 42nd Street
New York, New York 10017

MULTI-MEDIA RIGHTS LICENSE (MMERL)

License No. _____

Date of Issuance _____

The following provisions shall apply as indicated in the body of this License:

(A) Licensee: _____

(B) Musical Composition: _____

(C) Licensor(s) and percentage of ownership: _____

(D) License Date: _____

(E) Term: _____

(F) Advance: _____

(G) Units: _____

(H) Royalty Per Unit: "Two times the so-called 'statutory royalty rate' (provided pursuant to Section 115 of the United States Copyright Act for the making and distribution of phonorecords) [17 U.S.C. 115].", **OR**

(H) Royalty Per Unit: "_____ cents"

(I)  Territory: _____

(J) Software Serial Number: _____

## Definitions

1.  For the purposes hereof, the following terms shall have the following meanings:
    a)  "MULTI-MEDIA" shall mean the medium in which a musical composition will be utilized in conjunction with, but not limited to, computer monitor visual displays.
    b)  "MULTI-MEDIA DISK" which shall include, but not be limited to CD Rom or computer assisted laser disks, shall mean those Multimedia disks containing those musical recordings which is the subject of this license.
    c)  The term "MULTI-MEDIA DISK MARKET" shall refer to the sale, lease, license, use or other distribution of MULTI-MEDIA DISKS directly or indirectly to individuals for playback through, but not limited to, a personal computer, whether now in existence or hereafter developed.

d)   "Copy" or "copies" shall mean all MULTI-MEDIA DISK copies manufactured and distributed by Licensee.

Now it is therefore agreed as follows:

1.   Licensee is hereby applying to Licensor for a MULTI-MEDIA rights license to use the musical composition referred to in (B) (above) for the purposes of manufacturing, distributing and selling to the public throughout the territory [(I)], MULTI-MEDIA, embodying the musical composition.

2.   Licensor hereby grants to the Licensee the following non-exclusive rights with respect to MULTI-MEDIA DISK, in all respects subject to the terms and conditions herein provided:

a)   To record and re-record in digital, computer readable or other form consistent with the integral requirements of the MULTI-MEDIA, the musical composition for use in whole or in part in connection with and with respect to MULTI-MEDIA DISK;

b)   To make and distribute copies of the MULTI-MEDIA DISK program throughout the territory only [(I)];

c)   Licensee may make arrangements and orchestrations of the Composition for its recording purposes, however, this license does not include the right to alter the fundamental character of the Composition, to print sheet music or to make any other use of the Composition not expressly authorized hereunder, all rights to uses not expressly granted hereunder are hereby expressly reserved by the Licensor.

3.   Licensee covenants that it shall place on the outside of all containers or, where possible, in every MULTI-MEDIA DISK copy a conspicuous notice to clearly read as follows:

c    Title of Composition and Names of writers. Copyright © 19____ (owner of composition). International Rights Secured. Not for broadcast transmission. All rights reserved. DO NOT DUPLICATE. NOT FOR SEPARATE RENTAL.

*Warning:* "It is a violation of Federal Copyright Law to synchronize this MULTI-MEDIA DISK with video tape or film, or to print this MULTI-MEDIA DISK in the form of standard music notation without the express written permission of the copyright owner."

4.   The musical composition recorded as a MULTI-MEDIA DISK shall not exceed ____ minutes and ____ seconds.

5.   The use of the musical composition hereunder shall be:

_____

6.   The term during which the rights licensed hereunder may be exercised shall be [the number referred to in (E)] years from the License date (D).

7.  a)  Licensee shall make the royalty payments hereunder, which shall be accompanied by a detailed accounting statement listing units distributed within 45 days after the end of each calendar quarter during which the MULTI-MEDIA DISK copies are distributed, equal to [the amount referred to in (H)] per MULTI-MEDIA DISK copy of the work which is manufactured and distributed during each such respective calendar quarter. Within thirty (30) days after the execution of this license, Licensee shall make such payment and render such statement for all units distributed prior to the execution of this license.

    b)  In the event that Licensee fails to account and pay royalties as herein provided, Licensor shall have the right to give written notice to Licensee that unless the default is remedied within thirty (30) days from the date of the notice, this license shall be deemed terminated. Such failure to pay and cure default in such thirty (30) day period shall render either the making or the distribution, or both, of all MULTI-MEDIA DISK copies hereunder for which royalties have not been paid, actionable acts of infringement under, and fully subject to the remedies provided by the U.S. Copyright Act.

8.  Upon ten business days prior written notice, Licensor, by the Harry Fox Agency ("HFA"), shall have the right during reasonable business hours at Licensee's place of business and at HFA's sole expense to examine, and make copies and extracts from the books and records of Licensee relating to its production, making and distribution of MULTI-MEDIA copies hereunder for the purpose of verifying the accuracy of statements and payments and the performance of Licensee's obligations hereunder. Licensee shall not be required to submit to such an examination more than once during any twelve (12) month period.

9.  This license does not include the rights to:
    a)  Rent separately the musical composition included in the MULTI-MEDIA copies or to permit purchasers or others to do so;
    b)  Use the story of the musical composition or dramatically depict the musical composition;
    c)  Parody the lyrics and/or music of the musical composition in any way;
    d)  Publicly perform, broadcast/cablecast or transmit the work in any manner;
    e)  Make, sell or distribute audio phonorecords of the musical composition;
    f)  Utilize a sound recording and/or audiovisual master(s) not owned or separately licensed by Licensee.

10. All rights of every kind and nature with respect to the composition which are not expressly granted to Licensee hereunder are expressly reserved by Licensor.

11. Licensor warrants only that it has the right to grant this license, and this license is given and accepted without any other representation, warrant or recourse, express or implied, except for

Licensor's agreement to repay the consideration paid for this license if the aforesaid warranty should be breached. In no event shall the total liability of the Licensor exceed the total amount of consideration received by it hereunder.

12. Upon the expiration of this license, all rights herein granted shall cease and terminate and the right to make or authorize any further use or distribution of any recordings made hereunder shall also cease and terminate subject to Licensee's right to sell off its inventory of MULTI-MEDIA DISK for an additional period of one year subject to the continuing obligation to pay royalties therefor. No right to make, sell, or distribute MULTI-MEDIA DISK programs or copies embodying the composition shall survive the termination of this license pursuant to Paragraph 7(a) hereof.

13. This license does not include a grant of performing rights. The public performance of the musical composition as part of the MULTI-MEDIA DISK which is the subject of this license, is expressly conditioned upon such performers or places of performance thereof, having valid performing rights licenses from the respective copyright owners or their designated performing rights societies.

14. This license supersedes and renders null and void any prior agreements otherwise in effect respecting the Composition and those rights which are the subject of this license.

15. This license is being entered into on an experimental and nonprejudicial basis, shall apply for the term set forth herein only, and shall not be binding upon or prejudicial to any position taken by Licensor or Licensee for any period subsequent to the period of this license.

16. This license sets forth the entire understanding of the parties hereto with respect to the subject matter thereof, may not be altered, amended or assigned without an express written instrument to such effect accepted by Licensor and shall be governed and construed by and under the laws of the State of New York applicable to contracts wholly to be performed therein.

By: _____

By: _____
(Licensee)

By:   THE HARRY FOX AGENCY, INC. on behalf of:

By: _____
(Licensor)

## *16*  **Music and Sound Recording License**

This agreement is used to license a musical composition and the sound recording of the musical composition for use in a developer's multimedia product. It is most appropriate for music which is specially created for the developer. If the developer is using pre-existing music, the developer will probably have to use the license of the owner of such rights.

## MUSIC AND SOUND RECORDING LICENSE

THIS AGREEMENT ("Agreement") entered into as of _____, 19____, by and between Development Company, a _____ corporation with its principal place of business at _____ ("Devco"), and Composer Company, a _____ with its principal place of business at _____ ("Composer").

### Recitals

WHEREAS, Composer owns the right to a certain musical composition and the master recording thereof;

WHEREAS, Devco wishes to license rights to that musical composition and the master recording thereof as provided under the terms of this Agreement.

### Agreement

NOW, THEREFORE, the parties agree as follows:

1.  **Definitions.**  The terms used in this Agreement shall have the following definitions:
    *Audiovisual Work* means the Multimedia title _____ developed by Devco.
    *Master* means the master recording of the Musical Composition embodying the performance of [Composer].
    *Multimedia* means the medium in connection which the Musical Composition and Master will be utilized, which includes, but is not limited to, a software program involving film, photographs, music, or text.
    *Multimedia Disks* means those Multimedia disks containing the Musical Composition and/or the Master, including but not limited to, CD-ROMs, laser disks, and floppy disks for any computing platforms.
    *Musical Composition* means the musical composition entitled _____ written by _____.

2.  **License Grant.**  Composer hereby grants to Devco and Devco accepts, a worldwide, non-exclusive license, with the right to sublicense, during the term of this Agreement, to do the following:
    (a) reproduce and have reproduced, in digital, computer readable, or other form consistent with the integral requirements of the Multimedia, the Musical Composition for use in whole or in part in connection with the Multimedia Disk;
    (b) to synchronize the Master, or a portion thereof, in time-relation with the Audiovisual Work and in any promotions and advertisements of the Audiovisual Work;
    (c) to reproduce and have reproduced, distribute copies of, and publicly perform the Multimedia Disks;

(d) to create derivative works of the Musical Composition and Master in order to make arrangements and orchestrations for reproducing the Musical Composition or to promote or advertise the Audiovisual Work; *provided, however*, Devco does not have the right to alter the fundamental character of the Musical Composition or Master, to print sheet music of the Musical Composition, or to make any other use of the Musical Composition or Master except as expressly authorized under this Agreement;

(e) to publicly perform the Musical Composition and the Master in connection with the Audiovisual Work;

(f) to use or refer to Composer in the credits, and in any promotions, advertisements and publicity in connection with the Audiovisual Work.

3. **Payment.**   In consideration of the license and the rights granted herein, Devco shall pay to Composer the sum of _____ ($_____).

4. **Term.**
   (a) This license and grant of rights made herein shall subsist, at a minimum, for the remainder of the term of all copyrights in and to the Musical Composition and the Master, and any and all renewals or extensions thereof that Composer or its successors or assigns may now own or control or hereafter own or control without additional consideration therefor.
   (b) Upon the expiration of this license, all rights herein granted shall cease and terminate, and the right to make or authorize any further use or distribution of any recordings made hereunder shall also cease and terminate subject to Devco's right to sell off its inventory of Multimedia Disks for an additional period of two (2) years.

5. **No Obligation to Include Musical Composition or Master.**   Nothing herein shall obligate or require Devco to include the Musical Composition or Master in the Audiovisual Work.

6. **Representation and Warranty; Indemnity.**   Composer represents and warrants that it has the right to grant this license. Composer shall indemnify and hold harmless Devco, its officers, directors, employees, sublicensees, customers and agents against all claims, actions or demands, alleging that the reproduction, distribution, modification, or public performance of the Musical Composition or the Master libels, defames, infringes the copyright or trademarks, infringes the publicity or privacy rights of any individual, or violates other similar proprietary rights of third parties in any jurisdiction. Composer represents and warrants that Composer has paid any American Federation of Musicians or other union re-use fees to permit Devco to use the Musical Composition in Devco's Audiovisual Works.

7. **License Limitations.**   This license does not include the right to:
   (a) rent separately the Musical Composition or Master included in the Multimedia Disks or to permit purchasers or others to do so;
   (b) use the story of the Musical Composition or dramatically depict the Musical Composition;

(c) parody the lyrics and/or music of the Musical Composition in any way;

(d) make, sell or distribute audio phonorecords of the Musical Composition or Master.

8. **Miscellaneous.**   This Agreement sets forth the entire understanding of the parties hereto with respect to the subject matter hereof and supersedes all prior understandings, if any, whether oral or written pertaining thereto and may only be changed by mutual agreement of authorized representatives of the parties in writing. This Agreement shall bind and inure to the benefit of the parties and their successors and permitted assigns. This Agreement shall be governed in all respects by the laws of the State of California as applied to agreements entered into and performed entirely within California by California residents.

IN WITNESS WHEREOF, the parties have executed this Agreement as of the date indicated above.

DEVCO:

DEVELOPMENT COMPANY

By: _____

COMPOSER:

COMPOSER COMPANY

By: _____

## *17* **Model Release**

This model release is used to obtain the rights to use a person's image in a photograph. The release is general and permits the use of the image in all media and any product. Some releases are more limited: for example, they may limit the use of an image to a particular product or prevent the modification of the image.

## MODEL RELEASE

Job #: _____     Name: _____

Location: _____     Date: _____

### Model Release / Development Company ("DEVCO")

For valuable consideration received, I hereby grant to Devco the absolute and irrevocable right and permission, in respect of the photographs that it has taken or has had taken of me or in which I may be included with others, to copyright the same, in its own name or otherwise (and assign my rights throughout the world in such photograph), to use, re-use, publish, and re-publish, and otherwise reproduce, modify and display the same, in whole or in part, individually or in conjunction with other photographs, and in conjunction with any copyrighted matter, in any and all media now or hereafter known, for illustration, promotion, art, advertising and trade, or any other purpose whatsoever; and to use my name in connection therewith if it so chooses. I hereby release and discharge Devco from any and all claims and demands arising out of or in connection with the use of the photographs, including without limitation any and all claims for libel or invasion of privacy.

Devco may sell, assign, license or otherwise transfer all rights granted to it hereunder. This authorization and release shall also inure to the benefit of the heirs, legal representatives, licensees, and assigns of Devco, as well as the person(s) (if any) for whom it took the photographs.

I am of full age and have the right to contract in my own name. I have read the foregoing and fully understand the contents thereof. This release shall be binding upon me and my heirs, legal representatives and assigns. I further release Devco from any responsibility for injury incurred during the photography session.

Signed: _____

_____
Address

_____
City, State, Zip

_____
Phone

_____
Soc.Sec #

I, being the parent or guardian of the above named minor, hereby consent to and join in the foregoing release and consent on behalf of said minor.

Signed: _____

## *18*  Screen Actors Guild Interactive Media Agreement

This agreement is SAG's current collective bargaining agreement for multimedia developers. It is discussed in Chapter 14.

SCREEN ACTORS GUILD
STANDARD
INTERACTIVE MEDIA AGREEMENT

This AGREEMENT is made between SCREEN ACTORS GUILD, INC. a California non-profit corporation, herein called "SAG" AND _____ a corporation,
herein called "PRODUCER."

1. **Recognition**.   SAG is recognized by Producer as the exclusive bargaining agent for all principal
   performers (throughout the United States) and extra performers (only in the zones specified in
   Paragraph 9 below) in the production of audio-visual material for interactive use (except as provided in Paragraph 2, below) which may be played on home-type television or computer screens.
   Such audio-visual material shall hereafter be referred to as "Interactive Programs". The other
   capitalized terms in this Contract shall have the same meaning as those terms have in the SAG
   Theatrical and Television agreements.

2. **Contract Not Applicable**.   This Contract shall not apply to the following:
   a. Interactive Programs in which (1) part or all of the audio portion replicates a phonograph
      recording, tape, or disc or portion thereof, as those recordings are known under the AFTRA
      Phono Code and, (2) the video portion consists of concert-type footage which may or may
      not include performers other than the recording artists(s), and/or other visual information
      (e.g. lyrics, text, still photos, or biographical information).
   b. Interactive Programs consisting of still photographs with or without narration.
   c. Any tape production more than half of which is made up of excerpts or whole programs that
      were produced under an AFTRA agreement:
   d. Any tape production more than half of which is made up of news, games shows, quiz-panel
      type shows, or talk shows;
   e. Interactive Programs produced by a producer who is, or who has been, signatory to any col-
      lective bargaining agreement with AFTRA and provided such producer is party to an inter-
      active program production contract with AFTRA which provides no less favorable terms to
      principal performers and extras performers than those herein provided.

3. **Applicability of SAG Television Agreement**.   Except as otherwise herein expressly provided,
   all the terms and conditions of the 1992 Screen Actors Guild Television Agreement shall apply to
   this Contract.

4. **Effective Date and Terms**.   This Contract shall be effective for a term commencing June 1,
   1993 and continuing to June 30, 1995 and shall continue thereafter until terminated by either
   party by sixty days notice in writing to the other.

5. **Compensation.**   Except as set forth in the attached schedule, the minimum rates of compensation for all other performers shall be as provided in the 1992 Screen Actors Guild Television Agreement, and in the 1992 Screen Actor Guild Television Animation Agreement, whichever is applicable.  Such compensation shall cover the distribution of Interactive Programs for use on home-type television or computer screens.

The minimum wage rate for registered extra performers shall be $99.00 per day. Whenever Producer employs more than ten registered extra performers for work in an Interactive Program on any day, Producer may employ any number of non-registered persons to perform crowd work. This contract shall not be applicable to non-registered persons performing crowd work in the manner provided in the SAG 1992 Theatrical and Television Agreement.

6. **Sub-contracting.**   Producer agrees that if Producer finances the production of, or engages an independent contractor to produce an Interactive Program or any part thereof, then, with respect to such principal performers and extra performers employed by such independent contractor whose employment would have been covered by this contract had Producer employed them directly, Producer shall remain responsible under this Contract for the economic equivalent of wages, hours and work standards provided herein.  This shall not apply to the acquisition by Producer of stock footage.

This paragraph does not apply to any Interactive Programs which Producer distributes pursuant to a license from, or which Producer purchases from, an independent producer provided Producer did not finance or subcontract the production of such Interactive Program. Producer agrees to give SAG written notice of all licensing and purchase agreements, which shall identify the Interactive Program, the independent producer and, in the case of licensing, the term of the license to distribute.

7. **Reservation of Rights.**   It is expressly understood and agreed that SAG reserves the right to bargain for payment for extended rights to distribute Interactive Programs for use on home-type television or computer screens, in addition to the compensation herein provided for production services, in negotiations for renewal of this Contract after June 30, 1995.

8. **Pension and Health Contributions.**   Producer agrees to contribute to SAG Producers Pension Plan and the SAG Producers Health Plan (the "Plans") amounts equal to 12.65% of all gross compensation paid by Producer to all principal performers and extra performers hereunder.

9. **Extra Zones.**   The terms and conditions of this Contract with respect to extra performers shall apply in the extra zones as listed below:

    Los Angeles   (30 miles from the center of Beverly & La Cienega Blvd. with a second zone extending to 75 mile from that intersection)

    New York   (300 miles from Columbia Circle)

    San Francisco   (25 miles from Powell & Market Street)

    San Diego   (City limits of San Diego)

    Las Vegas   (City limits of Las Vegas including the "Strip")

    Hawaii   (Entire state of Hawaii)

## Interactive Contract Rates

|  | 7/1/92-<br>6/30/93 | 7/1/93-<br>6/30/94 | 7/1/94-<br>6/30/95 |
|---|---|---|---|
| Day Performers<br>(8 Hour Day) | $466.00 | $485.00 | $504.00 |
| Off-camera Performer<br>(First 4 Hours) | $466.00 | $485.00 | $504.00 |
| Animation/Voice Over<br>(Up to 3 voices per production)<br>Overtime applied after: | $466.00 | $485.00 | $504.00 |
| 4 Hours for episodic or non-episodic<br>programs less than 30 minutes in length |  |  |  |
| 6 Hours for non-episodic programs 30<br>minutes in length |  |  |  |
| Extra Performers | $99.00 | $99.00 | $99.00 |

## Consecutive Employment:

The lapse period during which no pay for intervening days shall be (5) days, rather than fourteen (14) or ten (10), as the case may be.

* (This provision applies to DAY PERFORMERS ONLY, and only ONE Drop/Pick-up per performer per production may occur).

Pension and Health Contribution is 12.65% on all work performed.

## Most Favored Nations

THE PARTIES HERETO RECOGNIZE THAT THE FIELD OF PRODUCING INTERACTIVE PRO-GRAMS IS DEVELOPING RAPIDLY AND THAT THIS AGREEMENT IS ONE OF THE EARLIEST SUCH AGREEMENTS BEING NEGOTIATED BY SAG.  IT IS THEREFORE AGREED THAT SHOULD SAG NEGOTIATE AN AGREEMENT WITH ANY OTHER PRODUCER OF INTERACTIVE PRO-GRAMS WHICH, IN THE OPINION OF THE PRODUCER, IS MORE FAVORABLE TO THE PRO-DUCER THAN THIS AGREEMENT, THE PRODUCER SHALL HAVE THE OPTION OF ADOPTING THE TERMS OF SUCH OTHER AGREEMENT IN THE PLACE AND STEAD OF THIS AGREEMENT WITH RESPECT TO ANY PRODUCTIONS WHICH ARE PRODUCED AFTER THE EFFECTIVE DATE OF SUCH OTHER AGREEMENT.  IN ORDER TO EFFECTUATE THE PURPOSES OF THIS AGREEMENT, SAG AGREES TO NOTIFY PRODUCER OF ANY TERMS OF ANY DIFFERENT INTERACTIVE AGREEMENT WHICH SAG NEGOTIATES DURING THE TERM OF THIS AGREEMENT.

IN WITNESS WHEREOF, the parties have each executed this Agreement.

SCREEN ACTORS GUILD, INC.

Date: _____

By: _____

By: _____

(Company Name)

_____

(Authorized Signature)                    (Date)

_____

(Print Name and Title)

_____

(Address)

_____

_____

_____

(Telephone)

## Appendix C

# Rights Clearance Agencies and Search Firms

This appendix lists rights clearance agencies, search firms, and professional organizations that can help you clear rights to use third-party content. (Clearing rights is covered in Chapter 10.)

Search firms help you find out who owns copyrights and other intellectual property rights in third-party works. They will not assist you in obtaining the rights to use third-party works in your project. Search firms should be used when you are performing the "clearance" work yourself. (See "Determining Who Owns the Copyright," Chapter 10.)

Rights clearance agencies will clear rights and obtain licenses for you. They are described in "Rights Clearance Agencies," Chapter 10.

The professional organizations listed in this appendix handle public performance right licenses for musical compositions. They are discussed in "Option #2: Using Preexisting Music," Chapter 12.

This list of agencies, firms, and individuals has been compiled from a variety of sources. None of these businesses paid to be listed in this book, and we don't endorse any of them. If you use them, make sure they have experience relevant to your particular project.

## Rights Clearance Agencies

Jill Arofs
Total Clearance
P.O. Box 836
Mill Valley, CA 94942
Telephone: 415-445-5800

The Content Company
171 East 74th Street
2nd Floor
New York, NY 10021
Telephone:    (212) 772-7363
Fax:            (212) 772-7393

deForest Research
1645 North Vine Street
Suite 532
Hollywood, CA 90028
Telephone:    (213) 469-2271
Fax:            (213) 856-0375

Music Clearing House Ltd.
6605 Hollywood Blvd.
Suite 200
Hollywood, CA 90028
Telephone:    (213) 469-3186
Fax:            (213) 469-1213

Betsy Strode
1109 Southdown Road
Hillsborough, CA 94010
Telephone:    (415) 340-1370
Fax:            (415) 340-1370

Barbara Zimmerman
BZ/Rights & Permissions, Inc.
125 West 72nd Street
New York, NY 10023
Telephone:    (212) 580-0615
Fax:            (212) 769-9224

## Copyright Search Firms

Government Liaison Services
3030 Clarendon Blvd., Suite 209
Arlington, Va. 22201
Telephone:    (800) 642-6564
              (703) 524-8200

Robert Roomian
P.O. Box 7111
Alexandria, VA 22307
Telephone:    (703) 690-6451
Fax:          (703) 690-0074

Thomson & Thomson Copyright Research Group
500 E. Street, Suite 970
Washington, D.C. 20024-2710
Telephone:    (202) 488-2900
              (800) 356-8630
Fax:          (202) 546-8069

XL Corporate Services
ATTN:  Mark Moel, Esq.
62 White St.
New York, NY  10013
Telephone:    (800) 221-2972
Fax:          (212) 431-1441

(Handles copyright filings and trademark
searches as well)

## Trademark Search Firms

Coresearch
16 West 22nd Street
8th Floor
New York, NY 10010
Telephone:    (800) 732-7241
              (212) 627-0330
Fax:          (800) 233-2986

Thomson & Thomson
500 Victory Road
N. Quincy, MA 02171
Telephone:    (800) 692-8833
Fax:          (617) 786-8273

# Appendix D

# Stock Houses and
# Other Content Sources

Stock houses and media libraries are described in "Stock Houses and Libraries," Chapter 10. This list was obtained from a variety of sources, including trade shows, advertisements, and recommendations. We have chosen to provide you the largest set of choices, rather than screening the entries. Consequently, you have the responsibility to ensure that they can provide you with the materials which you need for your project. None of these firms paid to be listed here, and we don't endorse any of them.

The standards for licensing these stock materials are still being established. If you license content from one of these sources, make sure your license covers all the rights you need for your intended use (see "Determining What Rights You Need," Chapter 10.)

## Sound Libraries

Associated Production Music
6255 Sunset Boulevard
Suite 820
Hollywood, CA 90028-9804
Telephone:    (213) 461-3211
              (800) 543-4276
Fax:          (213) 461-9102

Capitol Production Music
6922 Hollywood Blvd. #718
Hollywood, CA 90028
Telephone:    (213) 461-2701
Fax:          (213) 461-1543

Creative Support Services
1950 Riverside Drive
Los Angeles, CA 90039
Telephone:    (213) 666-7968
              (800) 468-6874

FirstCom/Music House
13747 Montfort, Suite 220
Dallas, TX 75240
Telephone:    (800) 858-8880

Hollywood Film Music Library
11684 Ventura Blvd. #850
Studio City, CA 91604
Telephone:    (800) 373-3256
Fax:          (818) 985-9997

Jasmine Multimedia
Publishing, Inc.
1888 Century Park East #300
Los Angeles, CA 90067
Telephone:    (310) 277-7523

Killer Tracks, the Production Music Library
6534 Sunset Blvd.
Hollywood, CA 90028
Telephone:    (800) 877-0078
              (213) 957-4455
Fax:          (213) 957-4470

More Media
853 Broadway
Suite 1516
New York, NY 10003
Telephone:    (212) 677-8815

MPI Multimedia
5525 West 159th Street
Oak Forest, IL 60452
Telephone:   (800) 777-2223
Fax:            (708) 535-1541

Outlaw Sound
1140 N. LaBrea Ave.
Los Angeles, CA 90038
Telephone:   (213) 462-1873
Fax:            (213) 856-4311

Passport Designs, Inc.
100 Stone Pine Road
Half Moon Bay, CA 94019
Telephone:   (415) 726-0280
Fax:            (415) 726-2254

Production Music Library Association
40 E. 49th Street
New York, NY 10017
Telephone:   (212) 832-1098

Pro Music
941-A Clint Moore Road
Boca Rotan, FL 33481
Telephone:   (800) 322-7879
                   (305) 776-2070
Fax:            (305) 776-2074

Quality Sound, Inc.
5625 Melrose Ave.
Hollywood, CA 90038
Telephone:   (213) 467-7154

Selected Sound Recorded Music Library/
   Southern Library of Recorded Music
6777 Hollywood Blvd. #209
Hollywood, CA 90028
Telephone:   (213) 469-9910
Fax:            (213) 656-3298

SoperSound Music Library
P.O. Box 498
Palo Alto, CA 94301
Telephone:   (415) 321-4022
                   (800) 227-9980
Fax:            (415) 321-9261

The Blue Ribbon Soundworks, Ltd.
Venture Center
1605 Chantilly Drive
Suite 200
Atlanta, GA 30324
Telephone:   (404) 315-0212
Fax:            (404) 315-0213

Valentino, Inc.
151 West 46th Street
New York, NY 10036
Telephone:   (800) 223-6278

Voyetra Technologies
333 Fifth Avenue
Delhain, NY 10803
Telephone:   (914) 738-4500
                   (800) 233-9377
Fax:            (914) 738-6946

## VideoClips/Film

Airboss
125 South Sixth Street
Louisville, KY 40202
Telephone:   (502) 585-9800
Fax:            (502) 589-5339

Alpha Technologies Group, Inc.
6921 Cable Drive
Suite 100
Marriottsville, MD 21104
Telephone:   (410) 781-4200
Order:         (800) 843-9497

Archive Films Stock Footage Library
530 West 25th Street
New York, NY 10001
Telephone:    (212) 620-3980
                    (800) 886-3980
Fax:              (212) 645-2137

Budget Films
4590 Santa Monica Blvd.
Los Angeles, CA 90029
Telephone:    (213) 660-0187
Fax:              (213) 660-5571

CBS News Archives
524 West 57th Street
New York, NY 10019
Telephone:    (212) 975-2875
Fax:              (212) 975-5442

Cinema Network (CINENET)
2235 First Street #111
Simi Valley, CA 93065
Telephone:    (805) 527-8700
Fax:              (805) 527-0305

Classic Images
1041 N. Formosa Avenue
West Hollywood, CA 90046
Telephone:    (213) 850-2980

Creative Digital, Inc.
1465 Northside Drive
Suite 110
Atlanta, GA 30318
Telephone:    (404) 355-5800
Fax:              (404) 350-9825

Dick Clark Media Archives
3003 W. Olive Avenue
Burbank, CA 91510
Telephone:    (818) 841-3003
Fax:              (818) 562-1621

Dreamlight
932 North LaBrea
Los Angeles, CA 90035
Telephone:    (213) 850-1996
Fax:              (213) 850-5318

Educorp
7434 Trade Street
San Diego, CA 92121
Telephone:    (800) 843-9497
Fax:              (619) 536-2345

Energy Productions
12700 Ventura Boulevard
Studio City, CA 91604
Telephone:    (818) 508-1444
Fax:              (818) 508-1923

Filmbank
425 South Victory Blvd.
Burbank, CA 91502
Telephone:    (818) 841-9176
Fax:              (818) 567-4235

Form and Function
1595 17th Street
San Francisco, CA 94111
Telephone:    (415) 664-4010
Order:            (800) 843-9497

Imageways
412 West 48th Street
New York, NY 10036
Telephone:    (800) 862-1118
Fax:              (212) 586-0339

Jasmine Multimedia Publishing, Inc.
1888 Century Park East #300
Los Angeles, CA 90067
Telephone:    (310) 277-7523

Macromedia
600 Townsend Street
Suite 310W
San Francisco, CA 94103
Telephone:    (415) 252-2000
Fax:              (415) 626-2843

Mediacom
P.O. Box 36173
Richmond, VA 23235
Telephone:     (804) 794-0700
Fax:              (804) 794-0799

MPI Multimedia (WPA Film Library)
5525 West 159th Street
Oak Forest, IL 60452
Telephone:     (800) 777-2223
Fax:              (708) 535-1541

NBC News Video Archive
30 Rockefeller Plaza
New York, NY 10112
Telephone:     (212) 664-3797
Fax:              (212) 957-8917

Petrified Films, Inc.
430 West 14th Street, Room 204
New York, NY 10014
Telephone:     (212) 242-5461
Fax:              (212) 691-8347

Prelinger Archives
430 West 14th Street
Suite 403
New York, NY 10014
Telephone:     (800) 243-2252,  ext 10
Fax:              (212) 255-5139

The Image Bank Films
*Los Angeles office:*
4526 Wilshire Blvd.
Los Angeles, CA 90010
Telephone:     (213) 930-0797
Fax:              (213) 930-1089

Video Tape Library, Ltd.
1509 N. Crescent Heights Blvd.
Suite 2
Los Angeles, CA 90045
Telephone:     (213) 656-4330
Fax:              (213) 656-8746

## Photo Stock Houses

After Image, Inc.
6100 Wilshire Boulevard
Los Angeles, CA 90048
Telephone:     (800) 825-8899

AllStock, Inc.
222 Dexter Ave. North
Seattle, WA 98109
Telephone:     (206) 622-6262
Fax:              (206) 622-6662

American Society of Picture Professionals
Box 5283
Grand Central Station
New York, NY 10163
Telephone:     (212) 685-3870

Archive Photos
530 W. 25th Street
New York, NY 10001
Telephone:     (800) 688-5656
                     (212) 594-8816
Fax:              (212) 675-0379

Bettman Archives
902 Broadway
Fifth Floor
New York, NY 10010
Telephone:     (212) 777-6200
Fax:              (212) 533-4034

Cosmotone, Inc.
24422 South Main Street
Suite 503
Carson City, CA 90745
Telephone:     (800) 872-7872
Fax:              (310) 513-6298

FPG International
32 Union Square East
New York, NY 10003
Telephone:     (212) 777-4210
Fax:              (212) 995-9652

Harris Design/The Digital Directory
301 Cathedral Parkway
Suite 2N
New York, NY 10026
Telephone:    (212) 864-8872

Historical Picture Services, Inc.
921 West Van Buren
Suite 201
Chicago, IL 60607
Telephone:    (312) 346-0599

Index Stock Photography, Inc.
126 Fifth Avenue
7th Floor
New York, NY 10011
Telephone:    (800) 729-7466
              (212) 929-4644
Fax:          (212) 633-1914

Liaison International, Inc.
11 East 26th Street
17th Floor
New York, NY 10010
Telephone:    (800) 488-0484
              (212) 447-2509
Fax:          (212) 447-2534

Natural Selection Stock Photography, Inc.
183 St. Paul Street
Rochester, NY 14604
Telephone:    (716) 232-1502
Fax:          (716) 232-6325

Photo 20-20
50 Kenyon Avenue
Kensington, CA 94708
Telephone:    (510) 526-0921
Fax:          (510) 527-7740

Photo Researchers, Inc.
60 East 56th Street
New York, NY 10022
Telephone:    (800) 833-9033
              (212) 758-3420
Fax:          (212) 355-0731

Picture Research
6107 Roseland Drive
Rockville, MD 20852-3642
Telephone:    (301) 230-0043

Sharpshooters, Inc.
4950 Southwest 72nd Avenue
Suite 114
Miami, FL 33155
Telephone:    (800) 666-1266
              (305) 666-1266
Fax:          (305) 666-5485

Stock Boston, Inc.
36 Gloucester Street
Boston, MA 02115
Telephone:    (617) 266-2300
Fax:          (617) 353-1262

Swanstock Agency
P.O. Box 2350
Tucson, AZ 85702
Telephone:    (602) 622-7133
Fax:          (602) 622-7180
Minn:         (612) 673-9382

The Image Bank

*Los Angeles office:*
4526 Wilshire Blvd.
Los Angeles, CA 90010
Telephone:    (213) 930-0797
Fax:          (213) 930-1089

*New York office:*
111 Fifth Avenue
New York, NY 10003
Telephone:    (212) 529-6700
Fax:          (212) 529-8886

The Image Bank, Inc.
5221 North O'Conner Blvd.
Suite 700
Irving, TX 75039
Telephone:    (214) 432-3960
Fax:          (214) 432-3960

The Stock Market Photo Agency
360 Park Ave. South
New York, NY 10010
Telephone:   (212) 684-7878
Fax:           (212) 532-6750

Time Picture Syndication
Time & Life Bldg. #23-52
Rockefeller Center
New York, NY 10020
Telephone:   (212) 522-3866

Tony Stone Worldwide Stock Agency
Chicago office:
233 E. Ontario Street
Suite 100
Chicago, IL 60611
Telephone:   (800) 234-7880
                (312) 787-7880
Fax:           (312) 787-8798

Los Angeles office:
6100 Wilshire Blvd. #240
Los Angeles, CA 90048
Telephone:   (800) 234-7880
                (213) 938-1700
Fax:           (213) 938-0731

Westlight
2223 So. Carmelina Avenue
Los Angeles, CA 90064
Telephone:   (800) 872-7872
                (310) 820-7077
Fax:           (310) 820-2687

Woodfin Camp & Associates, Inc.
116 E. 27th Street
New York, NY 10016
Telephone:   (212) 481-6900
Fax:           (212) 481-6909

# Text

Corporation for National Research Initiatives/
   The Digital Library Project
1895 Preston White Drive
Suite 100
Reston, VA 22091
Telephone:   (703) 620-8990
Fax:           (703) 620-0913

Copyright Clearance Center
27 Congress Street
Salem, MA 01970
Telephone:   (508) 744-3350
Fax:           (508) 741-2318

# Multimedia Organizations
# and Publications

## Organizations

Interactive Multimedia Association
3 Church Circle #800
Annapolis, MD 20401
Telephone:     (410) 626-1380

International Communications Industries
   Association
3150 Spring Street
Fairfax, VA 22301
Telephone:     (703) 273-7200
Fax:           (415) 278-8082

International Interactive Communications
   Society (IICS)
14657 SW Teal Boulevard, Suite 119
Beaverton, OR 97007
Telephone:     (503) 579-4427
Fax:           (503) 579-1075

San Francisco-Multimedia Development Group
2601 Mariposa Street
San Franciso CA 94110
Telephone:     (415) 553-2300
Fax:           (415) 553-2403

Software Publishers Association
1730 M Street, N.W. #700
Washington, D.C. 20036
Telephone:     (202) 452-1600

## Publications

*Converge* (formerly *The Quicktime Forum*)
Multi-Facet Communications, Inc.
P.O. Box 70758
Sunnyvale CA 94086
Telephone:     408-749-0549

A bimonthly newsletter on both technical and
business issues.

*Digital Media*
428 E. Baltimore Pike
P.O. Box 644
Media, PA 19063
Telephone:     (215) 565-2480
Fax:           (215) 565-4569

*San Francisco Office:*
444 De Haro Street, Suite 128
San Francisco, CA 94107
Telephone:     (415) 575-3775
Fax:           (415) 575-3780

A monthly magazine which provides in depth
coverage of trends in the multimedia industry.

*Film/Tape World*
461 Second Street, Suite 104
San Francisco, CA 94111
Telephone:     (415) 543-6100

A monthly tabloid for the film and video tape
industry in San Francisco.

*Hollywood Reporter*
5055 Wilshire Blvd.
Los Angeles, CA 90036
Telephone:     (213) 525-2000

A daily magazine of the entertainment industry.
They publish special issues on multimedia twice
each year.

*IICS Reporter*
14657 SW Teal Blvd, Suite 119
Beaverton OR 97007
Telephone:    (503) 579-4427
Fax:             (503) 579-6272

A monthly newsletter published by the IICS on
issues for multimedia developers.

*Inside Report on New Media*
30777 S. Highway 1
P.O. Box 1289
Gualala, CA 95445
Telephone:    (707) 884-4413

A monthly newsletter on business issues in the
multimedia industry.

*Media Letter*
44 Pleasant Street
Watertown, MA 02172

A monthly newsletter on interactive technologies
for creative applications.

*Morph's Outpost*
P.O. Box 578
Orinda, CA 94563
Telephone:    (510) 238-4545
Fax:             (510) 238-9459
Online:         (510) 238-4554

A monthly tabloid written by and for multimedia
developers.

*Multimedia Monitor*
P.O. Box 26
Falls Church, CA 22040
Telephone:    (703) 241-1799
Fax:             (703) 532-0529

A monthly magazine which provides summary of
developments in the multimedia industry and a
review of the many conventions.

*Multimedia Review*
11 Ferry Lane West
Westport, CT 06880
Telephone:    (203) 226-6967
Fax:             (203) 454-5840

A quarterly magazine which focuses on technical
and marketing issues.

*Multimedia Week*
Phillips Business Information, Inc.
1201 Seven Locks Rd.
P.O. Box 61130
Potomac MD 20854
Phone:          (301) 424-3338
Fax:             (301) 424-4297

A weekly newsletter on business developments
in the multimedia industry.

*Multimedia World*
501 2nd Street
San Francisco, CA 94107
Telephone:    415-281-8650
Fax:             415-281-3915

A monthly magazine targeted primarily at users
of multimedia which is currently included as part
of *PC World*.

*Nautilus CD*
Multimedia Magazine
7001 Discovery Blvd.
Dublin, OH 93017
Telephone:    (800) 448-2323
                    (614) 761-2000
Fax:             (614) 761-4110

A monthly CD-ROM magazine which includes a
wide variety of material, including demos, games
and calendars.

*New Media*
901 Mariners Blvd.
Suite 365
San Mateo, CA 94404
Telephone:    (415) 573-5170
Fax:             (415) 573-5131

A mass market magazine for the multimedia
industry, including both developers and users.

*SF-MDG Bulletin*
2601 Mariposa Street
San Francisco, CA 94110
Telephone:    (415) 553-2300
Fax:             (415) 553-2403

A monthly fax newsletter for members of the San
Francisco Multimedia Development Group.

## Guides to Multimedia Companies

*Multimedia Directory*
Carronade Group
717 S. Cochran Ave #9
P.O. Box 36157
Los Angeles CA 90036
Phone:       (213) 935-7600
Fax:         (213) 939-6705

*Multimedia Source Book*
Templin Bogen Associates
440 Davis Court Suite 709
San Francisco CA 94111
Phone:    (415) 281-3666

## Multimedia Books

*Creating Multimedia on Your PC* (1994)
Tom Badgett
Corey Sandler
John Wiley & Sons, Inc.
ISBN:        0-471-58928-4
Price:       $29.95

This book is not a broad introduction like many of the other books on this list. It is a very detailed guide on how to use the programs in the CD-ROM accompanying the book.

*Desktop Multimedia Bible* (1993)
Jeff Burger
Addison-Wesley Publishing Company
ISBN:        0-201-58112-4
Price:       $32.95

This book is a broad introduction to the development of multimedia products. It does not focus on specific programs, but reviews tools by function and category. After a review of the individual elements in multimedia productions, the book discusses the integration of such media in an actual multimedia productions. It does not include a diskette or CD-ROM.

*Demystifying Multimedia* (1993)
J. Sterling Hutto (editor)
vivid publishing inc.
    Call (415) 512-7200 to order
Price:         $25.00

This book is a detailed description on how to develop multimedia works. It includes many examples and interviews with well-known multimedia developers. It was written with the help of Apple Computer, Inc.It does not include a diskette or CD-ROM.

*A Guide to Multimedia* (1993)
Victoria Rosenburg
New Rider Publishing
ISBN:        1-56205-082-6
Price:       $29.95

This book is designed for multimedia production in the corporate environment. It gives detailed instructions on how to create multimedia works with several authoring tools. It includes a diskette of demos and programs.

*Instant Multimedia for Windows 3.1* (1993)
Kris Jamsa
John Wiley & Sons, Inc.
ISBN:        0-471-58972-1
Price:       $29.95

This book focuses on the ability to use sound, video, and other multimedia elements under Windows 3.1 without soundboards or other peripherals. It includes a basic overview of the multi-media capabilities of the Windows 3.1 program. The book has a detailed review of particular multimedia authoring software for Windows. It also includes a diskette with demos and programs.

*Multimedia: Making It Work* (1993)
Tay Vaughan
Osborne: McGraw-Hill
ISBN:        0-078-81869-9
Price:       $27.95

This book is a broad introduction to multimedia. First, it provides an overview of the various components of multimedia products. It includes numerous tips and "warnings." The book includes Tempra editing software and a special section on how to use such software.

*Multimedia Mania* (1993)
Harald Frater
Dick Paulissen
Abacus
ISBN:           1-557-55166-9
Price:          $49.95

This book is a broad introduction to multimedia. It includes detailed review of various systems and components. The book also describes how to develop presentations with particular tools. The book includes a CD-ROM with demos and software.

*Multimedia Power Tools* (1993)
Peter Jarran
Michael Gosney
Random House Electronic Publishing
ISBN:           0-679-79118-3
Price:          $50.00

This book provides a comprehensive overview of multimedia and the underlying technology. It focuses on creating multimedia on the MacIntosh computer. The book also discusses how to use the tools on the accompanying CD-ROM. The CD-ROM has tools and demos from commercial products.

*Multimedia Toolkit* (1992)
Russell Lipton
Random House Electronic Publishing
ISBN:           0-679-74084-8
Price:          $45.00

This book provides an introduction to multimedia concepts and technology. It reviews specific hardware and software products. It includes a copy of Bell-Atlantic's DocuSource program and detailed instructions on how to use it.

## Appendix F

# Unions, Guilds, and
# Other Organizations

## Unions and Guilds

American Federation of Musicians
1501 Broadway #600
New York, NY 10036
Telephone:   (212) 869-1330
              (800) 237-0988

American Federation of Television and
   Radio Artists (AFTRA)

*Chicago office:*
75 East Wacker Drive, 14th Floor
Chicago, IL 60601
Telephone:   (312) 372-8081

*Hollywood office:*
6922 Hollywood Blvd.
Hollywood, CA 90028
Telephone:   (213) 461-8111
Contact:     Karen Stuart, Ext. 400

*Nashville office:*
1108 17th Avenue South
Box 121087
Nashville, TN 37212
Telephone:   (615) 327-2944

*New York office:*
260 Madison Avenue
New York, NY 10016
Telephone:   (212) 532-0800

Directors Guild of America (DGA)
*Chicago office:*
400 North Michigan Avenue
Suite 307
Chicago, IL 60611
Telephone:   (312) 644-5050

*Los Angeles office:*
7920 Sunset Boulevard
Los Angeles, CA 90046
Telephone:   (310) 289-2000
Fax:          (310) 289-2029

*New York office:*
110 West 57th Street
New York, NY 10019
Telephone:   (212) 581-0370
Fax:          (212) 581-1441

Graphic Artists Guild
11 West 20th Street
8th Floor
New York, NY 10011-3704
Telephone:   (212) 463-7730

Picture Agency Council of America (PACA)
(U.S. & Canada)
1530 Westlake Avenue North
Suite 600
Seattle, WA 98109
Fax:          (206) 286-8502

Screen Actors Guild (SAG)
*Chicago office:*
75 East Wacker Drive
14th Floor
Chicago, IL 60601
Telephone:   (312) 372-8081

*Dallas office:*
6060 N. Central Expressway
Suite 302
LB604
Dallas, TX 75206
Telephone:   (214) 363-8300

*Los Angeles office:*
5757 Wilshire Blvd.
Los Angeles, CA 90036
Telephone:   (213) 954-1600
Contact:     Mike Prohaska
              (213) 549-6847

*New York office:*
1515 Broadway
44th Floor
New York, NY 10036
Telephone:    (212) 944-1030

*Nashville office:*
P.O. Box 121087
Nashville, TN 37212
Telephone:    (615) 327-2958

*San Francisco office:*
235 Pine Street
Suite 1100
San Francisco, CA 94104
Telephone:    (415) 391-7510

Society of European Stage Authors &
    Composers (SESAC)

*Nashville office:*
Telephone:    (615) 320-0055

*New York office:*
421 West 54th Street
New York, NY 10019
Telephone:    (212) 586-3450
Fax:               (212) 397-4682

Songwriters Guild of America (SGA)

*Hollywood office:*
6430 Sunset Blvd.
Hollywood, CA 90028
Telephone:    (213) 462-1108

*Nashville office:*
1222 Sixteenth Avenue S.
Nashville, TN 37212
Telephone:    (615) 329-1782

*New York office:*
276 Fifth Avenue
New York, NY
Telephone:    (212) 686-6820

Writers Guild of America (WGA)

*WGA West:*
8955 Beverly Blvd.
West Hollywood, CA 90048
Telephone:    (310) 550-1000
Fax:               (310) 550-8185

*WGA East:*
555 West 57th Street
New York, NY 10019
Telephone:    (212) 767-7800

## Professional Organizations

American Society of Composers, Authors &
    Publishers (ASCAP)

*Chicago office:*
Telephone:    (312) 527-9775
Fax:               (312) 527-9774

*Los Angeles office:*
Telephone:    (213) 466-7681
Fax:               (213) 466-6677

*Nashville office:*
Telephone:    (615) 742-5000
Fax:               (615) 327-0314

*New York office:*
1 Lincoln Plaza
New York, NY 10023
Telephone:    (212) 595-3050
Fax:               (212) 724-9024

Broadcast Music, Inc. (BMI)

*Hollywood office (song indexing):*
Telephone: (213) 659-9109

*New York office (headquarters and eastern
    U.S. licensing):*
320 W. 57th Street
New York, NY 10019
Telephone:    (212) 586-2000
                     (800) 326-4264

*Phoenix office (western U.S. licensing):*
410 North 44th Street
Suite 1140
Phoenix, AZ 85008
Telephone:    (800) 326-4264

Society of European Stage Authors &
 Composers (SESAC)

*Nashville office:*
Telephone:    (615) 320-0055

*New York office:*
421 West 54th Street
New York, NY 10019
Telephone:    (212) 586-3450
Fax:          (212) 397-4682

The Harry Fox Agency
205 East 42nd Street
New York, NY 10017
Telephone:    (212) 370-5330

## Other Agencies

*MPC Logo*
Multimedia PC Marketing Council
1730 M Street, N.W.
Suite 707
Washington D.C. 20036
Telephone:    (202) 331-0494
Fax:          (202) 785-3197

*Photo-CD Logo*
Rita S. Ignizio
License Administration
Eastman Kodak Company
1700 Dewey Avenue
Rochester, NY 14650-1924
Telephone:    (716) 588-4155
Fax:          (716) 722-9230

# Appendix G

# Copyright Office Forms

# search request form

Copyright Office
Library of Congress
Washington, D.C. 20559

Reference & Bibliograpy
Section
(202) 707-6850
8:30 a.m.-5 p.m. Monday-Friday
(Eastern time)

**Type of work:**

☐ Book ☐ Music ☐ Motion Picture ☐ Drama ☐ Sound Recording
☐ Photograph/Artwork ☐ Map ☐ Periodical ☐ Contribution ☐ Architectural Work

**Search information you require:**

☐ Registration ☐ Renewal ☐ Assignment ☐ Address

**Specifics of work to be searched:**

TITLE: _____

AUTHOR: _____

COPYRIGHT CLAIMANT (if known): _____
(name in © notice)

APPROXIMATE YEAR DATE OF PUBLICATION/CREATION: _____

REGISTRATION NUMBER (if known): _____

OTHER IDENTIFYING INFORMATION: _____

If you need more space please attach additional pages.

*Estimates are based on the Copyright Office fee of $20.00 an hour or fraction of an hour consumed. The more information you furnish as a basis for the search the better service we can provide.*

**Names, titles, and short phrases are not copyrightable.**

Please read Circular 22 for more information on copyright searches.

YOUR NAME: _____ DATE: _____

ADDRESS: _____

DAYTIME TELEPHONE NO. ( _____ ) _____

Convey results of estimate/search by telephone
☐ yes ☐ no

Fee enclosed? ☐ yes
☐ no

Amount $ _____

# DOCUMENT COVER SHEET

**For Recordation of Documents**
UNITED STATES COPYRIGHT OFFICE

DATE OF RECORDATION
(Assigned by Copyright Office)

Month _____ Day _____ Year _____

Volume _____ Page _____

Volume _____ Page _____

**DO NOT WRITE ABOVE THIS LINE.**

REMITTANCE _____

## To the Register of Copyrights:
*Please record the accompanying original document or copy thereof.*

FUNDS RECEIVED _____

**1** NAME OF THE PARTY OR PARTIES TO THE DOCUMENT, AS THEY APPEAR IN THE DOCUMENT.

Party 1: _____
(assignor, grantor, etc.)

_____
(address)

_____

Party 2: _____
(assignee, grantee, etc.)

_____
(address)

_____

**2** DESCRIPTION OF THE DOCUMENT:
- ☐ Transfer of Copyright
- ☐ Security Interest
- ☐ Change of Name of Owner
- ☐ Termination of Transfer(s) [Section 304]
- ☐ Shareware
- ☐ Life, Identity, Death Statement [Section 302]
- ☐ Transfer of Mask Works
- ☐ Other _____

**3** TITLE(S) OF WORK(S), REGISTRATION NUMBER(S), AUTHOR(S), AND OTHER INFORMATION TO IDENTIFY WORK.

Title                     Registration Number     Author

_____     _____     _____

_____     _____     _____

_____     _____     _____

Additional sheet(s) attached?
- ☐ yes
- ☐ no

If so, how many? _____

**4**
- ☐ Document is complete by its own terms.
- ☐ Document is not complete. Record "as is."

**5** Number of titles in Document: _____

**6** Amount of fee enclosed or authorized to be charged to a
Deposit Account _____ .

**7** Account number _____
Account name _____

**8** Date of execution and/or effective date of accompanying
document _____ .
(month)     (day)     (year)

**9** AFFIRMATION:* I hereby affirm to the Copyright Office that the information given on this form is a true and correct representation of the accompanying document. This affirmation will not suffice as a certification of a photocopy signature on the document.

_____
Signature

_____
Date

**10** CERTIFICATION: * Complete this certification if a photocopy of the original signed document is submitted in lieu of a document bearing the actual signature.

I certify under penalty of perjury under the laws of the United States of America that the accompanying document is a true copy of the original document.

_____
Signature

_____
Duly Authorized Agent of:

_____
Date

MAIL RECORDA-TION TO:

Name▼ _____

Number/Street/Apartment Number▼ _____

City/State/ZIP▼ _____

**YOU MUST:**
- Complete all necessary spaces
- Sign your cover sheet in space 9

**SEND ALL 3 ELEMENTS IN THE SAME PACKAGE:**
1. Two copies of the Document Cover Sheet
2. Fee in check or money order payable to *Register of Copyrights*
3. Document

**MAIL TO:**
Documents Unit, Cataloging Division, Copyright Office, Library of Congress Washington, D.C. 20559

The Copyright Office has the authority to adjust fees at 5-year intervals, based on changes in the Consumer Price Index. The next adjustment is due in 1996. Please contact the Copyright Office after July 1995 to determine the actual fee schedule.

*Knowingly and willfully falsifying material facts on this form may result in criminal liability. 18 U.S.C.§1001.

January 1993—50,000

☉ U.S. GOVERNMENT PRINTING OFFICE: 1993-342-582/60.032

# ⊘ Filling Out Application Form PA

*Detach and read these instructions before completing this form. Make sure all applicable spaces have been filled in before you return this form.*

## BASIC INFORMATION

**When to Use This Form:** Use Form PA for registration of published or unpublished works of the performing arts. This class includes works prepared for the purpose of being "performed" directly before an audience or indirectly "by means of any device or process." Works of the performing arts include: (1) musical works, including any accompanying words; (2) dramatic works, including any accompanying music; (3) pantomimes and choreographic works; and (4) motion pictures and other audiovisual works.

**Deposit to Accompany Application:** An application for copyright registration must be accompanied by a deposit consisting of copies or phonorecords representing the entire work for which registration is to be made. The following are the general deposit requirements as set forth in the statute:

**Unpublished Work:** Deposit one complete copy (or phonorecord).

**Published Work:** Deposit two complete copies or one phonorecord of the best edition.

**Work First Published Outside the United States:** Deposit one complete copy (or phonorecord) of the first foreign edition.

**Contribution to a Collective Work:** Deposit one complete copy (or phonorecord) of the best edition of the collective work.

**Motion Pictures:** Deposit *both* of the following: (1) a separate written description of the contents of the motion picture; and (2) for a published work, one complete copy of the best edition of the motion picture; or, for an unpublished work, one complete copy of the motion picture or identifying material. Identifying material may be either an audiorecording of the entire soundtrack or one frame enlargement or similar visual print from each 10-minute segment.

**The Copyright Notice:** For works first published on or after March 1, 1989, the law provides that a copyright notice in a specified form "may be placed on all publicly distributed copies from which the work can be visually perceived." Use of the copyright notice is the responsibility of the copyright owner and does not require advance permission from the Copyright Office. The required form of the notice for copies generally consists of three elements: (1) the symbol "©", or the word "Copyright," or the abbreviation "Copr."; (2) the year of first publication; and (3) the name of the owner of copyright. For example: "© 1989 Jane Cole." The notice is to be affixed to the copies "in such manner and location as to give reasonable notice of the claim of copyright." Works first published prior to March 1, 1989, **must** carry the notice or risk loss of copyright protection.

For information about notice requirements for works published before March 1, 1989, or other copyright information, write: Information Section, LM-401, Copyright Office, Library of Congress, Washington, D.C. 20559.

## LINE-BY-LINE INSTRUCTIONS

## 1 SPACE 1: Title

**Title of This Work:** Every work submitted for copyright registration must be given a title to identify that particular work. If the copies or phonorecords of the work bear a title (or an identifying phrase that could serve as a title), transcribe that wording *completely* and *exactly* on the application. Indexing of the registration and future identification of the work will depend on the information you give here. If the work you are registering is an entire "collective work" (such as a collection of plays or songs), give the overall title of the collection. If you are registering one or more individual contributions to a collective work, give the title of each contribution, followed by the title of the collection. Example: "'A Song for Elinda' in *Old and New Ballads for Old and New People.*"

**Previous or Alternative Titles:** Complete this space if there are any additional titles for the work under which someone searching for the registration might be likely to look, or under which a document pertaining to the work might be recorded.

**Nature of This Work:** Briefly describe the general nature or character of the work being registered for copyright. Examples: "Music"; "Song Lyrics"; "Words and Music"; "Drama"; "Musical Play"; "Choreography"; "Pantomime"; "Motion Picture"; "Audiovisual Work."

## 2 SPACE 2: Author(s)

**General Instructions:** After reading these instructions, decide who are the "authors" of this work for copyright purposes. Then, unless the work is a "collective work," give the requested information about every "author" who contributed any appreciable amount of copyrightable matter to this version of the work. If you need further space, request additional Continuation Sheets. In the case of a collective work, such as a songbook or a collection of plays, give information about the author of the collective work as a whole.

**Name of Author:** The fullest form of the author's name should be given. Unless the work was "made for hire," the individual who actually created the work is its "author." In the case of a work made for hire, the statute provides that "the employer or other person for whom the work was prepared is considered the author."

**What is a "Work Made for Hire"?** A "work made for hire" is defined as: (1) "a work prepared by an employee within the scope of his or her employment"; or (2) "a work specially ordered or commissioned for use as a contribution to a collective work, as a part of a motion picture or other audiovisual work, as a translation, as a supplementary work, as a compilation, as an instructional text, as a test, as answer material for a test, or as an atlas, if the parties expressly agree in a written instrument signed by them that the work shall be considered a work made for hire." If you have checked "Yes" to indicate that the work was "made for hire," you must give the full legal name of the employer (or other person for whom the work was prepared). You may also include the name of the employee along with the name of the employer (for example: "Elster Music Co., employer for hire of John Ferguson").

**"Anonymous" or "Pseudonymous" Work:** An author's contribution to a work is "anonymous" if that author is not identified on the copies or phonorecords of the work. An author's contribution to a work is "pseudonymous" if that author is identified on the copies or phonorecords under a fictitious name. If the work is "anonymous" you may: (1) leave the line blank; or (2) state "anonymous" on the line; or (3) reveal the author's identity. If the work is "pseudonymous" you may: (1) leave the line blank; or (2) give the pseudonym and identify it as such (for example: "Huntley Haverstock, pseudonym"); or (3) reveal the author's name, making clear which is the real name and which is the pseudonym (for example: "Judith Barton, whose pseudonym is Madeline Elster"). However, the citizenship or domicile of the author **must** be given in all cases.

**Dates of Birth and Death:** If the author is dead, the statute requires that the year of death be included in the application unless the work is anonymous or pseudonymous. The author's birth date is optional, but is useful as a form of identification. Leave this space blank if the author's contribution was a "work made for hire."

**Author's Nationality or Domicile:** Give the country of which the author is a citizen, or the country in which the author is domiciled. Nationality or domicile **must** be given in all cases.

**Nature of Authorship:** Give a brief general statement of the nature of this particular author's contribution to the work. Examples: "Words"; "Co-Author of Music"; "Words and Music"; "Arrangement"; "Co-Author of Book and Lyrics"; "Dramatization"; "Screen Play"; "Compilation and English Translation"; "Editorial Revisions."

# 3 SPACE 3: Creation and Publication

**General Instructions:** Do not confuse "creation" with "publication." Every application for copyright registration must state "the year in which creation of the work was completed." Give the date and nation of first publication only if the work has been published.

**Creation:** Under the statute, a work is "created" when it is fixed in a copy or phonorecord for the first time. Where a work has been prepared over a period of time, the part of the work existing in fixed form on a particular date constitutes the created work on that date. The date you give here should be the year in which the author completed the particular version for which registration is now being sought, even if other versions exist or if further changes or additions are planned.

**Publication:** The statute defines "publication" as "the distribution of copies or phonorecords of a work to the public by sale or other transfer of ownership, or by rental, lease, or lending"; a work is also "published" if there has been an "offering to distribute copies or phonorecords to a group of persons for purposes of further distribution, public performance, or public display." Give the full date (month, day, year) when, and the country where, publication first occurred. If first publication took place simultaneously in the United States and other countries, it is sufficient to state "U.S.A."

# 4 SPACE 4: Claimant(s)

**Name(s) and Address(es) of Copyright Claimant(s):** Give the name(s) and address(es) of the copyright claimant(s) in this work even if the claimant is the same as the author. Copyright in a work belongs initially to the author of the work (including, in the case of a work made for hire, the employer or other person for whom the work was prepared). The copyright claimant is either the author of the work or a person or organization to whom the copyright initially belonging to the author has been transferred.

**Transfer:** The statute provides that, if the copyright claimant is not the author, the application for registration must contain "a brief statement of how the claimant obtained ownership of the copyright." If any copyright claimant named in space 4 is not an author named in space 2, give a brief statement explaining how the claimant(s) obtained ownership of the copyright. Examples: "By written contract"; "Transfer of all rights by author"; "Assignment"; "By will." Do not attach transfer documents or other attachments or riders.

# 5 SPACE 5: Previous Registration

**General Instructions:** The questions in space 5 are intended to find out whether an earlier registration has been made for this work and, if so, whether there is any basis for a new registration. As a general rule, only one basic copyright registration can be made for the same version of a particular work.

**Same Version:** If this version is substantially the same as the work covered by a previous registration, a second registration is not generally possible unless: (1) the work has been registered in unpublished form and a second registration is now being sought to cover this first published edition; or (2) someone other than the author is identified as copyright claimant in the earlier registration, and the author is now seeking registration in his or her own name. If either of these two exceptions apply, check the appropriate box and give the earlier registration number and date. Otherwise, do not submit Form PA; instead, write the Copyright Office for information about supplementary registration or recordation of transfers of copyright ownership.

**Changed Version:** If the work has been changed, and you are now seeking registration to cover the additions or revisions, check the last box in space 5, give the earlier registration number and date, and complete both parts of space 6 in accordance with the instructions below.

**Previous Registration Number and Date:** If more than one previous registration has been made for the work, give the number and date of the latest registration.

# 6 SPACE 6: Derivative Work or Compilation

**General Instructions:** Complete space 6 if this work is a "changed version," "compilation," or "derivative work," and if it incorporates one or more earlier works that have already been published or registered for copyright, or that have fallen into the public domain. A "compilation" is defined as "a work formed by the collection and assembling of preexisting materials or of data that are selected, coordinated, or arranged in such a way that the resulting work as a whole constitutes an original work of authorship." A "derivative work" is "a work based on one or more preexisting works." Examples of derivative works include musical arrangements, dramatizations, translations, abridgments, condensations, motion picture versions, or "any other form in which a work may be recast, transformed, or adapted." Derivative works also include works "consisting of editorial revisions, annotations, or other modifications" if these changes, as a whole, represent an original work of authorship.

**Preexisting Material (space 6a):** Complete this space **and** space 6b for derivative works. In this space identify the preexisting work that has been recast, transformed, or adapted. For example, the preexisting material might be: "French version of Hugo's 'Le Roi s'amuse'." Do not complete this space for compilations.

**Material Added to This Work (space 6b):** Give a brief, general statement of the **additional** new material covered by the copyright claim for which registration is sought. In the case of a derivative work, identify this new material. Examples: "Arrangement for piano and orchestra"; "Dramatization for television"; "New film version"; "Revisions throughout; Act III completely new." If the work is a compilation, give a brief, general statement describing both the material that has been compiled **and** the compilation itself. Example: "Compilation of 19th Century Military Songs."

# 7,8,9 SPACE 7, 8, 9: Fee, Correspondence, Certification, Return Address

**Fee:** Copyright fees are adjusted at 5-year intervals, based on increases or decreases in the Consumer Price Index. The next adjustment is due in 1995. Contact the Copyright Office in January 1995 for the new fee schedule.

**Deposit Account:** If you maintain a Deposit Account in the Copyright Office, identify it in space 7. Otherwise leave the space blank and send the fee of $20 with your application and deposit.

**Correspondence (space 7):** This space should contain the name, address, area code, and telephone number of the person to be consulted if correspondence about this application becomes necessary.

**Certification (space 8):** The application cannot be accepted unless it bears the date and the **handwritten signature** of the author or other copyright claimant, or of the owner of exclusive right(s), or of the duly authorized agent of the author, claimant, or owner of exclusive right(s).

**Address for Return of Certificate (space 9):** The address box must be completed legibly since the certificate will be returned in a window envelope.

# MORE INFORMATION

**How To Register a Recorded Work:** If the musical or dramatic work that you are registering has been recorded (as a tape, disk, or cassette), you may choose either copyright application Form PA or Form SR, Performing Arts or Sound Recordings, depending on the purpose of the registration.

Form PA should be used to register the underlying musical composition or dramatic work. Form SR has been developed specifically to register a "sound recording" as defined by the Copyright Act—a work resulting from the "fixation of a series of sounds," separate and distinct from the underlying musical or dramatic work. Form SR should be used when the copyright claim is limited to the sound recording itself. (In one instance, Form SR may also be used to file for a copyright registration for both kinds of works—see (4) below.) Therefore:

**(1) File Form PA** if you are seeking to register the musical or dramatic work, not the "sound recording," even though what you deposit for copyright purposes may be in the form of a phonorecord.

**(2) File Form PA** if you are seeking to register the audio portion of an audiovisual work, such as a motion picture soundtrack; these are considered integral parts of the audiovisual work.

**(3) File Form SR** if you are seeking to register the "sound recording" itself, that is, the work that results from the fixation of a series of musical, spoken, or other sounds, but not the underlying musical or dramatic work.

**(4) File Form SR** if you are the copyright claimant for both the underlying musical or dramatic work and the sound recording, *and* you prefer to register both on the same form.

**(5) File both forms PA and SR** if the copyright claimant for the underlying work and sound recording differ, or you prefer to have separate registration for them.

**"Copies" and "Phonorecords":** To register for copyright, you are required to deposit "copies" or "phonorecords." These are defined as follows:

Musical compositions may be embodied (fixed) in "copies," objects from which a work can be read or visually perceived, directly or with the aid of a machine or device, such as manuscripts, books, sheet music, film, and videotape. They may also be fixed in "phonorecords," objects embodying fixations of sounds, such as tapes and phonograph disks, commonly known as phonograph records. For example, a song (the work to be registered) can be reproduced in sheet music ("copies") or phonograph records ("phonorecords"), or both.

# FORM PA
**For a Work of the Performing Arts**
UNITED STATES COPYRIGHT OFFICE

REGISTRATION NUMBER

_____

PA           PAU

EFFECTIVE DATE OF REGISTRATION

_____

Month      Day      Year

---

**DO NOT WRITE ABOVE THIS LINE. IF YOU NEED MORE SPACE, USE A SEPARATE CONTINUATION SHEET.**

## 1

**TITLE OF THIS WORK ▼**

_____

**PREVIOUS OR ALTERNATIVE TITLES ▼**

_____

**NATURE OF THIS WORK ▼** See instructions

## 2

**a**

**NAME OF AUTHOR ▼**

**DATES OF BIRTH AND DEATH**
Year Born ▼      Year Died ▼

Was this contribution to the work a "work made for hire"?
☐ Yes
☐ No

**AUTHOR'S NATIONALITY OR DOMICILE**
Name of Country
OR { Citizen of ▶ _____
Domiciled in ▶ _____

**WAS THIS AUTHOR'S CONTRIBUTION TO THE WORK**
Anonymous? ☐ Yes ☐ No
Pseudonymous? ☐ Yes ☐ No

If the answer to either of these questions is "Yes," see detailed instructions.

**NATURE OF AUTHORSHIP** Briefly describe nature of the material created by this author in which copyright is claimed. ▼

**NOTE**

Under the law, the "author" of a "work made for hire" is generally the employer, not the employee (see instructions). For any part of this work that was "made for hire" check "Yes" in the space provided, give the employer (or other person for whom the work was prepared) as "Author" of that part, and leave the space for dates of birth and death blank.

**b**

**NAME OF AUTHOR ▼**

**DATES OF BIRTH AND DEATH**
Year Born ▼      Year Died ▼

Was this contribution to the work a "work made for hire"?
☐ Yes
☐ No

**AUTHOR'S NATIONALITY OR DOMICILE**
Name of Country
OR { Citizen of ▶ _____
Domiciled in ▶ _____

**WAS THIS AUTHOR'S CONTRIBUTION TO THE WORK**
Anonymous? ☐ Yes ☐ No
Pseudonymous? ☐ Yes ☐ No

If the answer to either of these questions is "Yes," see detailed instructions.

**NATURE OF AUTHORSHIP** Briefly describe nature of the material created by this author in which copyright is claimed. ▼

**c**

**NAME OF AUTHOR ▼**

**DATES OF BIRTH AND DEATH**
Year Born ▼      Year Died ▼

Was this contribution to the work a "work made for hire"?
☐ Yes
☐ No

**AUTHOR'S NATIONALITY OR DOMICILE**
Name of Country
OR { Citizen of ▶ _____
Domiciled in ▶ _____

**WAS THIS AUTHOR'S CONTRIBUTION TO THE WORK**
Anonymous? ☐ Yes ☐ No
Pseudonymous? ☐ Yes ☐ No

If the answer to either of these questions is "Yes," see detailed instructions.

**NATURE OF AUTHORSHIP** Briefly describe nature of the material created by this author in which copyright is claimed. ▼

## 3

**a** **YEAR IN WHICH CREATION OF THIS WORK WAS COMPLETED** This information must be given in all cases.
◀ Year

**b** **DATE AND NATION OF FIRST PUBLICATION OF THIS PARTICULAR WORK** Complete this information ONLY if this work has been published.
Month ▶ _____ Day ▶ _____ Year ▶ _____
◀ Nation

## 4

See instructions before completing this space.

**COPYRIGHT CLAIMANT(S)** Name and address must be given even if the claimant is the same as the author given in space 2.▼

**TRANSFER** If the claimant(s) named here in space 4 are different from the author(s) named in space 2, give a brief statement of how the claimant(s) obtained ownership of the copyright.▼

**DO NOT WRITE HERE OFFICE USE ONLY**

APPLICATION RECEIVED

ONE DEPOSIT RECEIVED

TWO DEPOSITS RECEIVED

REMITTANCE NUMBER AND DATE

---

**MORE ON BACK ▶**
• Complete all applicable spaces (numbers 5-9) on the reverse side of this page.
• See detailed instructions.
• Sign the form at line 8.

**DO NOT WRITE HERE**

Page 1 of _____ pages

**DO NOT WRITE ABOVE THIS LINE. IF YOU NEED MORE SPACE, USE A SEPARATE CONTINUATION SHEET.**

**PREVIOUS REGISTRATION** Has registration for this work, or for an earlier version of this work, already been made in the Copyright Office?

☐ Yes ☐ No  If your answer is "Yes," why is another registration being sought? (Check appropriate box) ▼

a. ☐ This is the first published edition of a work previously registered in unpublished form.

b. ☐ This is the first application submitted by this author as copyright claimant.

c. ☐ This is a changed version of the work, as shown by space 6 on this application.

If your answer is "Yes," give: **Previous Registration Number** ▼          **Year of Registration** ▼

**5**

**DERIVATIVE WORK OR COMPILATION**   Complete both space 6a & 6b for a derivative work; complete only 6b for a compilation.

a.  **Preexisting Material**   Identify any preexisting work or works that this work is based on or incorporates. ▼

b.  **Material Added to This Work**   Give a brief, general statement of the material that has been added to this work and in which copyright is claimed. ▼

See instructions
before completing
this space.

**6**

**DEPOSIT ACCOUNT**   If the registration fee is to be charged to a Deposit Account established in the Copyright Office, give name and number of Account.
**Name** ▼                         **Account Number** ▼

**7**

**CORRESPONDENCE**   Give name and address to which correspondence about this application should be sent.   Name/Address/Apt/City/State/Zip ▼

Area Code & Telephone Number ▶

Be sure to
give your
daytime phone
◀ number

**CERTIFICATION\***   I, the undersigned, hereby certify that I am the

Check only one ▼

☐ author
☐ other copyright claimant
☐ owner of exclusive right(s)
☐ authorized agent of
          Name of author or other copyright claimant, or owner of exclusive right(s) ▲

**8**

of the work identified in this application and that the statements made
by me in this application are correct to the best of my knowledge.

**Typed or printed name and date** ▼ If this application gives a date of publication in space 3, do not sign and submit it before that date.

_____ date ▶ _____

☞          Handwritten signature (X) ▼

**MAIL CERTIFI-CATE TO**

Certificate
will be
mailed in
window
envelope

Name ▼

Number/Street/Apartment Number ▼

City/State/ZIP ▼

**9**

\* 17 U.S.C. § 506(e): Any person who knowingly makes a false representation of a material fact in the application for copyright registration provided for by section 409, or in any written statement filed in
connection with the application, shall be fined not more than $2,500.

▲ June 1992—100,000                                ☆U.S. GOVERNMENT PRINTING OFFICE: 1992-312-432/60,003

# Ⓛ Filling Out Application Form TX

*Detach and read these instructions before completing this form.*
*Make sure all applicable spaces have been filled in before you return this form.*

## BASIC INFORMATION

**When to Use This Form:** Use Form TX for registration of published or unpublished non-dramatic literary works, excluding periodicals or serial issues. This class includes a wide variety of works: fiction, nonfiction, poetry, textbooks, reference works, directories, catalogs, advertising copy, compilations of information, and computer programs. For periodicals and serials, use Form SE.

**Deposit to Accompany Application:** An application for copyright registration must be accompanied by a deposit consisting of copies or phonorecords representing the entire work for which registration is to be made. The following are the general deposit requirements as set forth in the statute:

**Unpublished Work:** Deposit one complete copy (or phonorecord).

**Published Work:** Deposit two complete copies (or one phonorecord) of the best edition.

**Work First Published Outside the United States:** Deposit one complete copy (or phonorecord) of the first foreign edition.

**Contribution to a Collective Work:** Deposit one complete copy (or phonorecord) of the best edition of the collective work.

**The Copyright Notice:** For works first published on or after March 1, 1989, the law provides that a copyright notice in a specified form "may be placed on all publicly distributed copies from which the work can be visually per-

ceived." Use of the copyright notice is the responsibility of the copyright owner and does not require advance permission from the Copyright Office. The required form of the notice for copies generally consists of three elements: (1) the symbol "©," or the word "Copyright," or the abbreviation "Copr."; (2) the year of first publication; and (3) the name of the owner of copyright. For example: "© 1993 Jane Cole." The notice is to be affixed to the copies "in such manner and location as to give reasonable notice of the claim of copyright." Works first published prior to March 1, 1989, **must** carry the notice or risk loss of copyright protection.

For information about notice requirements for works published before March 1, 1989, or other copyright information, write: Information Section, LM-401, Copyright Office, Library of Congress, Washington, D.C. 20559.

## LINE-BY-LINE INSTRUCTIONS

Please type or print using black ink.

## 1 SPACE 1: Title

**Title of This Work:** Every work submitted for copyright registration must be given a title to identify that particular work. If the copies or phonorecords of the work bear a title or an identifying phrase that could serve as a title, transcribe that wording *completely* and *exactly* on the application. Indexing of the registration and future identification of the work will depend on the information you give here.

**Previous or Alternative Titles:** Complete this space if there are any additional titles for the work under which someone searching for the registration might be likely to look or under which a document pertaining to the work might be recorded.

**Publication as a Contribution:** If the work being registered is a contribution to a periodical, serial, or collection, give the title of the contribution in the "Title of this Work" space. Then, in the line headed "Publication as a Contribution," give information about the collective work in which the contribution appeared.

## 2 SPACE 2: Author(s)

**General Instructions:** After reading these instructions, decide who are the "authors" of this work for copyright purposes. Then, unless the work is a "collective work," give the requested information about every "author" who contributed any appreciable amount of copyrightable matter to this version of the work. If you need further space, request Continuation sheets. In the case of a collective work such as an anthology, collection of essays, or encyclopedia, give information about the author of the collective work as a whole.

**Name of Author:** The fullest form of the author's name should be given. Unless the work was "made for hire," the individual who actually created the work is its "author." In the case of a work made for hire, the statute provides that "the employer or other person for whom the work was prepared is considered the author."

**What is a "Work Made for Hire"?** A "work made for hire" is defined as (1) "a work prepared by an employee within the scope of his or her employment"; or (2) "a work specially ordered or commissioned for use as a contribution to a collective work, as a part of a motion picture or other audiovisual work, as a translation, as a supplementary work, as a compilation, as an instructional text, as a test, as answer material for a test, or as an atlas, if the parties expressly agree in a written instrument signed by them that the works shall be considered a work made for hire." If you have checked "Yes" to indicate that the work was "made for hire," you must give the full legal name of the employer (or other person for whom the work was prepared). You may also include the name of the employee along with the name of the employer (for example: "Elster Publishing Co., employer for hire of John Ferguson").

**"Anonymous" or "Pseudonymous" Work:** An author's contribution to a work is "anonymous" if that author is not identified on the copies or phonorecords of the work. An author's contribution to a work is "pseudonymous" if that author is identified on the copies or phonorecords under a fictitious name. If the work is "anonymous" you may: (1) leave the line blank; or (2) state "anonymous" on the line; or (3) reveal the author's identity. If the work is "pseudonymous" you may: (1) leave the line blank; or (2) give the pseudonym and identify it as such (for example: "Huntley Haverstock, pseudonym"); or (3) reveal the author's name, making clear which is the real name and which is the pseudonym (for example, "Judith Barton, whose pseudonym is Madeline Elster"). However, the citizenship or domicile of the author **must** be given in all cases.

**Dates of Birth and Death:** If the author is dead, the statute requires that the year of death be included in the application unless the work is anonymous or pseudonymous. The author's birth date is optional but is useful as a form of identification. Leave this space blank if the author's contribution was a "work made for hire."

**Author's Nationality or Domicile:** Give the country of which the author is a citizen or the country in which the author is domiciled. Nationality or domicile **must** be given in all cases.

**Nature of Authorship:** After the words "Nature of Authorship," give a brief general statement of the nature of this particular author's contribution to the work. Examples: "Entire text"; "Coauthor of entire text"; "Chapters 11-14"; "Editorial revisions"; "Compilation and English translation"; "New text."

# 3 SPACE 3: Creation and Publication

**General Instructions:** Do not confuse "creation" with "publication." Every application for copyright registration must state "the year in which creation of the work was completed." Give the date and nation of first publication only if the work has been published.

**Creation:** Under the statute, a work is "created" when it is fixed in a copy or phonorecord for the first time. Where a work has been prepared over a period of time, the part of the work existing in fixed form on a particular date constitutes the created work on that date. The date you give here should be the year in which the author completed the particular version for which registration is now being sought, even if other versions exist or if further changes or additions are planned.

**Publication:** The statute defines "publication" as "the distribution of copies or phonorecords of a work to the public by sale or other transfer of ownership, or by rental, lease, or lending"; a work is also "published" if there has been an "offering to distribute copies or phonorecords to a group of persons for purposes of further distribution, public performance, or public display." Give the full date (month, day, year) when, and the country where, publication first occurred. If first publication took place simultaneously in the United States and other countries, it is sufficient to state "U.S.A."

# 4 SPACE 4: Claimant(s)

**Name(s) and Address(es) of Copyright Claimant(s):** Give the name(s) and address(es) of the copyright claimant(s) in this work even if the claimant is the same as the author. Copyright in a work belongs initially to the author of the work (including, in the case of a work made for hire, the employer or other person for whom the work was prepared). The copyright claimant is either the author of the work or a person or organization to whom the copyright initially belonging to the author has been transferred.

**Transfer:** The statute provides that, if the copyright claimant is not the author, the application for registration must contain "a brief statement of how the claimant obtained ownership of the copyright." If any copyright claimant named in space 4 is not an author named in space 2, give a brief statement explaining how the claimant(s) obtained ownership of the copyright. Examples: "By written contract"; "Transfer of all rights by author"; "Assignment"; "By will." Do not attach transfer documents or other attachments or riders.

# 5 SPACE 5: Previous Registration

**General Instructions:** The questions in space 5 are intended to show whether an earlier registration has been made for this work and, if so, whether there is any basis for a new registration. As a general rule, only one basic copyright registration can be made for the same version of a particular work.

**Same Version:** If this version is substantially the same as the work covered by a previous registration, a second registration is not generally possible unless: (1) the work has been registered in unpublished form and a second registration is now being sought to cover this first published edition; or (2) someone other than the author is identified as copyright claimant in the earlier registration, and the author is now seeking registration in his or her own name. If either of these two exceptions apply, check the appropriate box and give the earlier registration number and date. Otherwise, do not submit Form TX; instead, write the Copyright Office for information about supplementary registration or recordation of transfers of copyright ownership.

**Changed Version:** If the work has been changed and you are now seeking registration to cover the additions or revisions, check the last box in space 5, give the earlier registration number and date, and complete both parts of space 6 in accordance with the instructions below.

**Previous Registration Number and Date:** If more than one previous registration has been made for the work, give the number and date of the latest registration.

# 6 SPACE 6: Derivative Work or Compilation

**General Instructions:** Complete space 6 if this work is a "changed version," "compilation," or "derivative work" and if it incorporates one or more earlier works that have already been published or registered for copyright or that have fallen into the public domain. A "compilation" is defined as "a work formed by the collection and assembling of preexisting materials or of data that are selected, coordinated, or arranged in such a way that the resulting work as a whole constitutes an original work of authorship." A "derivative work" is "a work based on one or more preexisting works." Examples of derivative works include translations, fictionalizations, abridgments, condensations, or "any other form in which a work may be recast, transformed, or adapted." Derivative works also include works "consisting of editorial revisions, annotations, or other modifications" if these changes, as a whole, represent an original work of authorship.

**Preexisting Material (space 6a):** For derivative works, complete this space **and** space 6b. In space 6a identify the preexisting work that has been recast, transformed, or adapted. An example of preexisting material might be: "Russian version of Goncharov's 'Oblomov'." Do not complete space 6a for compilations.

**Material Added to This Work (space 6b):** Give a brief, general statement of the new material covered by the copyright claim for which registration is sought. **Derivative work** examples include: "Foreword, editing, critical annotations"; "Translation"; "Chapters 11-17." If the work is a **compilation**, describe both the compilation itself and the material that has been compiled. Example: "Compilation of certain 1917 Speeches by Woodrow Wilson." A work may be both a derivative work and compilation, in which case a sample statement might be: "Compilation and additional new material."

# 7 SPACE 7: Manufacturing Provisions

Due to the expiration of the Manufacturing Clause of the copyright law on June 30, 1986, this space has been deleted.

# 8 SPACE 8: Reproduction for Use of Blind or Physically Handicapped Individuals

**General Instructions:** One of the major programs of the Library of Congress is to provide Braille editions and special recordings of works for the exclusive use of the blind and physically handicapped. In an effort to simplify and speed up the copyright licensing procedures that are a necessary part of this program, section 710 of the copyright statute provides for the establishment of a voluntary licensing system to be tied in with copyright registration. Copyright Office regulations provide that you may grant a license for such reproduction and distribution solely for the use of persons who are certified by competent authority as unable to read normal printed material as a result of physical limitations. The license is entirely voluntary, nonexclusive, and may be terminated upon 90 days notice.

**How to Grant the License:** If you wish to grant it, check one of the three boxes in space 8. Your check in one of these boxes together with your signature in space 10 will mean that the Library of Congress can proceed to reproduce and distribute under the license without further paperwork. For further information, write for Circular 63.

# 9,10,11 SPACE 9,10,11: Fee, Correspondence, Certification, Return Address

**Fee:** The Copyright Office has the authority to adjust fees at 5-year intervals, based on changes in the Consumer Price Index. The next adjustment is due in 1996. Please contact the Copyright Office after July 1995 to determine the actual fee schedule.

**Deposit Account:** If you maintain a Deposit Account in the Copyright Office, identify it in space 9. Otherwise leave the space blank and send the fee of $20 with your application and deposit.

**Correspondence** (space 9) This space should contain the name, address, area code, and telephone number of the person to be consulted if correspondence about this application becomes necessary.

**Certification** (space 10): The application can not be accepted unless it bears the date and the **handwritten signature** of the author or other copyright claimant, or of the owner of exclusive right(s), or of the duly authorized agent of author, claimant, or owner of exclusive right(s).

**Address for Return of Certificate** (space 11): The address box must be completed legibly since the certificate will be returned in a window envelope.

**DO NOT WRITE ABOVE THIS LINE. IF YOU NEED MORE SPACE, USE A SEPARATE CONTINUATION SHEET.**

## 1

TITLE OF THIS WORK ▼

_____

PREVIOUS OR ALTERNATIVE TITLES ▼

_____

PUBLICATION AS A CONTRIBUTION If this work was published as a contribution to a periodical, serial, or collection, give information about the collective work in which the contribution appeared.    **Title of Collective Work ▼**

If published in a periodical or serial give:  **Volume ▼**        **Number ▼**        **Issue Date ▼**        **On Pages ▼**

## 2

**a**

NAME OF AUTHOR ▼

DATES OF BIRTH AND DEATH
Year Born ▼        Year Died ▼

Was this contribution to the work a "work made for hire"?
☐ Yes
☐ No

AUTHOR'S NATIONALITY OR DOMICILE
Name of Country
OR { Citizen of ▶ _____
     { Domiciled in ▶ _____

WAS THIS AUTHOR'S CONTRIBUTION TO THE WORK
Anonymous?        ☐ Yes  ☐ No
Pseudonymous?   ☐ Yes  ☐ No

If the answer to either of these questions is "Yes," see detailed instructions.

NATURE OF AUTHORSHIP Briefly describe nature of material created by this author in which copyright is claimed. ▼

**NOTE**

Under the law, the "author" of a "work made for hire" is generally the employer, not the employee (see instructions). For any part of this work that was "made for hire" check "Yes" in the space provided, give the employer (or other person for whom the work was prepared) as "Author" of that part, and leave the space for dates of birth and death blank.

**b**

NAME OF AUTHOR ▼

DATES OF BIRTH AND DEATH
Year Born ▼        Year Died ▼

Was this contribution to the work a "work made for hire"?
☐ Yes
☐ No

AUTHOR'S NATIONALITY OR DOMICILE
Name of Country
OR { Citizen of ▶ _____
     { Domiciled in ▶ _____

WAS THIS AUTHOR'S CONTRIBUTION TO THE WORK
Anonymous?        ☐ Yes  ☐ No
Pseudonymous?   ☐ Yes  ☐ No

If the answer to either of these questions is "Yes," see detailed instructions.

NATURE OF AUTHORSHIP Briefly describe nature of material created by this author in which copyright is claimed. ▼

**c**

NAME OF AUTHOR ▼

DATES OF BIRTH AND DEATH
Year Born ▼        Year Died ▼

Was this contribution to the work a "work made for hire"?
☐ Yes
☐ No

AUTHOR'S NATIONALITY OR DOMICILE
Name of Country
OR { Citizen of ▶ _____
     { Domiciled in ▶ _____

WAS THIS AUTHOR'S CONTRIBUTION TO THE WORK
Anonymous?        ☐ Yes  ☐ No
Pseudonymous?   ☐ Yes  ☐ No

If the answer to either of these questions is "Yes," see detailed instructions.

NATURE OF AUTHORSHIP Briefly describe nature of material created by this author in which copyright is claimed. ▼

## 3

**a** YEAR IN WHICH CREATION OF THIS WORK WAS COMPLETED  This information must be given ◀ Year in all cases.

**b** DATE AND NATION OF FIRST PUBLICATION OF THIS PARTICULAR WORK
Complete this information ONLY if this work has been published.    Month ▶ _____ Day ▶ _____ Year ▶ _____    ◀ Nation

## 4

See instructions before completing this space.

COPYRIGHT CLAIMANT(S) Name and address must be given even if the claimant is the same as the author given in space 2. ▼

TRANSFER If the claimant(s) named here in space 4 is (are) different from the author(s) named in space 2, give a brief statement of how the claimant(s) obtained ownership of the copyright. ▼

DO NOT WRITE HERE
OFFICE USE ONLY

APPLICATION RECEIVED

ONE DEPOSIT RECEIVED

TWO DEPOSITS RECEIVED

REMITTANCE NUMBER AND DATE

**MORE ON BACK ▶**  • Complete all applicable spaces (numbers 5-11) on the reverse side of this page.
• See detailed instructions.        • Sign the form at line 10.

DO NOT WRITE HERE

Page 1 of _____ pages

**DO NOT WRITE ABOVE THIS LINE. IF YOU NEED MORE SPACE, USE A SEPARATE CONTINUATION SHEET.**

**PREVIOUS REGISTRATION** Has registration for this work, or for an earlier version of this work, already been made in the Copyright Office?

☐ Yes ☐ No  If your answer is "Yes," why is another registration being sought? (Check appropriate box) ▼

a. ☐ This is the first published edition of a work previously registered in unpublished form.

b. ☐ This is the first application submitted by this author as copyright claimant.

c. ☐ This is a changed version of the work, as shown by space 6 on this application.

If your answer is "Yes," give: **Previous Registration Number ▼**          **Year of Registration ▼**

**5**

**DERIVATIVE WORK OR COMPILATION** Complete both space 6a and 6b for a derivative work; complete only 6b for a compilation.

a. **Preexisting Material** Identify any preexisting work or works that this work is based on or incorporates. ▼

b. **Material Added to This Work** Give a brief, general statement of the material that has been added to this work and in which copyright is claimed. ▼

**6**

See instructions
before completing
this space.

## —space deleted—

**7**

**REPRODUCTION FOR USE OF BLIND OR PHYSICALLY HANDICAPPED INDIVIDUALS** A signature on this form at space 10 and a check in one of the boxes here in space 8 constitutes a non-exclusive grant of permission to the Library of Congress to reproduce and distribute solely for the blind and physically handicapped and under the conditions and limitations prescribed by the regulations of the Copyright Office: (1) copies of the work identified in space 1 of this application in Braille (or similar tactile symbols); or (2) phonorecords embodying a fixation of a reading of that work; or (3) both.

a ☐ Copies and Phonorecords          b ☐ Copies Only          c ☐ Phonorecords Only

**8**

See instructions.

**DEPOSIT ACCOUNT** If the registration fee is to be charged to a Deposit Account established in the Copyright Office, give name and number of Account.
**Name ▼**                    **Account Number ▼**

**9**

**CORRESPONDENCE** Give name and address to which correspondence about this application should be sent.   Name/Address/Apt/City/State/ZIP ▼

Be sure to
give your
daytime phone
◄ number

Area Code and Telephone Number ▶

**CERTIFICATION\*** I, the undersigned, hereby certify that I am the

Check only one ▶ {
☐ author
☐ other copyright claimant
☐ owner of exclusive right(s)
☐ authorized agent of _____

of the work identified in this application and that the statements made
by me in this application are correct to the best of my knowledge.

Name of author or other copyright claimant, or owner of exclusive right(s) ▲

**10**

Typed or printed name and date ▼ If this application gives a date of publication in space 3, do not sign and submit it before that date.

_____ date ▶ _____

☞  Handwritten signature (X) ▼

**MAIL
CERTIFI-
CATE TO**

Name ▼

Number/Street/Apartment Number ▼

**Certificate
will be
mailed in
window
envelope**

City/State/ZIP ▼

**11**

\*17 U.S.C. § 506(e): Any person who knowingly makes a false representation of a material fact in the application for copyright registration provided for by section 409, or in any written statement filed in connection with the application, shall be fined not more than $2,500.

February 1993—100,000

☆U.S. GOVERNMENT PRINTING OFFICE: 1993-342-581/60,504

# Index